Special and Decorative Breads

Les Pains

Spéciaux

et

Décorés

Special
and
Decorative Breads

Roland Bilheux
Alain Escoffier
Daniel Hervé
Jean-Marie Pouradier

Under the direction of
Jean Chazalon and Pierre Michalet

Translated by Rhona Poritzky-Lauvand and James Peterson

A copublication of
CICEM (Compagnie Internationale
de Consultation *Education* et *Media*)
Paris

and

**Van Nostrand Reinhold
New York**

First published as *Pains spéciaux et décorés* by Editions St-Honoré, Paris, France; copyright © 1987.

English translation copyright © 1989 by Van Nostrand Reinhold for the United States and Canada; by CICEM (Compagnie Internationale de Consultation *Education* et *Media*) for the rest of the world.

Library of Congress Catalog Number 89-8999

ISBN 0-442-31954-1

Printed in the United States of America

Van Nostrand Reinhold
115 Fifth Avenue
New York, NY 10003

Nelson Canada
1120 Birchmount Road
Scarborough, Ontario
Canada M1K 5G4

16 15 14 13 12 11 10 9 8 7 6 5 4 3 2

Library of Congress Cataloging-in-Publication Data

Pains spéciaux et décorés. English.
    Special and decorative breads / Roland Bilheux . . . [et al.] ;
  under the direction of Jean Chazalon and Pierre Michalet ;
  translated by Rhona Poritzky-Lauvand and James Peterson.
        p.   cm.
    Translation of: Pains spéciaux et décorés.
    Includes index.
    ISBN 0-442-31954-1
    1. Bread. I. Bilheux, Roland, 1944–   . II. Chazalon, Jean.
III. Michalet, Pierre. IV. Decorative breads. V. Title.
TX769.P2313   1989
641.8′15—dc20   89-8999
                                                               CIP

About the Authors

Roland Bilheux

Roland Bilheux, born in 1944, first apprenticed to become a pastry chef in his childhood province of Mayenne in western France. His first formal training was at the French culinary school Centre Technologique Ferrandi in Paris, familiarly known as Ferrandi. He augmented his culinary abilities by fulfilling his military obligation (mandatory in France) as a chef for a general in the NATO forces.

At the age of twenty-three, Roland Bilheux opened his own pastry shop and bread bakery in a suburb of Paris. Here, he perfected many of his skills, including his mastery of special breads and bread decorating.

Mr. Bilheux now teaches pastry at the Ferrandi school and is co-author of the definitive four-volume series *Traité de Pâtisserie Artisanale*, published in English as the *Professional French Pastry Series* by Van Nostrand Reinhold.

Jean-Marie Pouradier

Jean-Marie Pouradier was born in Loiret and first apprenticed in bread baking and pastry making in Maisons-Alfort, a suburb of Paris. He then worked in a Viennese bakery in Paris, where he became a respected and experienced baker. After fulfilling his military service in Germany, Mr. Pouradier worked for twelve years in various Viennese bakeries in Val-de-Marne, just outside Paris. He then worked for nine years as a consultant and gave demonstrations on Viennese baking for a prestigious baking association. Mr. Pouradier joined the Ferrandi school in 1983 as an instructor of bread baking and continues to teach today.

Alain Escoffier

Born in 1947 in the Ardeche region of southeastern France, Alain Escoffier first apprenticed at the Ferrandi school, where he obtained his C.A.P. in pastry making and bread baking. He continued his training as a pastry chef's assistant in a well-known Parisian pastry shop, where he also perfected his bread-baking skills.

At the age of twenty-six, he became an instructor at the Ferrandi school, where he continues to combine his skills as an instructor with his talents as pastry chef and baker.

Mr. Escoffier is co-author of the four-volume series *Traité de Pâtisserie Artisanale*, published in English as the *Professional French Pastry Series* by Van Nostrand Reinhold.

Daniel Hervé

Daniel Hervé, born in 1935 in Sarthe, apprenticed in Paris as both a bread baker and pastry chef. After fulfilling his military obligation in Algeria as a chef, he returned to France, where he managed a bakery at which he was responsible for both bread baking and pastry making.

In 1963 Mr. Hervé joined the Ferrandi school as instructor and supervisor of the bread-baking department. Rising in position throughout the years, he now holds the distinguished post of head chef instructor of the bread-baking and pastry-making department.

Mr. Hervé is the recipient of numerous awards from various competitions, most notably the first-place prize at the Prix au Concours d'Arpajon.

Jean Chazalon

Born into a long line of bakers, Jean Chazalon has worked as a dedicated professional for over thirty-six years. In addition to his responsibilities as a baker, he heads the Syndicat Professional, one of France's most important bakers' unions.

Mr. Chazalon is also vice-president of the Paris branch of the well-known bakers' and pastry chefs' guild, the Syndicat des Boulangers-Pâtissiers. He provided the impetus for *Special and Decorative Breads* and is frequently called upon to judge breads and pastries for professional competitions and government-run licensing exams.

Pierre Michalet

Pierre Michalet received his formal education in economics. He has since specialized in communications and educational media and is currently the director of the respected educational publishing firm Editions St-Honoré. He is responsible for the editorial and pictorial organization of *Special and Decorative Breads,* as well as for numerous other publications in France and the United States.

Contents

About the Authors   5
Foreword   8
Translators' Notes   9
Acknowledgments 10

Chapter 1. Basic Bread-making Techniques . . . *11*

Introductory note 11
Glossary 12
Types of flour 14
Yeast 17
How bread is made 20
Making bread by hand 22
Hygrometry 26
Hydration 27
Machine kneading 28
Fermentation 30
Yeast starters 32
Weighing bread dough 33
Shaping long loaves 34
Shaping round loaves 35
Scoring 36
Baking 37
Rediscovering traditional breads 39

Chapter 2. Special Breads *41*

The various types and textures of breads 42
The great variety of special breads 44
Guide to the special breads 46
Country-style breads 47
Country-style bread with a mixed starter 48
Country-style bread with a natural starter 52
Country-style bread with a yeast starter 54
Country-style bread with a sponge starter 56
Rye breads 58
Rye bread with a fermented dough starter 60
Rye bread with a mixed starter 63
Rye bread with a sponge starter 64

Light rye bread 65
Rye breads and rolls with raisins 66
Whole-wheat breads 68
Whole-wheat bread with a mixed starter 69
Whole-wheat bread with a sponge starter 72
Whole-wheat bread with a fermented
    dough starter 74
Apricot, apple, and prune breads 75
Seaweed bread 78
Brown bread 79
Brié bread 80
Four-grain bread 81
Chorizo bread 82
Cumin bread 83
Carrot bread 84
Herb bread 85
Carrot-herb bread 86
Whole-wheat bread with dried fruits 88
Wheat-germ bread 89
High-gluten bread 90
Low-gluten bread 91
Gruau bread 92
Oyster bread 93
Italian bread 94
Corn bread 95
Méteil bread (Wheat/rye bread) 96
Pullman bread 98
Normandy cider bread 100
Hazelnut , walnut, and almond breads 102
Onion, bacon, and onion/bacon breads 104
Olive bread 106
Barley bread 107
Provençale fougasse 108
Sesame-seed bread 109
Soy bread 111
Bran bread 112
Surprise breads 113
Viennese breads 114

Chapter 3. Elaborate Breads and Viennese Breads 117

Auvergne-style loaves (L'auvergnat) 120
Pouches (La tabatière) 121
Tricorns (Le tricorne) 122
Caps (La casquette) 123
Braids (La boule tressée) 124
Ropes, Pithiviers, and spirals (Pain cordon,
    pain pithiviers, et pain spiral) 125
Crowns (Les couronnes) 126
Lyons-style crowns (Les couronnes lyonnaises) . . . 127
Bear claws (Les pattes d'ours) 128
Split loaves (Les fendus) 129
Horseshoes (Les fers à cheval) 130
Folded loaves (Les pains pliés) 131
Crescents (Les pains croissants) 132
Country-style flat bread (La fougasse) 133
Shaping loaves with scissors 134
Milk bread dough (La pâte à pain au lait) 138
Viennese breads 142
Using templates to prepare Viennese breads 143
Examples of cutout breads 145
Hand-shaped breads 158
Examples of hand-shaped breads 160
Displaying Viennese breads 168
Braided loaves 170
Braiding with three strands of dough 172
Braiding with four strands of dough 174

Chapter 4. Decorative Breads 178

Basic decorating dough 179
Preparations for bread decoration 182

Working with decorating dough 188
Grapevines 198
Handmade flowers 206
Ears of corn 210
Corn leaves 214
Ears of wheat 218
Leaves 222
Ribbons and bows 227
Scrolls 230
Assorted decorations 237
Candle holders 238
Rose branches 241
Grapevines 244
Sheaves of wheat 249

Chapter 5. Presentation Pieces 253

Constructing presentation pieces 254
Judging presentation pieces 256
Weaving 260
Straw hats 262
Peels 263
Harvest scenes 264
Details of the harvest presentation piece 266
Windmills, lanterns, and people 267
The grape harvest 270
Traditional grape harvester's basket 272
Wine press 274
Roosters 275
Examples of presentation pieces 279

Chapter 6. Marketing Breads 295

Practical tips for marketing breads 296

Units of Measure and Conversions 299

Index 301

Forewords

Without bread, there is no eating in France. This is true for an elaborate dinner at a three-star restaurant, a middle-class repast, or a simple country meal. Probably more than in any other country of the world, bread is truly the "staff of life" in France.

It is said that bread in its present form was discovered in ancient Egypt, probably from a piece of leftover fermented dough that, when combined with fresh flour and water, developed air bubbles, resulting in a lighter dough and, ultimately, an airier, crisper, and better-tasting bread.

The symbolism of bread is everywhere. In Christianity, bread is used as a simile for the flesh of Christ. When people talk about their "bread and butter," they are referring to the essential part of their income, and the "bread-winner" is that member of a family whose labor sustains it.

Bread permeates all activities in the life of a French person. It has always been a powerful political tool in France, where climatic conditions and government decisions may provoke a bad harvest or a large increase in the price of cereals and cause a political or social crisis. It was because of a lack of bread and the condescending *bon mot* of Marie Antoinette that the French Revolution started on July 14, 1789.

For many years bread indicated social status in France. The sophisticated people of the towns ate white bread, while the uneducated country farmer and his family consumed dark bread. Ironically, however, in recent years black bread has been recognized as the healthier, more chic alternative, and it is the poorer segment of the population that now eats the soft white bread once considered the best.

Wonderful memories of my childhood in Bourg-en-Bresse, near Lyons, are associated with bread. I remember the little *ficelle,* spread with butter and dunked in *café au lait* at breakfast, and the afternoon *quatre heure,* a snack that French children eat when they come home from school. This usually consists of a piece of crunchy baguette and a chunk of dark chocolate. The *pain au chocolat* so popular in the United States is made from croissant dough wrapped around a piece of chocolate, but I think this will never compare with the cruder and better-tasting original version I ate as a child.

Although people in rural areas in France used to make their own bread, with the advent of better roads and professional bakers in small villages, it became rare for housewives to make bread. In the last few years, however, there has been a renaissance of the traditional craft, and both the professional and the home cook are bringing back a skill that many thought was lost forever.

The simple bread made of only flour and water is truly difficult to make well, as are all basic products, such as wine, which is "simply" fermented grape juice, and cheese, which is "only" curdled milk. Somehow bread making is at once both extremely precise and imprecise. The paradox here is that the techniques must be performed precisely to work well, but since so much depends on variable factors such as humidity, atmospheric pressure, external temperature, quality of flour (amount of gluten), and type of oven used, successful bread making is contingent on the art of the baker, who must correct and adjust to these factors until the dough feels right in his or her hands. That in-depth knowledge of ingredients, equipment, and techniques is what enables the baker to produce the same good bread every day.

The making of bread is a relaxing, creative, convivial, and fulfilling operation. Nothing can compare with the satisfaction of kneading dough and, later, the aroma created in the kitchen by a tray of bread baking in the oven.

This extraordinary book on bread is thorough and professionally designed, giving a complete analysis of the different types of flour and types of leavening agents, as well as of the old, original method of making bread with naturally developed yeast present in pieces of previously fermented dough. Notice also the attention given to a variety of healthier breads made from barley, bran, buckwheat, whole wheat, rye, and other grains. These types of bread were common until the middle of the nineteenth century in France, when they gave way to bread made of pure white flour, considered more prestigious and classier.

The information on ingredients and basic processes of bread making are carefully explained herein, including the specific steps followed in the making of bread by hand and by machine, as well as discussions on water, kneading, fermentation, temperature, and proofing. This comprehensive approach makes this a superb book for the professional and the amateur alike.

Special and Decorative Breads will be a great addition to the library of those with a general interest in cooking and a particular interest in bread making, whether as an avocation or a vocation. I know that *Special and Decorative Breads* will make many people at my house happy for years to come.

JACQUES PEPIN

This is the only book of its kind, as far as I know. The first half describes and illustrates in full detail the fundamentals of bread making, from the mixing of the dough to the forming of the loaves, including the familiar long shapes, generous round country loaves, molded sandwich breads, rolls, horseshoe shapes, raisin breads, nut breads, whole-wheat and rye breads. It goes into the wrong way to do things as well as the right way, with close-ups of shapes, cuts, and bread textures. The second part illustrates fantasy breads, appliqués, and all manner of ideas, such as exactly how to form, glaze, and bake leaves and flowers, bunches of grapes, sheaves of wheat, miniature wheelbarrows, windmills, baskets, nameplates, and presentation assemblages. It seems to me that anything you can think of that might be made with bread dough is described and pictured here.

Although this is most definitely a book by and for professionals, it is a treasure for all of us passionate home bakers. How else could we discover these secrets of the trade?

JULIA CHILD

Translators' Notes

Flour: There are many types of white wheat flours, each having its own particular characteristics. Although the recipes in this book were originally based on French flours, we have tried to find the best possible substitutes for the flours called for in each recipe; but keep in mind these are meant to be substitutions and in no way are they to be considered direct correlations.

In France, flour tends to be softer and lower in gluten and protein than in the United States. Flour milled from soft wheat does not have the elasticity required for breads. Therefore the French wheat is sometimes milled with hard wheat imported from the United States or Canada. This makes it difficult to duplicate the same flour in another country. Flour in the United States with similar specifications as flour in France may respond very differently when used. This does not mean, as many frustrated bakers have thought in the past, that wonderful French breads are out of reach outside of France. Though identical results are difficult to re-create in another country, equally good bread can be achieved. We recommend that the reader try different brands and types of flours available to find the flour that works best for them.

Some bakers are requesting organic wheat, grown free of pesticides and additives in soil that is properly prepared, which results in a tastier, higher-quality flour. Though organically grown flours are more difficult to come by, the more bakers demand them, the more farmers will oblige. The only way to achieve the savor, perfume, and texture of the old-style breads is to use products and techniques that were used to make them, using modern methods only when they augment rather than diminish the quality of the final bread.

Below are descriptions of various types of white wheat flours available in the United States. The germ and bran are removed from the kernel when white flour is milled, even though they contain nearly all the fiber and B vitamins; they are removed because they also negate the elastic properties of the gluten, which is so vital to the texture and crumb of the bread. The flours discussed here are milled from soft spring and soft winter wheat, which are generally grown in

eastern states, and hard spring and hard winter wheat, which are grown in the northern Midwest and Canada. Soft flour contains 8.4 to 8.8 percent protein, 0.44 to 0.48 percent ash, 1 percent fat, and 76 to 77 percent starch. Hard flour contains 11.2 to 11.8 percent protein, 0.45 to 0.50 percent ash, 1.2 percent fat, and 74 to 75 percent starch. The higher protein found in hard flour indicates a higher level of gluten, which results in a more elastic, better-textured bread. The ash content is the quantity of ash resulting after burning a given amount of flour. The lower the ash content, the higher the quality of the flour. The hard wheat flours most concern the bread baker.

In the United States, the improver azodicarbonamide is often added to flours to mature them. It is activated when the flour is mixed into the dough. This helps strengthen the gluten and consequently improves the elasticity and rising of the dough. Natural maturing takes from two to three months.

Straight flour is considered a good flour to use for bread making. It is 100 percent extraction flour. The extraction rate is the amount of flour obtained from wheat after milling, when the bran and germ are removed, leaving the endosperm, which contains most of the protein and carbohydrates. For example, based on 100 pounds of wheat, approximately 72 pounds of flour remains after extraction; the other 28 pounds is used for feed. The entire 72 pounds or 100 percent, of the remaining flour is straight flour. Straight flour is used to make patent, clear, and low-grade flours.

Patent flour is the purest and highest-quality commercial wheat flour available. Patent flour is made from the center portion of the endosperm. Patent flour is classified in five categories, depending on the amount of straight flour it obtains. Extra short or fancy and first patent flours are made from soft wheat and are used for cake flours. Extra short or fancy patent contains 40 to 60 percent straight flour. First patent flour contains 60 to 70 percent straight flour. Short patent flour made from hard wheat is the most highly recommended commercially milled flour for bread baking. It contains 70 to 80 percent straight flour. Medium patent flour

contains 80 to 90 percent straight flour and is also excellent for bread baking, as is long patent flour, which is made with 90 to 95 percent straight flour. It is up to the baker to determine which of these flours best serves his or her purposes.

Clear flour is the by-product of straight flour that remains after patent flour is removed. Clear flour is graded into fancy, first clear, and second clear. Clear flour is darker in color than the other flours previously mentioned, as it is made from the part of the endosperm closest to the bran. Fancy clear flour, milled from soft wheat, is used to make pastry flour. First clear, milled from hard wheat, is often blended by the baker with low-gluten flours to lighten the texture of breads such as rye or whole-wheat yet maintain the deep color desirable in such breads. Second clear flour has a very high ash content, is very dark, and is not generally used for food.

Stuffed straight flour is straight flour with some clear flour added.

The following types of flours are made from some of the flours discussed above. They are often named by their application rather than how they are milled.

Cake flour has the least amount of gluten of all wheat flours, making it best for light, delicate products such as sponge cakes, génoise, and some cookie batters. Made from extra short or fancy patent flour, milled from soft wheat, cake flour often comes bleached, which gives it a bright, white appearance. In this book, flours are assumed to be unbleached unless otherwise indicated.

Pastry flour also has a low gluten content, though it contains a bit more than cake flour. Made from fancy clear flour, a soft wheat flour, it is used for making tart and pie doughs, some cookie batters, and muffins.

All-purpose flour is made from a blend of hard wheat flours or sometimes a blend of soft and hard wheat flours. All-purpose flour varies throughout regions in the United States; blends are often determined by the flours available and the cooking styles of the area. It is called all-purpose flour because it is intended for most baking needs for general household use, not commercial use, where having several different flours, each used for a specific purpose, is feasible.

High-gluten flour is milled from hard wheat and has an especially high protein content, making it high in gluten. It is often blended by the baker with other low-gluten flours to give them more strength and elasticity. It is also used for particularly crusty breads and pizza doughs. It does not darken the color of the final product, as does clear flour.

Gelatin: In France, gelatin is marketed in 2-gram sheets, whereas in the United States, gelatin sheets may vary greatly in weight. It is therefore important to weigh them. The equivalent weight of powdered gelatin can be used to replace the gelatin sheet called for in the recipes. Before using them in a recipe, gelatin sheets should always be softened in cold water for several minutes and then gently squeezed by hand to remove the excess water.

Measurements: French professional bakers customarily weigh their ingredients. For this reason volume measurements are used only for liquids; dry ingredients are difficult to measure accurately by volume. Both metric and U.S. units of measure are given in the text. It is recommended that those who are serious about bread making familiarize themselves with the metric system. The metric system is the most widely used system of measurement and is easier to use, as metric measurement is based on units of ten.

Most U.S. conversions have been rounded off to the nearest half-unit of measure. Quantities less than 15 grams (½ ounce) are given in teaspoons and tablespoons.

Sheet pans: French sheet pans measure 40 by 60 centimeters (16 by 24 inches) and are made of heavy blue steel. It is always preferable to use the heaviest sheet pans available.

Malt: Malt is added to yeast doughs to speed fermentation, as it contains diastase, an enzyme that converts starch into sugar, which helps activate the yeast as yeast feeds on sugars. Use malt only when indicated in the recipe, as it can convert an excess of starch into sugar, which would adversely affect the texture of the bread, making it gluey. Malt is extracted from sprouted barley and can be found in syrup or dried form. Use only diastatic malt for bread baking; nondiastatic malt is used to add color and flavor to bakery products and is prepared at a high temperature that kills the enzymes, rendering it useless for bread-baking purposes.

About the Translators

Rhona Poritzky-Lauvand trained professionally in the culinary arts in Paris, France, working as apprentice in such restaurants as the Michelin two-star Jacque Cagna and Gerard Panguad.

Ms. Lauvand returned to New York and worked in several restaurants, where her talent for instruction became evident. In 1986 she joined the staff of the French Culinary Institute in New York City, the sister school to Le Ferrandi in Paris. Ms. Lauvand currently heads up the pastry department at the French Culinary Institute and has contributed significantly to the development of the pastry curriculum there. In addition to her own professional activities as a pastry chef and free-lance pastry specialist, Ms. Lauvand seriously studies music in New York City.

Jim Peterson trained in the culinary arts as an apprentice in several restaurants in Paris and the French countryside, including Le Vivarois in Paris and Chez La Mère Blanc in Vonnas, both three-star Michelin restaurants.

In 1979, Mr. Peterson returned to the United States where he opened Le Petit Robert in New York to critical acclaim.

Since 1984 Mr. Peterson has taught French cooking in several of New York's cooking schools, including the French Culinary Institute, Peter Kump's New York Cooking School, and the New York Restaurant School. Besides his work as a restaurant consultant and translator, he is also writing a book on sauce making for Van Nostrand Reinhold.

Ms. Lauvand and Mr. Peterson are also the translators of *Traité de Pâtisserie Artisanale,* a four-volume series published in English as the *Professional French Pastry Series,* by Van Nostrand Reinhold.

Acknowledgments

The translators would like to thank the following people, who helped answer questions in an effort to bring the taste of French breads to the English-speaking baker. Ron Wirtz, Head Librarian at Emerson Library of the American Baking Institute in Manhattan, Kansas; Jean-Marie Cadot, baker at Le Panatier in Rye, New York; Frank Kitchen, president of Voila! bakery; Marcus Farbinger, pastry chef of Marquet pastry in Brooklyn, New York; and Christian Foucher, Head Chef/Instructor of the French Culinary Institute (and chef/instructor from Le Ferrandi, our sister school and home to the authors), who brought the *Professional French Pastry Series* and *Special and Decorative Breads* to our attention, and us to the authors'.

Much appreciation goes to VNR's ever-proficient associate editor Cynthia Zigmund and our ceaselessly meticulous editor, Linda Venator.

A deep and personal thank-you to Remi Lauvand and Tibi Fish for their enduring support and love.

Chapter 1
Basic bread-making techniques

~~~~~~~~~~~~

Introductory Note

The preparation of decorative breads requires considerable technical experience. This book is for the professional who already has basic baking experience and wishes to learn more about technique to make a wider variety of products. This first section is intended primarily as a review of the more fundamental bread-making techniques. Although the authors assume that the reader has some baking experience, this introduction includes a glossary of terms that will be used throughout the remainder of the text.

Although this opening section is meant to be as concise as possible, the less experienced baker will find helpful explanations of the more basic bread-making techniques. It is imperative that the less experienced reader study this section carefully before working on the recipes given in the rest of this book.

Glossary

Abaisse (sheet of dough)
A thin sheet of pastry dough that is rolled out with the aid of a rolling pin or electric rolling mill (sheeter) to the desired thickness.

Accoler (to piece together)
To attach two or more pieces of decorating dough together to form a particular shape or design.

Allonger (to roll out or lengthen)
To roll a section of dough in such a way as to enlarge it to the desired size or shape.

Apprêt (proofing/final fermentation)
The stage preceding the baking of the dough. Refers to the final fermentation, from the time the dough is shaped until the actual baking.

Bassiner (to moisten a dry dough)
To moisten dough with additional water if the dough appears dry, to achieve the proper consistency.

Buée (steam)
Steam that is introduced into the oven just before or during baking of breads.

Clé ou Soudure (seam)
The point where bread dough that is folded over itself meets and forms a seal.

Contrefraser (to firm a moist dough)
To add extra flour during the preliminary working of bread dough (frasage) to make the dough firmer if it seems too moist.

Corps (body or consistency)
A dough is said to have developed body or the proper consistency when it has become elastic after successful kneading. Working a dough develops its body by activating the gluten to obtain elasticity, smoothness, and malleability.

Corser (to add body to bread dough)
To work (knead) bread dough so as to strengthen it and give it more body.

Dessécher (to dry)
To reduce the moisture content of dough or cooked bread by placing it an oven or proof box.

Ebarber (to trim)
To trim an irregular border or edge of bread dough to even it out.

Etuver (to warm)
To place bread dough in a proof box to accelerate its proofing. This technique is sometimes used to decrease the moisture content of raw or cooked decorating dough.

Façonner ou Tourner (to shape)
To give bread dough a specific shape by working it with the hands.

Ferrer (to burn and stick)
Describes a dough that has stuck to the bottom of the baking sheet and has burned. This is caused by baking in an oven that was too hot.

Force (dough strength)
The tendency of bread dough to pull together during fermentation. During fermentation, dough loses elasticity. *Pas assez* de force (too elastic/insufficiently strong) refers to dough that is overly elastic (perhaps because of overkneading) and does not rise properly, rising flatly rather than to a rounded shape. *Trop* de force (excessively strong) refers to a dough that holds together too firmly, resulting in overly rounded loaves.

Fraser (to bring together or to crush dough)
To bring together the ingredients at the beginning of kneading.
   Also, to crush the components of a dough (usually a pastry dough) with the palm of the hand so that they are well combined without being overworked.

Grigne (crusty opening on bread surface)
A slice made on the surface of the bread with a sharp knife allows the bread to expand during fermentation. As the slice expands and browns during baking, the opening and crusty raised edge is referred to as the bloom.

Hydratation (moisture content)
The amount of water absorbed by a given quantity of flour, which results in a dough of the desired consistency.

Inciser (to score)
To make cuts of varying depth into the surface of a piece of bread dough. This can be accomplished with:
- a special blade designed for this purpose (for bread)
- a paring knife or pair of scissors (for decorating bread dough)

Levain (sourdough or natural starter)
A bread starter consisting only of a mixture of flour and water. The wild yeasts contained in the flour initiate the fermen-

tation of the starter and eventually the bread dough.

Levure biologique (commercial yeast)
Commercial yeast that is used for the fermentation and leavening of the bread dough.

Levain-levure (yeast starter made with commercial yeast)
A bread starter consisting of flour, water, and commercial yeast.

Modeler (to shape or mold)
To shape bread dough into a specific decorative shape, often referred to as molding.

Moulage (cutout)
A small piece of dough that has been cut out or decorated with a dough cutter or imprint.

Moulure (preliminary shaping or molding)
The middle stage of shaping bread dough into loaves, in which the dough is given several successive folds. It is performed just before the loaves are rolled to size. This technique is used to make baguettes and other long shaped breads (but not round loaves).

Pointage (fermentation of dough)
The first fermentation of the bread dough, which begins immediately after the completion of kneading and ends with the shaping of the loaves (the final stage of fermentation, the proofing, occurs after the shaping of the loaves).

Poolisch (sponge starter)
A particularly moist starter made from equal amounts of water and flour and all or some of the yeast in a recipe, used to initiate the fermentation of the finished dough.

Pousse (rising)
The expansion or rising of the dough during fermentation.

Ressuage (loss of moisture while cooling)
The moisture that bread loses from the time it is removed from the oven until it has completely cooled.

Rompre/Donner un tour (to punch down)
To punch down dough does not literally mean the dough is punched or hit. The risen dough is actually gently pushed down with the palms of the hands; then the sides of the dough are brought into the center, and the entire mass is turned over. This is sometimes also referred to as degassing. This technique eliminates carbon dioxide that has accumulated in the dough. It also helps stimulate the yeast cells by working additional oxygen into the dough, and it contributes to the final consistency of the dough.

Sabler (to give a sandy texture)
To work flour and butter together to obtain a fine granular mixture with the consistency of sand.

Taux d'extraction (flour-to-wheat ratio)
The quantity of flour that can be extracted from a given amount of wheat by milling.

Tolérance (tolerance)
The ability of a given bread dough to tolerate insufficient or excessive fermentation.

Types of flour

Definition

The term *flour,* when used alone, designates a product obtained exclusively from the milling of wheat. The term also implies that it has been purified and is designated for human consumption.

Flour that is obtained from other grains or nuts, such as rye, barley, corn, or oats, is always named as such—rye flour, barley flour, and the like.

Composition of Bread Flour

Water: less than 16 percent
Starch: 60 to 72 percent
Nitrogen compounds (proteins): 8 to 12 percent (7 to 10 percent gluten)
Minerals: 0.45 to 0.60 percent
Fats (lipids): 1.20 to 1.40 percent
Sugars: 1 to 2 percent
Natural acids: 0.02 to 0.05 percent
Fiber: traces
Vitamins: B and E

Wheat flour also contains enzymes such as alpha-amylase and beta-amylase, which play a vital role in bread making.

Classification of Flours for Baking

Most countries, including the United States, classify wheat flour into types based on ash content. In general, more refined flours produce less ash and are usually thought to be of higher quality. The ash content of flour is also directly related to the extraction ratio (the amount of flour extracted from a given quantity of wheat). Generally, the higher the extraction ratio, the higher the ash content.

The ash content of flour is determined by burning a given quantity of flour at an extremely high temperature and measuring the residue.

The bulk of the ash (minerals) contained in a grain of wheat is found in the germ (5.3 percent) and in the husk, or bran (4.7 percent). The nut (caryopsis or endosperm) of the wheat grain has a mineral content of only 0.32 percent.

Exact American equivalents for French flours do not exist, as different categories are used. American flours with approximately the same qualities as specific French flours are indicated in the table below and are substituted throughout this book (see the translators' notes at the beginning of this book).

Type (American/French)	Ash Content	Approximate Extraction Ratio
cake & pastry/45	less than 0.50%	70% (65–75%)
all-purpose & bread/55	0.50 to 0.60%	75% (70–78%)
high-gluten/65	0.62 to 0.75%	80% (74–82%)
light whole-wheat/80	0.75 to 0.90%	82% (72–85%)
whole-wheat/110	1.00 to 1.20%	85% (79–87%)
dark whole-wheat/150	more than 1.40%	90% (90–95%)

Criteria for Judging Quality

When selecting an appropriate flour for bread making, it is important not only to be aware of its chemical and physical composition (these figures should be made available by the manufacturer) but also to keep in mind certain other criteria.

1. Whiteness

To get a clear look at the color of different types of flour, it is helpful to press a small quantity under a sheet of glass. This can be done with more than one flour at a time. This method not only facilitates a comparison of the whiteness of different flours but allows for an inspection for impurities. The flour should have a perfectly regular consistency and not contain any specks.

2. Texture and Feel

The texture and size of the grains play an important role in kneading and also determine the speed at which the dough rises.

3. Rising Ability and Elasticity

Several factors determine the rising ability and elasticity of a particular flour. In France the Chopin *alvéograph* is used to determine the relationship between the elasticity and rising power. The letter P represents the tenacity or holding power of the flour. Flours with a high P value tend to have a high gluten content and absorb a relatively large quantity of water. The letter L is used to represent the ability of the flour to rise. The relationship between L and P is represented by the letter W, which indicates the overall elasticity, strength, and ability of the flour to expand. (The G factor in the table at the right indicates how much the flour swells when tested with the Chopin *alvéograph*.)

4. Fermenting Ability and Enzyme Content

The quantity of enzymes (specifically amylases) contained in flour determines the rate at which starch is converted to sugar and thus rendered accessible to the yeasts.

5. Moisture Content

The moisture content of flour must not exceed 16 percent, or the flour will have a shorter shelf life and lower yield.

6. Absorption Ability

This is a measure of the amount of water that can be absorbed by a given quantity of flour. In bread making, it is usually preferable to have flour that can absorb a large amount of water.

Varieties of Flour

1. Oat Flour

Oats are a cereal from a plant in the grass family (Gramineae). They are widely cultivated in the United States, France, Germany, and the Soviet Union. Oat flour is obtained from the milling of oats. Oat flour tends to be flaky in texture.

Oat breads are becoming increasingly popular in the United States, especially since oat bran has been found to lower cholesterol. Because oat flour has a low gluten content, it must be combined with wheat flour when used in bread making. It also often enters into porridge (oatmeal), soups, and various purees. Oats are also used for animal fodder, grain alcohol, and dietary products.

2. Whole-Wheat Flour

Whole-wheat flour is prepared by milling the entire kernel of wheat, including the germ.

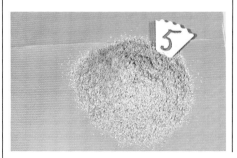

3. White Wheat Flour

White wheat flour comes in many varieties and is the flour most frequently used in bread making. Many types of white flour are used for baking in the United States, but bread flour is by far the most common.

4. High-Gluten Bread Flour

Gluten flour is extracted from wheat using a special industrial process. It is sometimes combined with flour that contains insufficient gluten to make it more suitable for bread making. It is also used in the preparation of gluten bread (see page 90).

5. Patent Flour

Certain breads and pastries require flour that is extremely pure and high in gluten. Special flours, milled only from the central part of the endosperm, are available for this purpose. These flours are usually extremely high in gluten and form extremely elastic bread dough. The W factor for these flours is at least 220.

These flours are reserved for bread and pastry recipes requiring high-quality, high-gluten flour with high elasticity and rising power, such as brioches.

Type (American/ French)	Minimum Protein	Minimum W Factor	Minimum G Factor	Ash Content
Cake & pastry flour/45	11%	220	19	less than 0.5%
All-purpose & bread flour/55	11.5%	220	19	0.5 to 0.6%

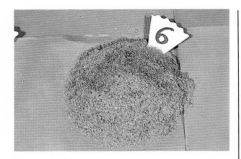

6. Cornmeal

Corn is a member of the family of grasses, Gramineae, and is widely cultivated throughout the world, principally in the United States, China, Brazil, Mexico, France, Argentina, Romania, and the Soviet Union. Cornmeal has a higher starch content than flour made from any other grain.

Because cornmeal has a relatively high fat content, it has a somewhat shorter shelf life than other flours. When used in bread making, it must be combined with other flours.

Cornstarch, which is derived from cornmeal, is often used in pastry making for thickening various creams and sauces.

7. Rye/Wheat Flour

Originally this flour was prepared by milling together grain that came from fields planted equally in rye and wheat. Today it is simply an equal mixture of wheat and rye flours.

8. Barley Flour

Barley, a cereal in the grass family, Gramineae, is widely cultivated, especially in China, the United States, France, and the Soviet Union. Barley flour is obtained by milling barley grains. Other barley products include malt, whiskey, beer, baby cereal, orgeat, and animal fodder.

9. Rice Flour

Rice, a cereal in the family of grasses, Gramineae, is cultivated primarily in Asia (95 percent of the current production). A small amount is cultivated in Italy, Spain, Portugal, France, Australia, South America, the Soviet Union, and the United States. Rice requires a warm climate and high humidity. It is extremely rich in starch but contains relatively little gluten.

Rice flour cannot be used for bread making unless it is combined with other flour with a higher gluten content. Rice flour is very fine and hence useful for dusting the pastry marble and pin when rolling out or shaping dough. Rice is also used for alcoholic beverages (such as sake and rice wine) and breakfast cereals.

10. Buckwheat Flour

Buckwheat is cultivated primarily in China, the Soviet Union, and the United States. A small amount is cultivated in Brittany, France. Unlike most cereals, buckwheat is not part of the grass family but is a member of the Polygonaceae family.

Buckwheat flour is prepared by milling the triangular seeds of the buckwheat plant. Because of its extremely low gluten content, buckwheat is rarely used in bread making and can never be used alone. However, it is much appreciated in crêpes, blinis, and Brittany-style cakes. Buckwheat is also used for grain alcohol and animal fodder.

11. Rye Flour

Rye is a cereal in the grass family (Gramineae). It is grown primarily in the United States, eastern Europe, and the Soviet Union. A small amount is also cultivated in France.

Rye flour is often used in bread making —only wheat flour is used more frequently. Rye flour has a very low gluten content (2 percent maximum), which is insufficient for bread making. Rye flour also contains an extremely viscous, starchy substance that becomes gluelike when combined with water. This substance interferes with the activation of the gluten in the dough and makes it difficult to handle.

In order to compensate for rye flour's low gluten content and viscosity, it is usually combined with a high-gluten wheat flour before being worked into dough. When using rye flour for bread making, it is also important to select one with a low ash content (low ash content is a sign of quality).

When fermenting rye bread dough, it is advisable to begin with a quantity of already fermented dough or to prepare a starter (levain). In this way, the fermentation is begun before the yeasts come in contact with the sticky rye bread dough.

Like wheat flour, rye flour is classified into several types based on ash content and extraction ratio, as shown below.

Rye is also used for grain alcohol and whiskey.

Type (American/French)	Ash Content (% Residue)
light rye/70	0.60 to 1.00% (lowest available)
medium–dark rye/ 85	0.75 to 1.25%
light pumpernickel/ 130	1.20 to 1.50% (grayish hue)
dark pumpernickel/170	above 1.50% (dark; almost whole rye)

12. Soy Flour

The soybean plant, a member of the legume family, Leguminosae, is a bushy annual that grows to a height of almost 1 meter (3 feet.). It is primarily cultivated in China, the United States, the Soviet Union, Brazil, and Argentina.

Soy flour is manufactured by milling soybeans. Soy flour contains very little starch but is extremely high in protein and quite high in natural fats, which makes it a nutritious and valuable food.

Soy flour is used in breads for the nutrition-minded consumer and for diabetics (because of its low starch content). Soybeans are also used for soybean oil, lecithin, soy sauce, and baby formula.

13. Bran

Bran is sometimes used in bread making. Because it contains little gluten, it must be combined with other flours before being worked into dough.

14. Wheat Germ

The germ of the wheat is extracted during milling and has an extremely high fat content. If flour is incorrectly or insufficiently milled, small flakes of wheat germ will remain in the flour and cause the bread to be greasy and heavy. For this reason, it is essential to select a good-quality flour that has been correctly and thoroughly milled.

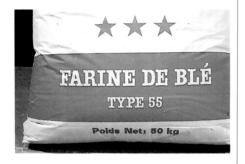

Yeast

Definition

Yeast is a monocellular microorganism which, under the right conditions, reproduces very rapidly. A single species of yeast, *Saccharomyces cerevisiae*, is used in bread making. It has either round or oval cells and converts sugar into alcohol and carbon dioxide. It is this ability that makes it so useful to the baker.

Industrial Manufacture of Yeast

Budding yeast cells require certain conditions to reproduce. A primary necessity, of course, is food and essential elements. These foods and elements are:

- sugars
- minerals
- nitrogen compounds
- oxygen

In industrial yeast manufacture, molasses, a by-product of sugar production, is used to supply the necessary sugar and nitrogen compounds.

It is possible to produce an unlimited quantity of yeast by starting with a single cell, which under the right conditions will produce infinitely. The reproduction of the yeast cells is usually begun under carefully controlled laboratory conditions before the cells are combined with molasses in large culture vats. It is imperative that the yeast cells be supplied with plenty of sugar (molasses) and oxygen while they are in the vats. Molasses, because it is a by-product of sugar production, is an excellent, low-cost source of food for the yeasts.

When the yeasts have reproduced to the desired quantity, they are skimmed off the surface of the molasses and carefully washed. The yeasts are then filtered to remove liquid before being compacted and wrapped in packets.

Yeast can also be manufactured from beer, as a by-product of brewing.

Function of Yeast in Bread Making

The primary function of yeast in baking is to generate carbon dioxide, which causes the dough to rise and give the bread a light texture. Yeast cells bring about the conversion of sugar into alcohol and carbon dioxide by secreting enzyme complexes, sometimes called zymase and cozymase, that catalyze the process.

The variety of yeast used in baking influences the flavor of the bread and the color of the final crust.

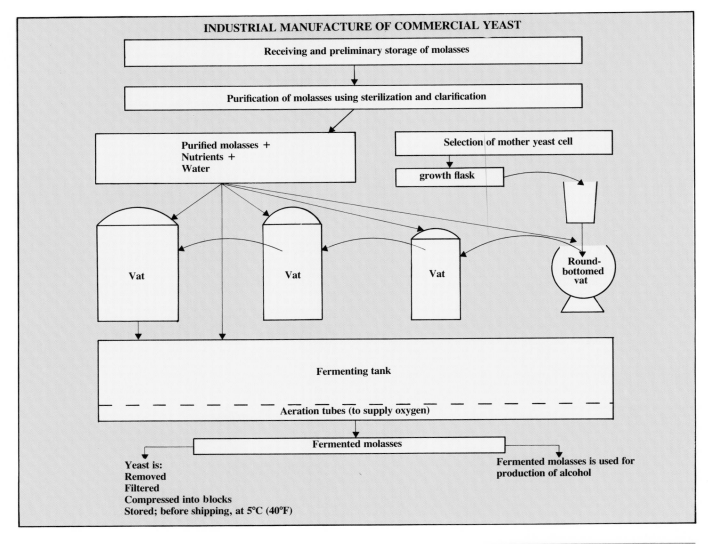

INDUSTRIAL MANUFACTURE OF COMMERCIAL YEAST

Receiving and preliminary storage of molasses

Purification of molasses using sterilization and clarification

Purified molasses +
Nutrients +
Water

Selection of mother yeast cell

growth flask

Vat

Vat

Vat

Round-bottomed vat

Fermenting tank

Aeration tubes (to supply oxygen)

Fermented molasses

Yeast is:
Removed
Filtered
Compressed into blocks
Stored; before shipping, at 5°C (40°F)

Fermented molasses is used for production of alcohol

Dried Yeast

As bread consumption increases in countries with tropical climates, the need for dried yeast has increased.

Because moist yeast is extremely perishable, dried yeast makes an excellent substitute in areas where storage conditions are hard to control. Dried yeast is prepared industrially using a sophisticated air-drying process.

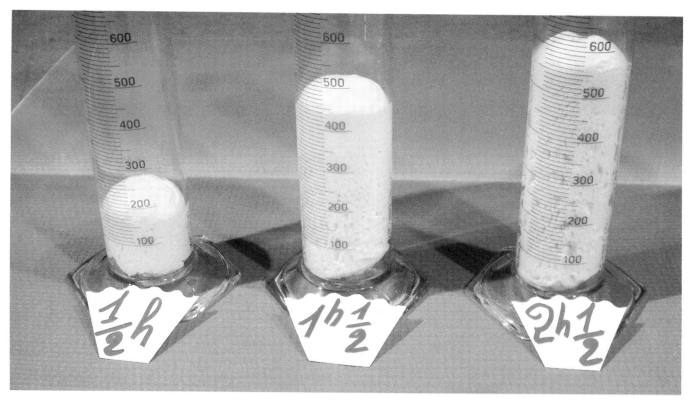

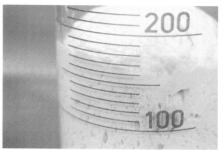

A Few Facts

Because dried yeast is more expensive than moist yeast, it is not often used in larger establishments in temperate climates. It is, however, recommended for use in hot climates.

1 gram (1/30 of an ounce) of yeast contains from 5 to 10 billion yeast cells. Active yeast cells have a life span of from 1 to 7 hours, depending on their environment and the age of the particular culture. The diameter of a yeast cell is several thousandths of a millimeter.

Dried yeast is usually available in powder, flake, or granular form. Dried yeast maintains 90 percent of its potency if stored under the following conditions:

1 year at	20°C (68°F)
6 months at	25°C (77°F)
3 months at	30°C (86°F)
2 months at	35°C (95°F)

How Bread Is Made

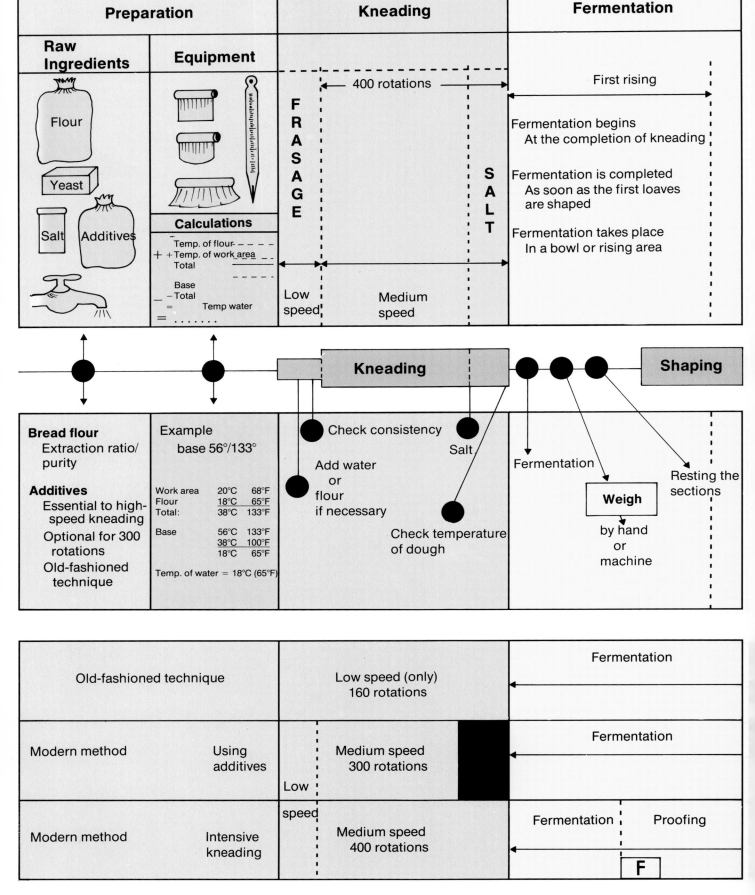

Preparation		Kneading	Fermentation
Raw Ingredients	**Equipment**		

Flour
Yeast
Salt   Additives

Calculations

- Temp. of flour - - - -
+ + Temp. of work area
    Total - - - -

    Base
- – Total
  = ... Temp water

FRASAGE

← 400 rotations →

SALT

Low speed | Medium speed

First rising

Fermentation begins
  At the completion of kneading

Fermentation is completed
  As soon as the first loaves
  are shaped

Fermentation takes place
  In a bowl or rising area

Kneading → Shaping

Bread flour
  Extraction ratio/
  purity

Additives
  Essential to high-
  speed kneading
  Optional for 300
  rotations
  Old-fashioned
  technique

Example
base 56°/133°

Work area	20°C	68°F
Flour	18°C	65°F
Total:	38°C	133°F
Base	56°C	133°F
	38°C	100°F
	18°C	65°F

Temp. of water = 18°C (65°F)

Check consistency

Add water
or
flour
if necessary

Salt

Check temperature
of dough

Fermentation

Weigh

by hand
or
machine

Resting the
sections

			Fermentation
Old-fashioned technique		Low speed (only) 160 rotations	
Modern method	Using additives	Low speed / Medium speed 300 rotations	Fermentation
Modern method	Intensive kneading	Low speed / Medium speed 400 rotations	Fermentation : Proofing F

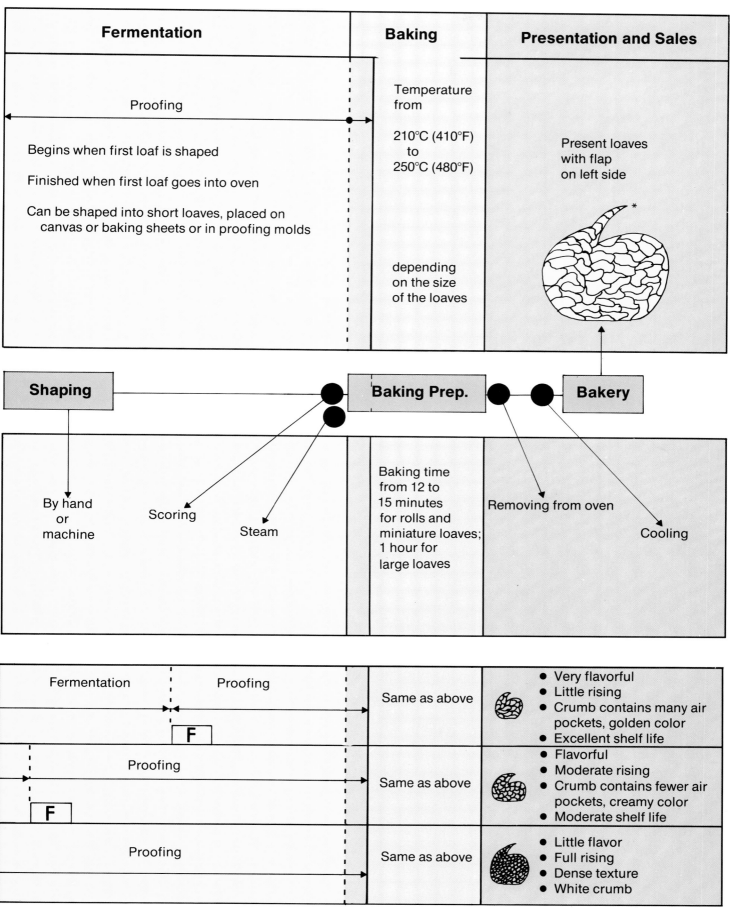

Fermentation	Baking	Presentation and Sales
Proofing Begins when first loaf is shaped Finished when first loaf goes into oven Can be shaped into short loaves, placed on canvas or baking sheets or in proofing molds	Temperature from 210°C (410°F) to 250°C (480°F) depending on the size of the loaves	Present loaves with flap on left side

Shaping		**Baking Prep.**		**Bakery**
By hand or machine	Scoring Steam	Baking time from 12 to 15 minutes for rolls and miniature loaves; 1 hour for large loaves	Removing from oven Cooling	

Fermentation / Proofing	Same as above		• Very flavorful • Little rising • Crumb contains many air pockets, golden color • Excellent shelf life
F			
Proofing	Same as above		• Flavorful • Moderate rising • Crumb contains fewer air pockets, creamy color • Moderate shelf life
F			
Proofing	Same as above		• Little flavor • Full rising • Dense texture • White crumb

Making bread by hand

Kneading by Hand

Preliminary Steps

Equipment
Drum sieve
Pastry cutter
Flour container
Measuring cups
Thermometer

Ingredients
Bread flour
Salt
Yeast
Water

Recipe

For approximately 8 kg (17 lb. 10 oz.) of dough

5 kg bread flour (11 lb.)
3 L water (3 qt. 6 oz.), which provides 60 to 63 percent hydration, depending on the flour
90 g salt (3 oz.)
100 g yeast (3.5 oz.)

Allow 2 hours for the first rising, punching down the dough after 1 hour, followed by a proofing for 1 hour after shaping.

Preparation

Sift the flour. Place the flour on the marble and make a well in the center. Place the salt and yeast in the well. Make sure that the yeast and salt are in different parts of the well and do not touch each other. Add the water.

Note

In order to regulate the temperature of the bread dough during kneading, the temperature of the water is adjusted as a function of the temperature of the flour and of the work area. To establish the desired water temperature, a base figure is provided in each recipe. The following example uses a base temperature of 70° for Celsius calculations and 222° for Fahrenheit calculations.

flour	21°C	70°F
work area	25°C	77°F
total	46°C	147°F
base	70°C	222°F
total, flour/work area	−46°C	−147°C
water temperature	24°C	75°F

Frasage

Kneading

Hand kneading is divided into five stages:

- Dividing
- Working
- Stretching
- Aerating
- Final sectioning and rolling

Dissolve the salt and yeast in the water in the center of the well. Gradually work the flour in from the sides of the well. Mix the flour and water until the ingredients are combined. Do not begin kneading at this stage. This initial stage, called the frasage, is now complete.

amount to be added depends on the type of flour but usually ranges from 1 to 5 percent of the amount of flour used.

Work the flour long enough to incorporate the additional water (usually about 5 minutes).

Dividing and Working the Dough

Divide the dough with both hands into sections (each section constituting about

one-fourth of the dough). As each section is pulled away from the dough, throw it rapidly back against the mass of dough remaining on the pastry marble.

Adding Additional Water

After the initial combining of ingredients (frasage), it may be necessary to add a small amount of extra water to the dough if it seems dry and crumbly. The

Continue this process of dividing and working the dough for about 5 minutes. This procedure is physically tiring, so the time needed depends on the baker. Usually about 5 minutes is required.

Stretching the Dough

This process consists of sliding the hands under the center of the dough, palms up, and lifting a part of the mass. With the dough held above the marble, pull the hands apart and stretch the dough. This stretching process helps activate the gluten, which in turn traps carbon dioxide and helps the bread to rise.

Stretch the dough for about 5 minutes.

Aeration

The purpose of this stage is to incorporate oxygen into the dough, which is important for fermentation. Keep this in mind while working the dough.

Grab the dough in the middle with both hands. Lift up the mass and flip it over and drop it onto the marble. As the dough falls back on the marble, bubbles of oxygen are trapped. As the process continues, the oxygen bubbles become progressively finer and more evenly distributed throughout the dough.

This procedure of incorporating air lightens the dough, makes it more malleable, and gives it a smoother texture.

Aerate the dough for approximately 5 minutes.

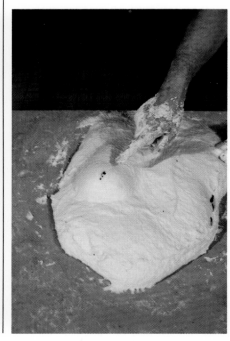

Final Sectioning and Rolling

This process consists of pulling the dough apart into sections of about 2 kilograms (4.5 pounds) and pressing and rolling each section to work the gluten for one last time.

Press and roll each section for approximately 2 to 3 minutes.

Preparation for First Rising

Put the dough into a plastic tub and cover with plastic wrap, with the wrap touching the dough, to prevent a skin from forming.

The total time needed for hand kneading should be from 15 to 20 minutes. The bread is now ready for its first rising, called the fermentation.

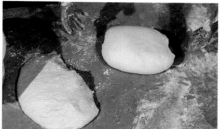

Hygrometry

Hygrometers

Principle

Hygrometers are instruments designed to measure humidity. Traditionally, their design is based on the fact that a hair or fiber contracts or stretches as the humidity changes.

Types of Hygrometers

Most hygrometers are designed with a hair or fiber attached to a needle. The needle then rotates against the surface of a dial as the fiber expands and contracts. The hygrometer is calibrated using standard atmospheric conditions. In this way, the humidity can be read at a glance.

Some hygrometers come equipped with an additional needle that can be rotated manually around the dial. This fixed needle serves as a reference point so it is easy to determine if the humidity is increasing or decreasing.

Recording hygrometers are also available. They can monitor humidity changes 24 hours a day.

It should be noted that the relative humidity is not directly proportional to the movement of the needle on the dial of a traditional hygrometer. The movement of the needle tends to change less as the humidity increases.

The photos shows a variety of hygrometers, including both traditional and modern types.

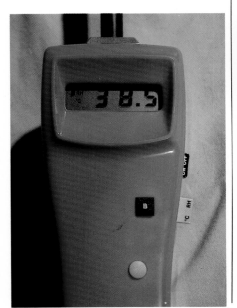

Hydration

Hydration (Water Content)

The consistency of bread dough is a function of its moisture content. Below is a rough chart relating consistency with percentage water content.

Consistency	Water Content
Stiff, dry	*58 to 60%*
Firm and tight	*60 to 62%*
Moderately firm	*62 to 63%*
Malleable	*63 to 64%*
Soft	*64 to 65%*
Soft and sticky	*65 to 67%*

The table below indicates the amount of flour, in kilograms/**ounces**, required to achieve the percentage of hydration specified based on the given quantity of liquid, in liters/**fluid ounces**.

Amount of Liquid		60%		61%		62%		63%		64%		65%		66%	
1	33.8	1.66	58.6	1.64	57.8	1.61	56.8	1.59	56.1	1.56	55.0	1.54	54.3	1.51	53.3
2	67.6	3.33	117.5	3.28	115.7	3.22	113.6	3.17	111.8	3.12	110.1	3.07	108.3	3.03	106.9
3	101.4	5.00	176.4	4.92	173.5	4.84	170.7	4.76	167.9	4.68	165.1	4.61	162.6	4.54	160.1
4	135.3	6.66	234.9	6.56	231.4	6.45	227.5	6.40	225.7	6.25	220.5	6.15	216.9	6.07	214.1
5	169.1	8.33	293.8	8.19	288.9	8.06	284.3	7.94	280.1	7.81	275.5	7.69	271.2	7.57	267.0
6	202.9	10.00	352.7	9.84	347.1	9.67	341.1	9.52	335.8	9.37	330.5	9.23	325.6	9.09	320.6
7	236.7	11.67	411.6	11.47	404.6	11.29	398.2	11.11	391.9	10.94	385.9	10.77	379.9	10.61	374.2
8	270.5	13.33	470.2	13.11	462.4	12.90	455.0	12.70	448.0	12.50	440.9	12.31	434.2	12.12	427.5
9	304.3	15.00	529.1	14.75	520.3	14.52	512.2	14.28	503.7	14.06	495.9	13.85	488.5	13.64	481.1
10	338.1	16.67	588.0	16.39	578.1	16.13	569.0	15.87	559.8	15.62	551.0	15.38	542.5	15.15	534.4
15	507.2	25.00	881.8	24.59	867.4	24.19	853.3	23.81	839.9	23.44	826.8	23.08	814.1	22.72	801.4
20	676.3	33.33	1,175.6	32.79	1,156.6	32.25	1,137.6	31.74	1,119.6	31.25	1,102.3	30.77	1,085.4	30.30	1,068.8
25	845.4	41.67	1,469.8	40.98	1,445.5	40.32	1,422.2	39.68	1,399.6	39.06	1,377.8	38.46	1,356.6	37.88	1,336.1
30	1,014.4	50.00	1,763.7	49.18	1,734.7	48.39	1,706.9	47.62	1,679.7	46.87	1,653.2	46.15	1,627.8	45.45	1,603.2
35	1,183.5	58.33	2,057.5	57.38	2,024.0	56.45	1,991.2	55.55	1,959.4	54.69	1,929.1	53.85	1,889.5	53.03	1,870.5

Machine kneading

Important

The steps used in machine kneading are divided into three stages:

1. Calculation of temperatures and preparation of the raw ingredients.

2. Preliminary kneading (frasage), which requires careful control of temperatures and the consistency of the dough. At this stage, the mixer is run at slow speed.

3. Final kneading, using the mixer at medium speed.

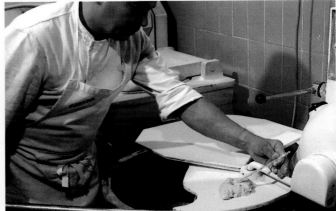

Determining the Kneading Time Required

Necessary information:

- The number of kneadings required for a specific type of dough (*kneading* refers to a single working of the entire mass of dough):

    Intensive kneading: 400 kneadings at medium speed

    Medium kneading time: 300 kneadings at medium speed

    Ordinary kneading time: 160 kneadings at slow speed

- The amount of dough worked by the dough hook in each rotation (in general, from one-quarter to one-third of the dough)
- The rotation speed of the mixer (in rpm). Most professional machines have the following speeds:

    40 rpm at slow speed

    80 rpm at medium speed

    110 rpm (on some models) at medium speed

Kneading Times Using Medium Speed

(with dough hook attachment)

Required Kneadings	Amount of Dough Kneaded	Mixer Rotation at Medium Speed (rpm)	Kneading Time	
			Calculations	Time
Intensive kneading 400	¼	80 rpm	$\dfrac{400 \div \frac{1}{4}}{80}$	20 min.
Medium kneading 300	⅓	110 rpm	$\dfrac{300 \div \frac{1}{3}}{110}$	8 min.
Ordinary kneading 160	¼	40 rpm (slow speed)	$\dfrac{160 \div \frac{1}{4}}{40}$	16 min.

The time required for kneading is then calculated using the following formula:

$$\text{Time required} = \frac{\text{number of kneadings} \div \text{amount of dough worked}}{\text{mixer rotation speed (rpm)}}$$

Preparation of Raw Ingredients

a. Water

b. Additional ingredients

c. Flour

d. Yeast

Kneading Stages

Slow speed:

1. Preliminary kneading (frasage)
2. Checking consistency

Medium Speed:

Required kneading time (see table above)

Salt is generally added to the dough 5 minutes before the end of kneading.

At the End of Kneading:

When the kneading is complete, check the temperature of the dough.

Increase in Temperature of Dough during Kneading at Medium Speed

Kneading machine (80 rpm/medium speed)

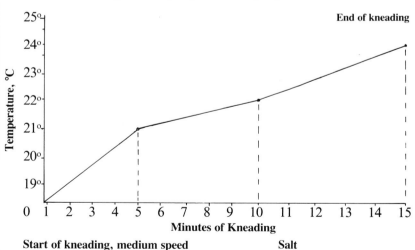

Graph starts with dough after preliminary kneading (frasage) at 19°C (66°F)

During the first 10 minutes of kneading, the temperature of the dough increases by 3°C (5.5°F). Once salt has been added, the rate increases to about 2°C (3.5°F) every five minutes.

Note

To adjust the temperature of the finished dough, it is necessary to anticipate the temperature of the dough at the end of the preliminary kneading. This may require some adjustment of the base temperature. For example, in order to have a dough with a final temperature of 1°C (1.8°F) more than the example given here, the base temperature should be increased by 3. For example:

Base 54: for a temperature at the end of kneading of 24°C (75°F).

Base 57: for a temperature at the end of kneading of 25°C (77°F).

Fermentation

Alcoholic Fermentation in Baking

Fermentation refers to the transformation of certain organic compounds into simpler related compounds. In bread making, fermentation is performed by living yeast.

In bread making, fermentation refers specifically to the conversion of sugars into alcohol and carbon dioxide through enzymatic action.

Fermentation Process

During fermentation, sugars are converted into alcohol and carbon dioxide in two stages:

First fermentation

(lasts approximately 3 hours)

Second fermentation

(amylase dependent)

(see chart at right)

First Fermentation *(duration: 3 hours)*

Yeast enzymes	Sugar already present	Production CO$_2$ + alcohol
Sucrase	*converts* **sucrose**	
	— — — *into* — —	
Zymase/ cozymase	*converts* **glucose and fructose into**	CO$_2$ + alcohol

Second Fermentation *(of starch-derived sugars)*

	Sugars formed by starch breakdown	
Maltase	*converts* **maltose**	
	— — *into* — —	
Zymase/ cozymase	*converts* **glucose into**	CO$_2$ + alcohol

Sugar Involved in Fermentation

The first fermentation depends on sugars that are already present in flour (from 1 to 2 percent). These sugars are composed mostly of sucrose (table sugar) and glucose.

The second fermentation depends on the action of the enzyme amylase on the flour. Amylase converts starch contained in the flour into maltose, a compound sugar made up of two molecules of glucose. The maltose is in turn converted into glucose through the action of another enzyme, maltase. Once this enzymatic process is completed, enzyme complexes in the yeast, sometimes referred to as zymase and cozymase, catalyze the breakdown of glucose into carbon dioxide and alcohol.

Retention Power

Retention power refers to the ability of a particular dough to entrap carbon dioxide. It is largely a function of the gluten content of the flour, which contributes an elastic quality to the dough.

Tolerance

The tolerance of a dough is its ability to withstand problems during fermentation (such as sudden changes in temperature) without damaging the quality of the finished bread. Dough with high retention power and fermenting power (high enzyme content) usually has a higher tolerance.

External Factors Influencing Fermentation

Two external factors affect fermentation:

- the humidity of the rising area
- the temperature of the rising area

First Rising/Fermentation (Pointage)

The first rising, or fermentation, is the period during which the dough is allowed to rise before it is shaped into loaves. The time required for the first rising depends on several factors:
- the amount and quality of the yeast used
- work methods
- the temperature of the dough at the completion of kneading
- the temperature and humidity of the work area

Proofing/Final Rising (Apprêt)

The final rising, called *proofing,* takes place between the shaping of the dough into loaves and the baking of the bread, when the heat of the oven kills the yeast cells and finishes the fermentation process. The time required for proofing depends on several factors:
- the amount of yeast used in the dough
- the time allowed for the fermentation
- the method of fermentation
- the temperature and humidity of the rising area

Factors That Reduce the Time Needed for Fermentation

- quicker kneading of the dough—20 to 25 minutes on high speed

- too high a temperature in the rising area—higher than 26°C (79°F)

- insufficient water added to the dough, so it is too firm and stiff

- use of a starter to initiate the fermentation (sourdough starter, mixed starter, or sponge starter)

- excessive yeast added at the beginning of fermentation

- use of certain additives that accelerate fermentation

Factors That Increase the Time Needed for the Fermentation

- slow kneading of the dough, with the mixer set on slow speed

- kneading of the dough on medium speed for a maximum of 15 minutes

- too low a dough temperature after kneading; the temperature of the dough should not drop below 22°C (77°F)

- the addition of too much water during the preliminary kneading, making the dough too wet

- use of dough that is too loose and lacks the necessary elasticity for rising

- use of too little yeast

- failure to use additives that accelerate fermentation

- failure to use a starter to initiate fermentation

Yeast starters

History

The discovery of natural yeast starters is usually attributed to the Egyptians, who probably made the discovery by accident. A piece of soured bread dough was simply added to a new batch. The first leavened bread was no doubt much appreciated compared to the heavy unleavened breads that were the only types available before its discovery.

dough). Natural starters often have a more complex sourdough quality than dough made with commercial yeast. This is because of the accumulation of lactic- and acetic-acid-forming bacteria, which work symbiotically with the active yeast cells. Until the discovery and systematic production of baker's yeast in the seventeenth century, a natural starter was the only method available to the baker to initiate fermentation of bread dough.

Working with a Natural Starter

When using a natural or sourdough starter, the baker uses a piece of fermented dough called the "chef." In English it is sometimes referred to as the "mother." In order to reactivate and convert the mother into a workable quantity of dough, it is refreshed through a series of kneadings with additional water and flour. Enough water, flour, and salt are added to the mother to double its weight. This process is repeated until the desired quantity of dough is obtained. This cycle is then repeated indefinitely.

A modern baker rarely prepares dough using a natural yeast starter but will more likely use one of the methods described below. In most bakeries it is far simpler to inoculate bread dough using a previously made batch than to initiate fermentation each time. When fermentation is begun from scratch, commercial yeast is used, rather than the natural wild yeasts contained in the flour.

Natural Yeast Starter (Levain Naturel)

Natural yeast starter, also known as sourdough starter, is a dough made of a simple combination of flour and water that has begun to sour without the addition of manufactured yeast: the bread dough is inoculated with natural "wild" yeasts simply by being left in a warm, humid place. Fermentation is caused by these wild yeasts.

The natural yeast starter is kept active by periodically adding fresh flour and water (this is referred to as *refreshing* the

Yeast Starter (Levain Levure)

After the discovery of yeast in the seventeenth century, bakers began to prepare starters with manufactured yeast. A starter is simply a small batch of dough that contains no salt and is allowed to ferment; it is then added to the rest of the dough.

In general, a yeast-inoculated, starter is prepared with one-third of the total amount of water needed for the entire batch of dough. The amount of yeast used is based on the total amount of water used for the entire batch, about $\frac{1}{100}$, or 10 grams per liter (½ ounce per 50 fluid ounces). The rising time of the starter depends on the amount of the yeast, the humidity, and the temperature of the bakery or pastry kitchen, but normally it takes from 3 to 5 hours. After the starter has risen, the salt is added to the remaining water, the remaining flour is added, and the mixture is kneaded in the usual way. The fermentation of the finished dough is a function of the starter, the humidity, and the temperature of the dough and the kitchen. Normally this fermentation takes about an hour.

Combined Method: Using Mixed Starter and Refreshed Dough (Levain Mixte sur Rafraîchi)

Today bakers rarely use only a yeast starter. Usually they begin with a piece of finished bread dough (made with commercial yeast) taken from the previous batch. The finished bread dough should be fermented for at least 3 or 4 hours (or 16 to 18 hours in a cool place) before being worked into a new batch. To the piece of finished bread dough, the baker then adds more yeast, salt, water, and flour. It is generally recommended to use 100 grams of fermented dough per liter of water used in the new batch (3.5 ounces of dough per 34 fluid ounces of water). This combined method (already fermented dough plus fresh ingredients) ensures consistency in the flavor and texture of the finished product.

Sponge Starter (Poolisch)

The use of a sponge starter was popular in Viennese pastry making before it was introduced in France near the beginning of the eighteenth century.

A sponge starter can be prepared several hours before the kneading of the final dough. It is composed of equal quantities of flour and water (about one-third the total of each) taken from the total recipe. All the yeast from the recipe is also added. No salt is added to sponge starters; salt is added when the starter is combined with the rest of the dough.

The amount of yeast varies according to how much time the starter is given to rise. For example:

- For a 2-hour fermentation, use 35 grams of yeast per liter of water (1.2 ounces yeast per 34 fluid ounces water)
- For a 4-hour fermentation, use 18 grams yeast per liter of water (0.7 ounces yeast per 34 fluid ounces water)
- For an 8-hour fermentation, use 9 grams yeast per liter of water (0.2 ounces yeast per 34 fluid ounces water)

Using a semiliquid starter contributes to the flavor and holding power of the finished products and also allows greater flexibility in working with fermented dough.

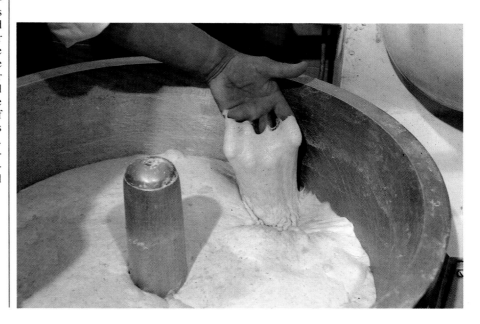

Weighing bread dough

Method

After the bread dough has risen for the first time (pointage), it must be weighed into sections that correspond to the final loaf sizes.

When sectioning and weighing the bread dough, use as little flour as possible. Use a metal pastry cutter. Cut the dough as quickly as possible to keep it from forming a crust on the surface. Form each of the sections of dough into evenly rounded mounds. Carefully weigh each of the mounds (flat side facing the scale). When removing each of the mounds from the scale, round their surface slightly before placing them back on the marble or work surface. Cover the individual mounds of dough with plastic wrap to prevent the formation of a crust.

Shaping long loaves

Method

Shaping bread dough (sometimes called *rounding*) into loaves requires careful attention at each stage. The bread's final appearance, so important to the customer, is directly affected by the care and skill used during shaping. Correct shaping will also contribute to the texture and lightness of the finished bread.

Initial Shaping

Use as little flour as possible.

Take a section of dough and roll it toward you on the work surface. Press on the dough with the palms of the hands to eliminate the carbon dioxide that has accumulated during fermentation. Be sure to press on the dough so that it keeps a slightly rounded form.

Take one side of the dough and fold it over the center. Press gently on the loaf to attach the fold. Fold the other side of the dough in the same way so the two folds attach along the center of the loaf. Press gently once more to eliminate carbon dioxide.

Rolling the Dough

Fold the dough once again over itself by rolling it toward you. Using both hands, roll the dough in the other direction (away from you) while pressing gently.

With the fold running down the middle, gently press on the loaf to help seal it.

Final Folding

Make a well along the center of the dough by pressing firmly with the two thumbs. Fold the bread over this well by rolling it over the work surface or marble.

Final Shaping

Using both hands, roll the loaves to the desired length. They can then be shaped as desired.

Shaping round loaves

Forming a Round Loaf

After the bread dough is sectioned and weighed, place the sections on the work surface. Press them with the palms of the hands to force out the carbon dioxide that has accumulated. Keep the smooth, rounded surfaces of the loaves facing upward, and gently push the sides on the bottom toward the loaf's center. Make sure the loaves are lightly dusted with flour as they are worked.

As the loaves begin to take shape, rotate them with the palms of the hands, just as if rotating a turned-over bowl. Continue turning the loaves until they are smooth, even, and the right size.

When the round loaves are formed, they should always be kept flat side down on the work surface. Occasionally, before the final shaping, bakers will gently roll the weighed dough into round loaves to help make the dough somewhat more dense and firm. The loaves are then shaped a second time.

More frequently, round loaves are prepared directly for baking. Remember that it is particularly important that the small seam formed on the bottom surface of the loaf be as small and as close to the center as possible. The loaf should be perfectly even and have no tears or breaks in the surface.

Scoring

The slices and markings on the surface of a loaf of bread are so decorative and individual that they can be thought of as the baker's signature. However, these incisions on the bread's surface are more than just decorative; they help the bread rise and develop into the desired shape during baking.

It is best to score the bread using an extremely sharp blade, which must be kept perfectly clean at all times. Many professionals use razor blades for this purpose, but remember that it is necessary to fashion some kind of handle to make the blade easy and safe to manipulate. An artist's razor knife can also be used.

When cutting into a loaf's surface, stand back somewhat from the work surface. This makes it easier to cut even, parallel lines.

Cutting a Loaf: Three Slices

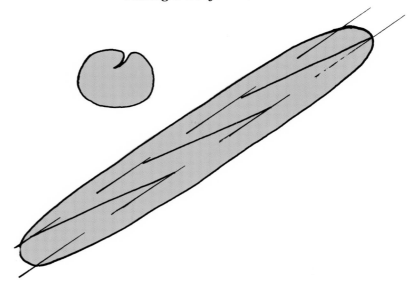

The number of cuts made on a loaf's surface depends on the baker's style and the traditions of the particular bread-making region.

When scoring a baguette diagonally, hold the blade almost flat against the surface of the dough: a 20- to 30-degree angle is optimal. The blade should cut sideways into the dough.

Make sure that the incisions are clean and crisp. Keep them evenly spaced. Each incision should be the same length and depth.

Each cut should be made about 2 centimeters (1 inch) up from the cut before it. Keep the incisions from 1 to 2 centimeters (½ to 1 inch) apart.

When scoring, it is helpful to visualize the cuts dividing the length of the loaf into equal sections. For example, if four cuts are being made, each should have a length of one-quarter of the total length of the loaf.

Sausage Cut

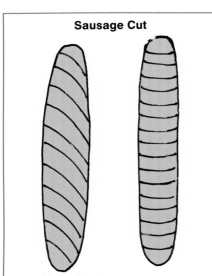

Hold the blade vertically, directly above the loaf to be cut. Do not cut too deeply. The cuts should be evenly spaced and parallel. Make cuts along the entire length of the loaf.

Polka Cut

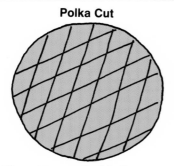

The cutting method is the same as for the sausage cut, but here the cuts are made in a crisscross pattern, forming a decorative diamond pattern on the surface of the bread.

Examples of Incorrect Bread Cuts

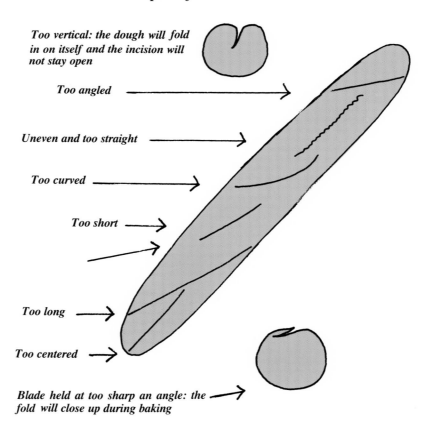

Too vertical: the dough will fold in on itself and the incision will not stay open

Too angled

Uneven and too straight

Too curved

Too short

Too long

Too centered

Blade held at too sharp an angle: the fold will close up during baking

Baking

Ovens and Temperature Control

The final baking of bread is the culmination of the baker's art. It is imperative that the baker be familiar with his or her particular oven and be able to control its temperature closely.

Because every oven is different, it is difficult to establish rules that work in every situation. Below are some general guidelines that will be especially helpful to the beginning baker. Baker's ovens are categorized into three major types: old-style, deck ovens, and convection.

Old-style Ovens

Old-style ovens are usually made of brick, have a single heating chamber, and are heated with either wood or coal. Controlling the temperature of these ovens requires considerable experience.

Over the centuries bakers have invented a variety of techniques for judging the temperatures of these old-style ovens. One technique is to place a small amount of flour either directly on the floor of the oven or on a small baking sheet placed in a particular spot in the oven and watch how quickly it browns. A piece of parchment paper is sometimes placed in the oven and the temperature judged by the length of time needed for it to brown. Seasoned professionals often judge the oven temperature simply by feeling the temperature at the mouth of the oven with their hand. When bakers use any of these techniques, they rarely talk about specific oven temperatures but in general terms, such as a low, medium, or hot oven.

Multiple-chamber Deck Ovens

These ovens have gradually replaced the old-style brick ovens. They have several baking chambers and are heated indirectly with moving air or steam. The temperature of these ovens is controlled with a thermostat and monitored by a thermometer visible from the outside. Because thermometers on commercial ovens measure the temperature in different parts of the oven or near the heat source itself, it is impossible to give precise temperatures for baking. For this reason, the terms *low oven, medium oven*, and *hot oven* are used in this book.

Most types of multiple-chamber deck ovens have a mechanism for introducing steam into each baking chamber. These ovens enable the baker to bake several types of bread at the same time.

Convection Baking Ovens

These ovens are designed so that it is not necessary to bake bread on the oven floor in the traditional way. For this reason, these ovens can accommodate larger quantities of bread, making them particularly useful in industrial bakeries. Because it is rare for a bakery to prepare large quantities of the breads discussed in this book, this type of large industrial oven is not often needed.

Other Types of Ovens

The three types of ovens discussed above are professional bakery ovens and are not always available in a restaurant or home kitchen. A number of the specialties discussed in the following chapters can be baked in restaurant pastry ovens or even in regular ovens.

The biggest problem in using an oven that is not specifically designed for bread baking is that it has no mechanism for producing steam, which is so important in baking bread. One method of producing steam for a small batch of bread is to place hot, wet baking sheets in the oven several minutes before putting in the bread. This creates a moist enough environment for the majority of special and decorative breads.

Another method of maintaining a moist environment during baking is to place a small container of boiling water on the oven floor when putting the bread into the oven. Never splash the inside of the oven directly with water. This can damage the heat coils of an electric oven and can even cause the oven floor to crack (floors of professional ovens are usually made of a ceramic material).

Generally, for bread baking, the terms *low oven, medium oven, hot oven,* and

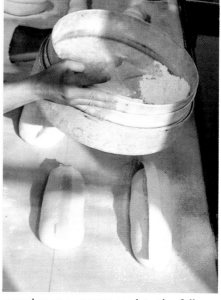

very hot oven correspond to the following temperatures:

Very hot	240°–250°C (465°–480°F)
Hot	230°–240°C (445°–465°F)
Medium	220°–230°C (430°–445°F)
Low	200°–210°C (390°–410°F)

Note

Some ovens (primarily in Europe) are regulated on a 1-to-10 thermostat system, which corresponds to specific temperatures. To determine the Celsius temperature of a given thermostat setting, multiply the setting by 30. For example: thermostat setting $7 = 7 \times 30 = 210°C$. To convert Celsius degress to Fahrenheit, multiply by 1.8 and add 32. For example: $210°C = 210 \times 1.8 = 378$; $+ 32 = 410°F$.

Placing Bread in the Oven

Precautions

The preparation of the ovens and the arrangement of the loaves during baking are important factors in successful baking and require careful attention.

Preliminary Steps

- The oven temperature should be carefully regulated. The oven should always be preheated to the correct temperature before baking.
- Make sure that an oven is available.
- The exact time for the beginning of baking should be carefully calculated. Remember that bread can be allowed to rise too long before baking.
- In some cases it is necessary to introduce stream into the oven just before or during baking.
- Always make sure that the floor of the oven (the baking surface) is clean. Brush off any flour or burnt crumbs left from the previous baking. The oven floor can also be quickly wiped with a moist cloth.

Placing the Loaves in the Oven

In most bakeries, the bread loaves are placed directly on the oven floor. Traditionally the loaves of dough are arranged in the oven with a flat wooden pallet called a peel. It requires a certain amount of skill to place the dough in the correct position quickly without misshaping it. Some ovens have an oven-loading conveyor (see photo above). This makes it far easier to arrange the breads before they are slid into the oven.

Arranging the Loaves

The loaves need to be carefully arranged either directly in the oven or on the conveyor in front of the oven. It is important that they be evenly spaced and that enough distance is left between each loaf. This helps the heat circulate freely and evenly.

Once the loaves have been placed on the baker's peel or on the conveyor, several last steps must be taken before the loaves are placed in the oven:

- Lightly dust the surfaces of the loaves with a small amount of flour. This can be done either by hand or with a drum sieve.
- It may be necessary to moisten certain parts of the loaves with a pastry brush to bring them into better relief.
- For certain special breads, last-minute incisions should be made with scissors.

- Some bread loaves are decorated with strips of dough at this point. Such decoration requires experience and sound technique.

Baking

Baking changes raw dough into finished bread. Several transformations take place as the heat penetrates the dough:
- The fermentation is completed. As the heat penetrates the bread, active yeast cells are killed.
- The starch contained in the dough coagulates.
- Sugars contained in the dough are caramelized. This action is responsible for the coloring of the bread's crust.

Baking Time

The types and sizes of bread are so varied that it is impossible to specify exact baking times. Several factors do, however, influence the time required to bake a loaf of bread, and awareness of them will help in making individual determinations:

- Size of the loaves: the larger the loaf, the more time will be required for baking. Larger loaves should be baked at a lower temperature than smaller loaves.
- Humidity of the work area: moisture in the air slightly lengthens baking times.
- Type of flour used: not only do recipes use different types of flour, but flours vary from country to country and region to region. The type of flour used will affect the baking time.

- Shape of the loaves: round loaves require longer baking than baguette or elongated shapes.

Verifying Doneness

Determining when loaves are finished baking requires considerable experience. A number of techniques can be used to judge when the bread is done:

- length of time in the oven
- appearance
- texture and feel
- sound

Length of time in the oven: This gives an approximate idea of whether the bread is done.

Appearance: The color of the bread gives some idea of how the bread is baking, but use this method carefully: breads can be perfectly browned but not cooked through if the oven is too hot or overcooked and not brown enough if the oven is not hot enough.

Texture: The bread should feel firm to the touch without seeming hard.

Sound: When the loaves are properly cooked, they should sound slightly hollow when tapped on the underside.

Taking the Loaves from the Oven

This is a straightforward, easy process provided the breads have been properly prepared and baked. It is important, however, to remember that all the loaves in a particular batch may not be finished at the same time.

Before removing the loaves from the oven, make sure that baskets or racks are available and ready for use. The finished loaves should never be stacked before they have cooled, or they can be crushed.

Cooling the Loaves

As the hot loaves cool, water vapor contained in the middle of the loaf gradually works its way out toward the crust, causing the crust to soften slightly, which is normal.

Loss of Moisture

Even after the loaves of bread have completely cooled, they still contain moisture, which gradually evaporates into the surrounding environment. This gradual drying is natural but should not be excessive. The tendency of bread to lose or retain moisture depends on several factors. Bread dough that has been fermented very slowly and has hence undergone considerable enzymatic breakdown of starch into sugar tends to remain moist for longer periods. Using flour with a higher fat content will also help finished breads retain moisture.

The Importance of Steam

Water vapor plays an essential role in bread making and is usually introduced into the oven just before and/or during baking.

Depending on the type of oven used, steam can be produced by evaporation of hot water or injected directly into the oven during baking if the oven has a steam-generating attachment.

Because so many factors influence the amount of steam needed during baking, it can be extremely difficult to estimate the quantity to be generated. The size of the oven, the amount of bread being baked, and the degree to which the oven is hermetically sealed are all factors that influence the amount of steam required. It is essential that the baker be familiar with his or her oven in order to balance these factors and correctly judge the amount of steam to use.

The moisture content of the air surrounding the bread during baking has a direct effect on the texture and appearance of the finished loaves. Moisture helps soften the bread's crust during baking and allows the carbon dioxide trapped in the dough to expand fully and cause the bread to rise. If the crust were to dry out too quickly, it would prematurely hold the bread in shape and prevent the dough from rising, resulting in a dense, heavy loaf.

Moisture also helps caramelize the natural sugars contained in the bread. This caramelization is responsible for the appealing brown crust of correctly baked bread. If the air surrounding the bread during baking contains insufficient moisture, the bread itself is liable to dry out. This results in a lighter loaf that will become stale more quickly.

Signs of Insufficient Steam
- thick, hard crust
- diminished rising
- grayish appearance
- incisions on loaf's surface pull and tear

Signs of Too Much Steam
- the incisions on the bread's surface stick together
- the incisions on the bread's surface fail to open and do not allow the loaf to expand
- the bread, once out of the oven, collapses or shrinks because of excessive moisture content

Not all types of bread require the same amount of steam during baking. Certain types, such as pain de mie (pullman bread), can be baked with no steam at all. Regardless of the amount of steam used, make sure that the steam is not under pressure just before putting the loaves in the oven. Otherwise the steam will condense into water droplets as soon as the oven door is opened, which could interfere with correct baking.

The amount of steam that should be introduced during baking is also a function of the number of loaves being baked. The greater the number of loaves being baked, the less steam required, because the loaves will contribute their own moisture.

Rediscovering traditional breads

For millennia, bread has been such an important food source that it has taken on almost mythical qualities. Such expressions as "earning one's daily bread," "man does not live by bread alone," and "know on which side your bread is buttered" all attest to the importance of bread in Western culture.

What Is Bread?

Eaten practically every day by most Europeans and Americans, bread's composition is striking in its simplicity—flour, water, and sometimes yeast and salt are usually its only ingredients.

It is amazing that such an array of different-looking and different-tasting breads can be made with so few raw ingredients. This diversity is partially due to the fact that bread dough is a living thing. Anyone who has hand-kneaded bread dough remembers the comforting satisfaction of working with such a vital substance. Bread's diversity also stems from the traditional baker's care and interaction with the ingredients and the finished product. No machine will ever master the subtlety of traditional bread making, nor will one ever replace the baker who can feel, smell, touch, and experience the satisfaction of this almost magical process.

What Is a Baker?

The baking profession holds many paradoxes—it is both simple and complex, banal to some but at the same time timeless and fundamental. It is the baker who transforms grain, one of man's most fundamental foods, into digestible and edible food. This is no small responsibility, and it is the baker's duty to do it well.

Professional bakers must be adaptable to the needs of their clientele and should have mastered the necessary skills of baking. Understanding the fundamentals of bread making is essential. These include:

- correct kneading technique and all necessary calculations
- fermentation and its control
- the baking process, with the almost innumerable factors that influence its outcome

Successful bakers will always question and seek to perfect their knowledge and technique. They will take satisfaction in work well done while always seeking to improve.

Traditional baking is finally being appreciated by a public that has grown tired of mass-produced flavorless bread and is eager to eat something produced by an artisan rather than a machine.

Chapter 2
Special breads

~~~~~~~~~~~~~~~~~~~~

Presented here are some of the more uncommon, fanciful, and decorative breads that have been made over the centuries

There is much to admire in the work of those who developed the breads of the fourteenth century. The talemeliers or boulengiers (old French titles for bakers) offered a surprising assortment of breads despite the difficulties of the profession during this period in history. Some of the early breads presented below are discussed in Ambroise Morel's Histoire illustrée de la boulangerie en France *(Illustrated History of French Baking).*

Standard bread: made with flour, water, salt, and yeast. In France, the best of this type of bread was found in Chailly and Gonesse.

Hot baked bread (pain échaude): baked in hot water.

Ground bread: made with wheat flour beaten between two blades for a long period.

Soft bread: made with the purest flour available and lightly baked.

Sheep's bread: made with flour kneaded with butter and sprinkled with wheat grains.

Christmas butter bread: made with wheat flour, eggs, and milk

Spice bread: made with rye flour kneaded with spices and honey.

Chapitre (chapter) bread, also called "choîne" or "choesne": a superior white bread offered to a member belonging to the chapter in the Notre-Dame cathedral.

Shell bread: with a blistered crust. A statute written in March 1659 made this the standard bread for the middle class.

Ornamental bread: brown bread made with equal parts rye and wheat flour

Corbeil bread: appears in statutes dated from 1367. It was an ordinary bread easily found in the Maubert market in Paris.

Gentilly bread: made with butter.

Melun bread: highly valued during the fourteenth century

Saint-Brice bread: found in the statutes from 1367.

Tranchoirs or tailloir bread: "tranche" is the French word for "slice," which describes this round, brown bread that was cut into thick slices and used as a plate, or trencher. The bread was used in this fashion until the eighteenth century.

Rousset bread: made with a mixture of wheat and rye flours and served with soups.

Table breads: usually found on the tables of the rich, very hearty and filling. Traditionally women removed the crust before dunking the bread in broth.

Common bread: an inferior bread, reserved for servants.

Barley, oat, millet bread: made with a combination of flours based on what was available, producing a substandard bread that was usually eaten only during times of famine.

The various types and textures of breads

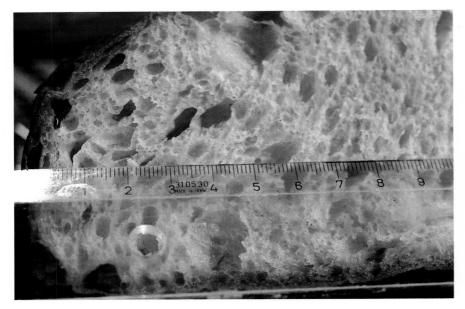

How does white bread differ from country-style breads?

Why do the same types of breads vary amongst themselves?

White Bread

White bread is kneaded more quickly and over a longer period of time than most breads. This extra kneading yields a high oxygen level that whitens the dough. The crumb is firm with an even texture and contains numerous small air pockets. The technique for making this bread requires a short, direct fermentation and therefore a large quantity of yeast. Only a very small amount of starch is transformed into simple sugars.

Results:
- a large bread
- white crumb
- blandness, lack of character
- short shelf life

Preferred Method

Although more difficult to make than white bread, there is a method that is a good compromise between the way breads were made using old-style techniques and those described for today's white bread above.

The bread is not kneaded for as long as today's white bread so the dough is less tough and elastic. Because the bread is given a longer rising period, less yeast is required.

More starch is transformed into simple sugars because of improved fermentation, which results in a bread that stays fresher longer.

Results:
- an attractive crust
- a medium-size crumb with an appealing light straw color
- irregular air pockets
- a rich flavor and smell

Old-style Bread-making Techniques

Old-fashioned techniques are considerably less practical than the two preceding methods and are more difficult and time consuming.

This method requires a fairly short but slow kneading to develop a softer dough. Usually a starter based on fermented dough or a sponge starter is used.

The fermentation or first rising is considerably longer than the two preceding methods and demands careful attention.

The least possible amount of yeast is used in this method. The dough must be worked under particular conditions and temperatures. The natural fermentation of the flour activates the fermentation of the sugars, caused by the formation of

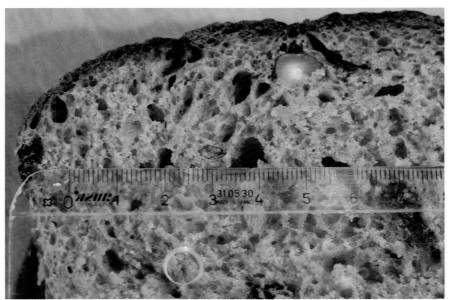

alcohol and carbon gases. The resulting bread has a fuller flavor with a pleasant, rich, slightly acid taste and smell. It is also easier to digest.

Results:
- rustic appearance
- fairly good rising
- large, straw-color crumb
- very irregular air pockets
- slightly acid taste
- good storage

Country-style Bread

Country-style breads are the first breads examined in detail in this volume. The techniques for making country-style bread are very particular and differ from those for ordinary breads.

It is important to understand the difference in technique and result between a true country-style bread and the poor imitations given the same name. A real country-style bread closely resembles the classic breads that were dusted with flour just before baking. A true country-style bread is considered the king of all breads.

The process for making country breads is incompatible with modern machinery. It is up to the baker to bring back this bread and the techniques needed to produce it. At the same time, the baker needs to educate the consumer to appreciate the difference between an exceptional bread and an ordinary bread.

This is why the first recipes here are devoted to country-style breads.

Making Country-style Breads

A good country-style bread begins with the starter or a sponge, the making of which demands a long and exacting procedure that requires training and mastery.

Making a starter, its fermentation and refreshing, a slow first rising, shaping by hand, and long proofing are the factors that influence the resulting bread. The flavor of the bread is determined by enzymes breaking down a large quantity of starch and transforming it into sugar; the sugar in turn naturally ferments, releasing alcohol and carbon dioxide. This chemical reaction gives country-style bread its characteristic slightly acid taste reminiscent of classic breads.

Results:
- thick golden brown crust
- blond-colored supple crumb
- large, irregular air pockets
- appealing, slightly acid scent and strong, rich flavor
- good storage
- easy digestibility

The great variety of special breads

Guide to the special breads

Traditional Breads

(by category)

Country-style Breads

1. based on a mixed starter 48
2. based on a natural starter (sourdough) 52
3. based on a yeast starter 54
4. based on a sponge starter 56

Rye Breads

1. based on a fermented dough starter 60
2. based on a mixed starter 63
3. based on a sponge starter 64
4. light rye bread 65
5. with raisins, and small rolls 66

Whole-wheat Breads

1. based on a mixed starter 69
2. based on a sponge starter 72
3. based on a fermented dough starter 74

Specialty Breads

Apricots, apples, prunes 75	Italian 94
Seaweed 78	Corn 95
Brown 79	Méteil 96
Brié 80	Pullman...................... 98
Four-grain 81	Normandy cider 100
Chorizo 82	Hazelnut, walnut, almond 102
Cumin 83	Onion/bacon 104
Carrot 84	Olive 106
Herb 85	Barley 107
Carrot-herb 86	Provençale fougasse 108
Dried fruit.................. 88	Sesame seed 109
Wheat-germ 89	Soy......................... 111
High-gluten................. 91	Bran 112
Low-gluten 90	Surprise 113
Gruau 92	Viennese 114
Oyster 93	

Country-style breads

Introduction

The country-style bread, sometimes referred to as peasant bread, has an attractive, rustic appearance usually made by dusting flour over a shaped loaf before baking, giving the bread its characteristic two-toned crust. Country-style bread is formed in various shapes and sizes. It is possible to imagine the flavor of a beautifully made country-style bread before actually biting into it.

It is very important that this type of bread be made with a starter to allow for a long, slow fermentation.

The fermented starter can be made using one of four methods:

● mixed starter
● natural, or sourdough, starter

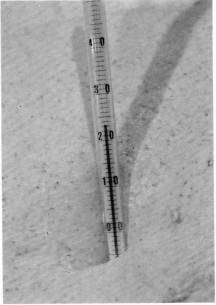

● yeast starter
● sponge (semiliquid starter)

Whichever type of fermentation method is chosen, country-style breads are usually based on pure wheat bread flour, without additives, or a mixture of bread flour and a brown flour (light whole-wheat) with a high extraction rate (80 to 85 percent). Sometimes a very small quantity of rye flour is added. (The extraction rate is the amount of flour obtained from the wheat kernel by milling.)

Bread making is exacting work and requires attentiveness, a good general knowledge, and practical experience with working with flour and its fermentation, which determines the final baked bread's flavor, appearance, scent, and storage. Country-style bread can be found throughout France and is becoming a staple in many parts of America and various European countries as well.

Storage

Country-style bread has a good shelf life, due to the starter or sponge.

Shapes

Each region in France shapes bread differently. Country-style bread can be shaped into short loaves, couronnes (crowns), rounds with crusty tops called tabatières (pouches), and countless other shapes, each expressive of its native region. Large round loaves can range from 700 grams (25 ounces) to 1.5 kilograms (53 ounces) each.

Appearance

The color of the crust should be more or less golden brown, depending on how it was scored and how much flour was dusted on the loaf before baking. The crust should always be thick and crisp.

Depending on the type of starter used, the bread should be well rounded and not be allowed to rise excessively. The crumb, or interior, of a loaf of baked bread should be creamy or lightly golden in color with a slightly airy, supple texture, without being overly crumbly.

Uses

A good country-style bread goes well with all foods prepared with or without sauces, including meat, game, chicken, fish, charcuterie (cold and smoked meats), and all cheeses.

Country-style bread is also delicious cut in slices, toasted, and buttered for breakfast.

Country-style bread with a mixed starter

Introduction

Using a mixed starter is one of the most popular methods for bread making today, as the resulting dough is very supple and easy to work with. A mixed starter is based on a section of dough reserved from a previously made kneaded batch of dough. This piece of dough is set aside to ferment for as long as necessary, usually a minimum of 3 to 4 hours. After fermenting, it is added to a batch of bread dough before kneading.

This method of fermentation makes for an excellent-tasting, appealing bread with a good shelf life.

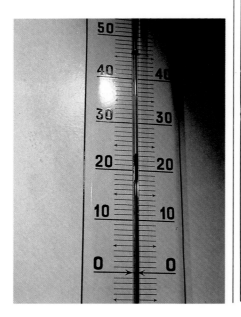

Preparing a Mixed Starter

Ready the starter by taking 500 grams (17.5 ounces) of bread dough from a batch of dough with a fermentation (first rising) of 3 to 4 hours minimum.

Prepare, weigh, and measure the raw ingredients for the mixed starter.

Calculate the temperature needed for the water used for the refreshing dough, which is determined by the temperature of the work space (see the chart below).

Allow time for the mixed starter to ferment, which is also determined by the temperature of the work space.

Temperatures and fermentation times at room temperature based on the temperature of the work space			
T° work space	T° flour	T° water	Fermentation time
22°C (71.5°F)	22°C (71.5°F)	14°C (57°F)	17 hours
23°C (73.5°F)	23°C (73.5°F)	12°C (53.5°F)	16 hours
24°C (75°F)	24°C (75°F)	8°C (46.5°F)	15 hours
25°C (77°F)	25°C (77°F)	6°F (43°F)	14 hours
26°C (79°F)	26°C (79°F)	4°C (39°F)	13 hours

A mixed starter can be fermented in a regulated proof box at 20°C (68°F) for 18 to 20 hours.

For a more even fermentation, adding 80 grams (3 ounces) of malt is recommended.

Recipe for Mixed Starter with Fermented and Refreshing Doughs

500 g fermented dough (17.5 oz.)
5 L water (169 fl. oz.)
150 g salt (5 oz.)
8.3 kg bread flour (18¼ lb.)
Hydration: 60 percent water based on flour measure

Kneading the Mixed Starter

Knead the above ingredients together, either in an electric mixer on low speed for 4 minutes, or in a kneading machine on low speed for 5 minutes.

Immediately transfer the mixed starter to one or several plastic containers (if using a kneading machine, it can be kept there).

Cover the starter to prevent a crust from forming during fermentation at room temperature. Refer to the chart on this page for duration of fermentation.

Preparing the Final Dough

Measure and verify the temperature of the water. If using a kneading machine, use a base temperature of 65° to 68°C (213° to 219°F); if using an electric mixer, use a base temperature of 62° to 64°C (208° to 211°F).

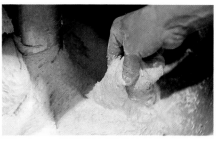

211°F). Knead the dough for 8 minutes on low speed or 6 minutes on low speed plus 2 minutes on medium speed.

The texture of the dough after kneading should be supple. The dough should be between 23° and 24°C (73.5° and 75°F).

Prepare, weigh, and measure the raw ingredients for the final dough.

Recipe for the Finished Dough

For approximately 27.5 kg (60.6 lb.) of dough, making 55 loaves of 500 g (17.5 oz.) of dough

5 L water (169 fl. oz.) at calculated temperature
150 g salt (5 oz.)
8.3 kg bread flour (18 lb. 5 oz.)
or
7 kg bread flour (15.5 lb.) plus 1,300 g rye flour (46 oz.)

Final Kneading of the Dough

Place the mixed starter in the kneading machine or electric mixer.

Add the remaining ingredients and knead together. If using the kneading machine, the base temperature should be between 65° and 68°C (213° and 219°F). Knead the dough for 10 minutes on low speed or 7 minutes on low speed plus 3 minutes on medium speed. If using an electric mixer, the base temperature should be between 62° and 64°C (208° and

Cover the dough with a sheet of plastic wrap.

Note the time the kneading was stopped.

Fermenting

The dough should be set in an area free of drafts.

The duration of fermentation is based on:
● the temperature of the work area
● the temperature of the dough
● the humidity of the work area

For example, allow 2 hours and 40 minutes for the dough to rise if the room temperature is between 22° and 24°C (71.5° and 75°F), the temperature of the dough is 23°C (73.5°F), and the humidity is approximately 75 percent. Rising times will vary; when the dough has doubled in volume, it has risen sufficiently.

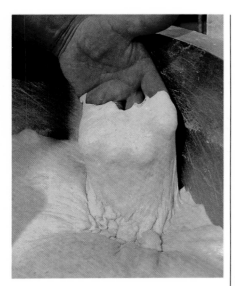

If the dough was made in a kneading machine, give the dough one rotation. If not using a kneading machine, turn it over by hand 1 hour after the fermentation has started. Turning the dough is often referred to as "punching down the dough." The dough is not really punched, but pulled up at the sides, gently pressed with the fingertips, and turned over to release some of the carbon dioxide that occur during fermentation and to give the dough a more uniform temperature.

An hour after punching down the dough, punch it down a second time. At this point the dough will have developed body.

Allow the dough to rest for 40 minutes more.

Note

The rising time is shortened if the temperature of the work area is over 25°C (77°F).

On the other hand, lengthen the rising time if the temperature of the work area is under 21°C (70°F).

Weighing

Using a minimum of flour, section and weigh the desired amount of dough needed for each loaf (this step is also referred to as scaling). Usually between 500 g and 1 kg (17.5 to 35 oz.) of dough is used per loaf. Shape the dough without overworking it after weighing each sec-

tion. Cover the weighed sections of dough, and allow each to rest for 5 to 10 minutes. Keep the sections in the order in which they were weighed so the first pieces will be covered first and timed accordingly.

Country-style Bread with a Mixed Starter

1st DAY			
Preparation	**5** min	**0** min	• Ready the fermented dough, which has fermented for a minimum of 3 to 4 hours.
Prepare the mixed starter	**5** min		
Knead the mixed starter	**13** min	**17** hr (approx.)	• Fermentation time ranges from approximately 13 to 17 hours after the mixed starter is made.
2nd DAY			
Preparing the final dough	**15** min	**0** min	• Prepare, weigh, and measure the raw ingredients. • Calculate the temperatures needed.
Kneading	**10** min	**25** min	• Verify the temperature, 23° to 24°C (73.5° to 75°F).
Fermenting	**2** hr **40**	**3** hr **05**	• Punch the dough down twice at 1-hour intervals during fermentation.
Weighing	**10** min	**3** hr **15**	• Use the least amount of flour possible to weigh and section the dough.
Resting	**10** min	**3** hr **25**	• Allow the dough to rest in a draft-free area
Shaping	**10** min	**3** hr **35**	• Using the least flour possible for dusting, shape the loaves as desired.
Proofing	**1** hr **30**	**5** hr **05**	• Proof the loaves until they have doubled in volume.
Preparing for baking	**5** min	**5** hr **10**	• Check the oven temperature and steam, which should not be excessive.
Baking	**35** to **40** min	**5** hr **50**	• Remove or turn off the source of steam 5 minutes before removing the loaves from the oven.
Cooling	**5** min	**5** hr **55**	• Immediately place the loaves in a wicker basket or on a cooling rack.

Shaping

When shaping the dough, dust with the least flour possible. Pull it somewhat firmly while shaping; the degree of pulling depends on the elasticity of the dough. Be careful not to tear the dough during this step. The dough can be

formed into any number of shapes, such as rounds, crowns, short baguettes, and large rounds. Place the shaped loaves, seam side down, on a cloth lightly dusted with either wheat or rye flour. Cover the loaves with plastic wrap.

Proofing

Place the shaped loaves in a warm area free from drafts. Proofing can take from 1 to 1½ hours, depending on the temperature of the dough, the duration of fermentation, and the temperature and humidity of the work area.

The loaves have been successfully proofed when they have doubled in size and are supple. When pressed with the fingertips, the dough should bounce back quickly.

Preparing for Baking

Verify the temperature of the oven, which should be between 220° and 230°C (425° and 450°F), depending on the size of the loaves. Smaller loaves must be baked at higher temperatures so that the crust can form before the inside is overcooked.

Carefully score the breads with decorative incisions, then place them in the oven. There should not be an excess of steam, which could cause the crust to become too thin.

Baking

Turn off or remove the steam (depending on how it is generated) 5 minutes before removing the bread from the oven.

For a loaf weighing 500 grams (17.5 ounces), allow 30 to 35 minutes of baking. For a loaf weighing 800 grams to 1 kilogram (28 to 35 ounces), allow 40 to 50 minutes.

Verifying Doneness

It takes considerable experience to determine when a bread is finished baking.

Some of the signs to look for are a deep golden brown crust, resistance of the crust when pressed, and a hollow sound when the heel of the bread is tapped with the fingertips.

Cooling

After removing the loaves from the oven, immediately place them on end in a wicker basket or on a cooling rack.

Placing them on end rather than on top of each other will prevent the top layer of loaves from crushing the loaves beneath. If using a cooling rack, cool the breads in single layers.

Storage

The baked, cooled breads can be wrapped in towels and kept in a slightly humid area at room temperature.

Country-style bread with a natural starter

Definition

A natural starter, often called a sourdough starter, is dough that has fermented from a simple mixture of flour and water, without the addition of a commercial (baker's) yeast. Although this type of starter works well in theory, in practice this type of naturally cultivated starter is difficult to control, as many environmental factors can alter its fermentation.

The manufacture of yeast has largely replaced natural starters made with yeast starters. Although a natural starter is difficult to control for commercial baking, if properly prepared, it can produce a wonderful-tasting bread with a crispy crust, delicious dough, and excellent shelf life.

About 9 kilograms (20 pounds) of final bread dough will yield approximately 18 loaves of bread weighing 500 grams (17.5 ounces) each.

Procedure

Preparing the Mother Starter
Prepare, weigh, and measure the raw ingredients:
400 g bread flour (14 oz.)
100 g whole-wheat flour (3.5 oz.)
300 ml water (10 fl. oz.), room temperature

Kneading the Mother Starter
In an electric mixer, knead the ingredients together at low speed for 5 minutes. Transfer the mixture to a plastic container and cover with a sheet of plastic wrap (touching the dough) to prevent a crust from forming.

Fermenting the Mother Starter
The mother starter should double in volume, which will take approximately 24 hours at room temperature or in a proof box or other area no warmer than 22° to 23°C (71.5° to 73.5°F). Be sure it is kept in an area free from drafts.

Recipe for First Refreshing Dough
500 g bread flour (17.5 oz.)
10 g salt (2 tsp.)
300 ml water (10 fl. oz.), room temperature

Kneading the First Refreshing Dough
Place the mother starter in the bowl of an electric mixer and add the ingredients for the first refreshing dough. Knead at low speed for 5 minutes. Transfer the mixture to a plastic container and cover with a clean sheet of plastic wrap. Leave the container and its contents at room temperature in an area free from drafts.

Fermenting the Refreshed Starter
Depending on the temperature of the

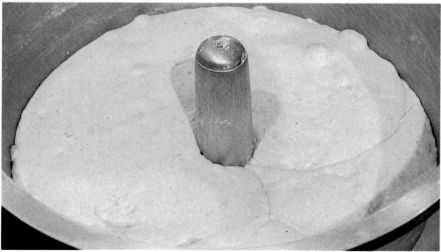

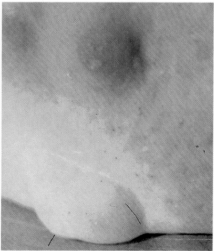

work area, which should be no warmer than 22°C (71.5°F), allow 20 to 24 hours for the dough to ferment. The starter should at least double in size, at most triple in size.

Recipe for Second Refreshing Dough

1 kg bread flour (35 oz.)
20 g salt (1½ Tbsp.)
600 ml water (20 fl. oz.), room temperature

Kneading the Second Refreshing Dough

Place the fermented, refreshed starter in the bowl of an electric mixer and add the ingredients for the second refreshing dough. Knead together for 5 minutes on low speed.

Transfer the now twice-refreshed starter to a plastic container, cover with clean plastic wrap, and allow to ferment in an area free from drafts.

Fermenting the Twice-Refreshed Starter

The starter is now referred to as "levain de tout point," or ripe starter. At 20°C (68°F) maximum, allow between 20 and 24 hours for the dough to ferment. The dough should again at least double in volume and no more than triple. It is important the dough does not fall just before kneading.

Recipe for the Final Bread Dough

2,300 ml water (78 fl. oz.)
90 g salt (3 oz.)
3 kg bread flour (6.5 lbs.) plus 500 g whole-wheat flour (17.5 oz.) *or* 3.5 kg bread flour (7 lbs. 11 oz.)

Kneading the Final Dough

Place the ripe starter in either a kneading machine or in the bowl of an electric mixer. Add the remaining ingredients and mix as follows:

Electric mixer: 8 minutes on low speed or 6 minutes on low speed and 2 minutes on medium speed. Use a base temperature of 62° to 68°C (208° to 219°F) to calculate the temperature of the water.

Kneading machine: 10 minutes on low speed or 7 minutes on low speed and 3 minutes on medium speed. Use a base temperature of 65° to 68°C (213° to 219°F) to calculate the temperature of the water.

The dough should feel supple after kneading. Check the temperature of the dough: it should be no more than 23° to 24°C (73.5° to 75°F). Cover the dough with a sheet of plastic wrap. Note the time the kneading was stopped.

Fermenting

The dough should be placed in an area at room temperature free from drafts to ferment for 2½ hours (see Fermentation of mixed starter, pages 49 to 50). One hour after kneading, turn the dough once if using the kneading machine; otherwise, punch the dough down by hand. One hour later repeat the procedure, and rest the dough for one hour more before sectioning and weighing.

Weighing and Rounding

Follow the procedure given for country-style bread based on a mixed starter (pages 50 to 51).

Proofing

Proof the dough for 1½ hours at room temperature. Punch down the dough two more times at 1-hour intervals.

Preparing for Baking, Baking, Verifying Doneness, Cooling, and Storing

Follow the procedures given for country-style bread based on a mixed starter (page 51).

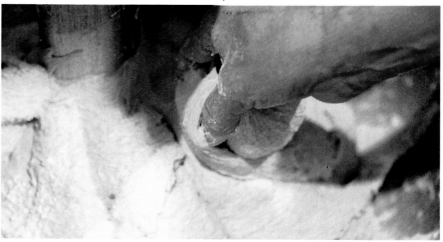

Country-style Bread with a Natural Starter

1st DAY			
Preparing the mother starter Prepare and knead the mother starter Ferment the mother starter		**10** min **24** hr	• Prepare, weigh, and measure the raw ingredients. • Place the mother starter in an area free of drafts until doubled in volume.
2nd DAY			
Preparing the first refreshing dough Prepare and knead the first refreshing dough Ferment the starter		**10** min **24** hr	• Knead the mother starter and refreshing dough on low speed. • Allow the starter to ferment in an area free of drafts.
3rd DAY			
Preparing the second refreshing dough Prepare and knead the second refreshing dough Ferment the twice-refreshed dough		**10** min **24** hr	• Knead the second refreshing dough and starter on low speed. • Allow the starter to ferment in an area free of drafts.
4th DAY			
Preparing and kneading the dough	**15** min	**0** min	• Prepare, weigh, and measure the raw ingredients. • Check the consistency and temperature of the dough.
Fermenting	**2** hr **30**	**2** hr **45**	• Place dough in an area free of drafts. • Punch down the dough twice at 1-hour intervals.
Weighing	**5** min	**2** hr **50**	• Section and weigh dough.
Resting	**10** min	**3** hr	• Cover the sections with plastic wrap.
Shaping	**10** min	**3** hr **10**	• Dust with as little flour as possible when shaping the dough.
Proofing	**1** hr **30**	**4** hr **40**	• The proofing time will be determined by the temperature of the work area, which should be free of drafts.
Preparing for baking	**5** min	**4** hr **45**	• Verify the temperature of the oven.
Baking	**35** to **40** min	**5** hr **25**	• Remove or turn off the steam 5 minutes before removing the bread.
Cooling	**5** min	**5** hr **30**	• Immediately place the bread in wicker baskets or on cooling racks.

Country-style bread with a yeast starter

Introduction

Breads based on yeast starters were first made after the discovery of cultured yeast during the middle of the seventeenth century.

Definition

The starter used for this method contains all the yeast that is required for the dough. This type of starter has a somewhat firm consistency. The fermentation of the starter is totally dependent on the quality of the yeast and the humidity and the temperature of the work area (refer to the fermentation chart on the opposite page).

The method of using a preliminary fermentation based on a yeast starter results in a somewhat more easily controlled bread dough, although it is important to use just the right amount of yeast and calibrate the required temperatures carefully. This method of bread making demands a good deal of professional experience because of the complexity of the fermentation.

Yield

About 27 kilograms (59.5 pounds) of dough will yield approximately 54 loaves weighing 500 grams (17.5 ounces) each.

Preparing the Yeast Starter

Prepare, weigh, and measure the raw ingredients for the yeast starter, listed below.

Calculate the temperature of the water to be used in the starter, which is determined by the temperature of the work area.

In a controlled fermentation area, such as a proof box, that is set at 20°C (68°F), allow between 18 and 20 hours for the fermentation of the yeast starter.

Recipe for the Yeast Starter

5 L water (169 fl. oz.)
8.3 kg bread flour (18 lb. 3 oz.)
150 g salt (5 oz.)
7 g yeast (¼ oz.), dissolved in a little water

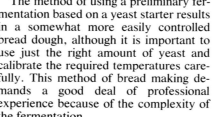

Kneading the Yeast Starter

Knead the ingredients either in an electric mixer on low speed for 4 minutes or in a kneading machine on low speed for 5 minutes.

Immediately transfer the starter into one or several plastic containers, or it can remain in the kneading machine, if available.

Cover the starter with plastic wrap to prevent a crust from forming during the fermentation period, which should take place at room temperature (refer to the chart on the opposite page).

Temperatures and fermentation times based on room temperature			
Temp. of work area	Temp. of flour	Temp. of water	Fermentation time of yeast starter
22°C (71.5°F)	22°C (71.5°F)	14°C (57°F)	17 hours
23°C (73.5°F)	23°C 73.5°F)	12°C (53.5°F)	16 hours
24°C (75°F)	24°C (75°F)	8°C (46.5°F)	15 hours
25°C (77°F)	25°C (77°F)	6°C (43°F)	14 hours
26°C (79°F)	26°C (79°F)	4°C (39°F)	13 hours

Prepare the Final Dough

Calculate the temperature of the water:

- for a kneading machine, use a base temperature of 65° to 68°C (213° to 219°F)
- for an electric mixer, use a base temperature of 62° to 64°C (208° to 211°F)

Prepare, weigh, and measure the raw ingredients.

Yield

About 27 kilograms (59 pounds 6.5 ounces) of dough will yield 54 loaves, 500 grams (17.5 ounces) each.

Recipe for the Final Dough

5 L water (169 fl. oz.)
150 g salt (5 oz.)
8.3 kg bread flour *or* 7.3 kg bread flour (16 lb. 1.5 oz.) and 1 kg rye flour (35 oz.)

Kneading

In the work bowl of the machine to be used, place the starter, and add the ingredients for the final dough. If using a kneading machine, knead on low speed for 10 minutes, or knead on low speed for 7 minutes and then on medium speed for 3 minutes. If using an electric mixer, knead on low speed for 8 minutes, or knead for 6 minutes on low speed and then for 2 minutes on medium speed.

After kneading, the dough should feel supple. The temperature of the dough should be no more than 23° to 24°C (73.5° to 75°F) after kneading.

Cover the dough with a sheet of plastic wrap to prevent a crust from forming.

Make note of the time the kneading was finished.

Ferment, Weighing, Shaping, Proofing, Preparing for Baking, Baking, Verifying Doneness, Cooling, and Storing

Follow the procedures given for using a mixed starter (pages 49 to 51).

Country-style Bread with a Yeast Starter

1st DAY

Preparation Prepare the yeast starter	5 min	0 min	• Prepare and knead the yeast starter.
Ferment the starter	5 min	17 hr (approx.)	• The fermentation time for the starter will be determined by the temperature of the work area, ranging from 13 to 17 hours.

2nd DAY

Preparing the dough	15 min	0 min	• Prepare, weigh, and measure the final raw ingredients. • Calculate the necessary temperatures.
Kneading	10 min	25 min	• Check the consistency and temperature of the dough, which should be 23° to 24° (73.5° to 75°F).
Proofing	2 hr 40	3 hr 05	• Punch down the dough twice at 1-hour intervals.
Weighing	10 min	3 hr 15	• Use as little flour as possible for dusting.
Resting	10 min	3 hr 25	• Rest the dough in an area free of drafts.
Shaping	10 min	3 hr 35	• Dust with a minimum of flour, and shape the dough as desired.
Proofing	1 hr 30	5 hr 05	• The loaves should double in volume.
Preparing for baking	5 min	5 hr 10	• Check the temperature of the oven. • Do not use too much steam.
Baking	35 to 40 min	5 hr 50	• Verify the doneness. Remove or stop the steam 5 minutes before removing the bread.
Cooling	5 min	5 hr 55	• Immediately place the baked bread in wicker baskets or on cooling racks.

Country-style bread with a sponge starter

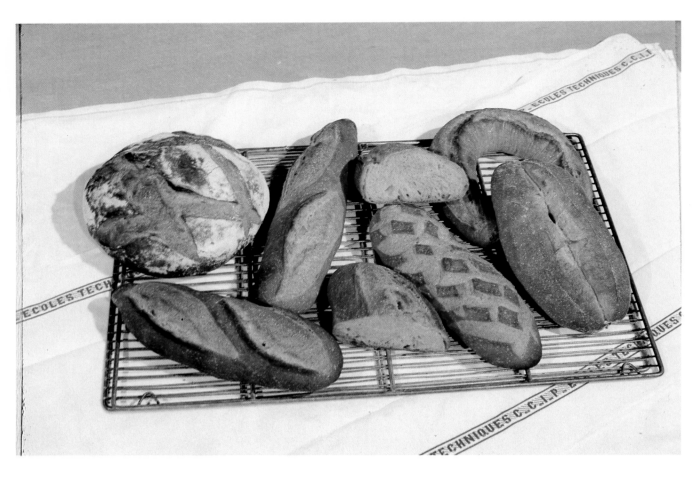

Introduction

A sponge, which is the most moist of all the starters, originated in Poland. This type of fermentation was brought to France by Viennese bakers during the reign of Queen Marie-Antoinette.

Definition

The sponge, a preliminary culture, is a semiliquid starter prepared several hours before the dough is kneaded. The sponge is composed of equal quantities of flour and water kneaded with a part or all of the yeast to be used in the recipe. No salt is added to the sponge. The fermentation of this starter depends on the quantity of the yeast and the humidity and temperature of the work area.

The sponge contributes to the flavor and shelf life of the bread. Although a sponge is more delicate than other starters, it requires the least fermentation and so requires the least time.

Yield

About 10 kilograms (22 pounds) of dough will yield 20 loaves of bread, 500 grams (17.5 ounces) each.

Recipe for the Sponge

2 kilograms bread flour (70.5 oz.)
2 L water (67.5 fl. oz.), approximately 15°C (59°F)
100 g yeast (3.5 oz.), dissolved in water

Preparing the Sponge

Prepare, weigh, and measure the raw ingredients. Thoroughly mix the ingredients together with a whisk.

Cover the mixture with a sheet of plastic wrap and let it ferment in an area free of drafts.

Allow approximately 2 hours for the sponge to ferment, depending on the temperature and humidity of the work area.

Recipe for the Final Dough

2 L water (67.5 fl. oz.)
120 g salt (4 oz.)
4 kg bread flour (8 lb. 13 oz.) *or* 3.5 kg bread flour (7 lb. 11 oz.) plus 500 g rye flour (17.5 oz.)

Preparing the Final Dough

Regulate the temperature of the water, establishing a base temperature. Using a kneading machine, the base temperature is 65° to 68°C (213° to 219°F). Using an electric mixer, the base temperature is 62° to 64°C (208° to 211°F)

Prepare, weigh, and measure the raw ingredients for the final dough.

Check the consistency of the dough at the beginning of kneading.

Check the temperature of the dough at the end of kneading.

Cover the dough with a sheet of plastic wrap.

Note the time the kneading was stopped.

Fermenting

Allow between 1 and 1½ hours for the dough to rise at room temperature, in an area free of drafts.

Weighing

Section and weigh out the amount of dough needed for each loaf. Round each section.

Resting

Allow the rounded sections of dough to rest, covered, for approximately 10 minutes.

Shaping

Shape the rounds of dough into the forms desired, being careful not to tear the dough while shaping it.

Proofing

Depending on the temperature and humidity of the work area, allow approximately 1 to 1½ hours to proof the dough in an area free of drafts.

Follow the same procedures given for country-style bread with a mixed starter (pages 50 to 51) to finish the bread.

Country-style Bread with a Sponge Starter			
Preparation	5 min	0 min	• Prepare and weigh the raw ingredients.
Kneading the sponge	5 min	10 min	• Thoroughly mix the ingredients with a whisk.
Fermenting the sponge	2 hr 30	2 hr 40	• The fermentation time depends on the temperature of the work area, which should be free of drafts.
Preparing and kneading the final dough	15 min	2 hr 55	• Prepare, weigh, and measure the raw ingredients. • Calculate the temperatures needed. • Check the consistency and the temperature of the dough.
Fermenting	1 hr	3 hr 55	• Fermentation time will vary according to the temperature of the work area.
Weighing	5 min	4 hr	• Dust with a minimum of flour
Resting	10 min	4 hr 10	• Rest the dough in an area free of drafts.
Shaping	10 min	4 hr 20	• Shape the dough as desired, dusting with a minimum of flour.
Proofing	1 hr 30	5 hr 50	• Duration of proofing will depend on the temperature and humidity of the work area.
Preparing for baking	5 min	5 hr 55	• Verify the temperature, and start filling the oven with steam.
Baking	35 to 40 min	6 hr 35	• Remove or turn off the source of steam 5 minutes before taking the bread out of the oven.
Cooling	5 min	6 hr 40	• Place the loaves in a wicker basket or on cooling racks.

Rye breads

Introduction

In France rye bread originated in mountainous regions such as the Alps, Pyrénées, Vosges, and central France, where it was the standard bread. It was also very popular in Brittany.

Today in France rye bread is less fre-quently eaten and more often reserved as an accompaniment to shellfish dishes such as oysters.

Rye bread is based on rye flour, with the addition of a maximum of 35 percent wheat flour.

Either a fermented dough or yeast starter is used, which makes the dough easier to handle. The procedure for mak-ing rye bread poses no particular difficul-ties.

Storage

Rye bread is usually not eaten just after baking, as it stays soft and fresh for a period of time and has a long shelf life.

Shapes

In France rye bread is shaped differently according to region. Outside cities, it is often shaped into large rounds or large flattened rounds weighing from 1.5 to 4 kilograms (3 to 9 pounds).

In Paris and other major French cities, it is more common to find smaller rounds or short baguettes ranging in weight from 300 to 500 grams (10.5 to 17.5 ounces). Small rye bread rolls are also popular.

Appearance

Rye bread has a smooth crust with a golden brown color if not dusted with flour just before baking.

The bread has a firm texture with small, regular air pockets and a supple crumb that adheres firmly to the crust.

Uses

Rye bread goes well with fish, shellfish, smoked or dry-cured ham, sauerkraut, white and black radishes, and strong cheeses from eastern France such as Munster. It is also popular to spread honey on toasted, buttered slices.

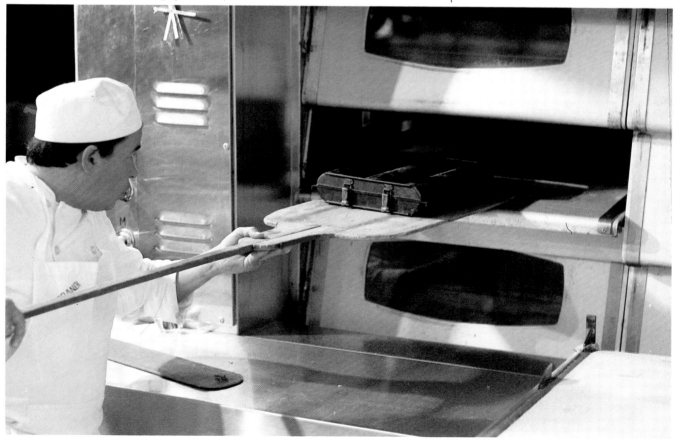

Rye bread with a fermented dough starter

Introduction

Rye flour is very low in gluten, with no more than 2 percent, and has a mediocre quality for bread making. It is therefore necessary to add wheat flour, such as bread flour, to it. In France, the proportions of rye and wheat flour are defined by law.

Rye bread made with a wheat-flour fermented dough starter will produce a less sticky dough, with a good texture and body. The resulting bread will have a good appearance, rises well, and has long shelf life and a superior taste.

Yield

About 5 kilograms (11 pounds) of dough yields 14 loaves, 350 grams (12.5 ounces) each.

If using a kneading machine, the base temperature should be between 65° and 68°C (213° and 219°F). The dough is kneaded for 10 minutes on low speed.

If using an electric mixer, the base temperature should be between 62° and 64°C (208° and 211°F). The dough is kneaded for 10 minutes on low speed.

Recipe

1.7 kg fermented dough starter (3 lb. 11 oz.), taken from a previous batch of dough fermented for a minimum of 3 to 4 hours
1.9 kg rye flour (4 lb. 1.5 oz.)
1.3 L water (44 fl. oz.)
45 g salt (1.5 oz.)
40 g gluten flour (1.5 oz.), optional
30 g yeast (1 oz.)

Kneading

In the bowl of a kneading machine or electric mixer, combine the yeast and the water; add the rye flour, salt, and gluten flour (if used). Knead the mixture for 5

minutes on low speed. Once the ingredients are blended, add small pieces of the fermented dough starter bit by bit, and knead the mixture for 5 more minutes on low speed.

Remove the dough from the machine.

The temperature of the dough should be no more than 23° to 24°C (73.5° to 75°F).

Cover the dough with a sheet of plastic wrap that touches the dough, to prevent a crust from forming.

Fermenting

Depending on the temperature and humidity of the work area, allow approximately 20 to 30 minutes for the dough to rise.

Weighing

Weigh out 350-gram (12.5-ounce) sections of dough. Round the sections, dusting with a minimum of flour. Cover the rounded sections with plastic wrap and allow them to rest for 15 minutes.

Shaping

Shape the sections by hand, dusting with rye flour to avoid the formation of white patches on the baked loaves.

Being careful not to tear the dough, shape the loaves into rounds or short loaves. Place the shaped loaves in floured long bread molds with the seam on top, or on canvas with the seam on the bottom.

If using canvas, the loaves can be dusted with flour sifted through a drum sieve. Score the loaves with sausage cuts (see page 36) after dusting with flour.

Proofing

Proof the loaves for approximately 1 hour, depending on the temperature and humidity of the work area. The loaves should nearly double in volume. Do not overproof the loaves, or they may tear and a crust may form.

Preparing for Baking

The oven should be between 220° and 230°C (425° and 450°F). Loaves in molds are decoratively scored at the last moment and are given a deep incision. Loaves proofed on canvas are gently placed on the floor of the oven, evenly and loosely spaced.

Baking

The ovens should be filled with plenty of steam before the loaves are placed inside.

Remove or turn off the source of steam 5 minutes before the breads are taken out of the oven. Depending on the size of the breads, allow approximately 30 to 35 minutes for baking.

Cooling

After removing the breads from the oven, place them in a wicker basket or on a cooling rack to allow them to cool quickly.

Storage

Wrapped in a clean towel, rye bread made with fermented dough will stay fresh for 2 to 3 days at room temperature.

To truly appreciate rye bread at its best, it is recommended to consume it no sooner than 2 hours after baking.

Rye Bread with a Fermented Dough Starter

Preparation	15 min	0 min	• Calculate the necessary temperatures. • Prepare, weigh, and measure the raw ingredients and the fermented dough (3 to 4 hours) taken from a previous batch.
Kneading	10 min	25 min	• Knead the dough on low speed.
Fermenting	30 min	55 min	• Allow the dough to rise, covered, in an area free of drafts.
Weighing	5 min	1 hr	• Weigh and round the dough, dusting with a minimum of flour.
Resting	15 min	1 hr 15	• Cover the sections of rounded dough with plastic wrap.
Shaping	10 min	1 hr 25	• Dust with a minimum of flour.
Proofing	1 hr	2 hr 25	• The proofing time depends on the temperature and humidity of the work area. • Be careful not to overproof the breads.
Preparing for baking	5 min	2 hr 30	• Verify the temperature of the oven. • Fill the oven with steam.
Baking	35 min	3 hr 05	• Remove or turn off the steam 5 minutes before taking the bread out of the oven. • Verify doneness.
Cooling	5 min	3 hr 10	• Immediately place the bread in wicker baskets or on cooling racks.

Rye bread with a mixed starter

Introduction

The mixed starter is an indirect method of fermentation based on a previously cultured dough. It is a reliable and relatively easy method for making rye bread.

Using a yeast starter results in an appetizing, slightly acidic bread that rises well, with a loose crumb and a nicely rounded loaf.

Yield

About 5 kilograms (11 pounds) of dough will yield 14 loaves, 350 grams (12.5 ounces) each.

Procedure for Preparing the Yeast Starter

See country-style bread with a mixed Starter (page 46).

Recipe

2 kg yeast starter (4 lb. 6.5 oz.)
1.9 kg rye flour (4 lb. 1.5 oz.)
40 g gluten flour (1.5 oz.), optional
1.1 L water (37 fl. oz.)
30 g yeast (1 oz.)
40 g salt (1.5 oz.)

Final Kneading of the Finished Dough

If using a kneading machine, use a base temperature of 65° to 68°C (213° to 219°F).

If using an electric mixer, use a base temperature of 62° to 64°C (208° to 211°F).

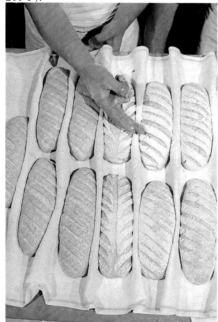

Dissolve the yeast with the water warmed to the appropriate temperature in the bowl of the kneading machine or the electric mixer. Add the rye flour, gluten flour, salt, and all of the starter.

If using an electric mixer, spattering can be prevented by starting the machine on low speed with the bowl in the down position. Then slowly raise the bowl and knead the dough for 10 minutes. If using a kneading machine, knead on low speed for 10 minutes as usual.

After kneading, the dough should have a firm texture. The dough should be between 23° and 24°C (73.5° and 75°F) after kneading.

Cover the dough with a sheet of plastic wrap touching the dough to prevent a crust from forming.

The remaining procedure is the same as for rye bread based on a fermented starter (page 62).

Rye Bread with a Mixed Starter

1st DAY			
Preparation Prepare the yeast starter Knead the yeast starter Ferment the starter	**5** min	**0** min **17** hr (approx.)	• The fermentation of the starter will vary depending on the temperature of the work area (between 13 and 17 hours).

2nd DAY			
Preparing the final dough	**15** min	**0** min	• Prepare, weigh, and measure the raw ingredients. • Calculate the necessary temperatures.
Kneading	**10** min	**25** min	• Check the consistency and temperature of the dough.
Fermenting	**30** min	**55** min	• Ferment the dough in an area free of drafts.
Weighing	**5** min	**1** hr	• Weigh and round the dough, using the least amount of flour possible.
Resting	**15** min	**1** hr **15**	• Cover the sections of dough with plastic wrap to prevent a crust from forming.
Shaping	**10** min	**1** hr **25**	• Dust with a minimum of flour when shaping.
Proofing	**1** hr	**2** hr **25**	• The proofing time is determined by the temperature and humidity of the work area. • Avoid overproofing the dough.
Preparing for baking	**5** min	**2** hr **30**	• Verify the temperature of the oven. • Fill the oven with steam.
Baking	**35** min	**3** hr **05**	• Remove or turn off steam toward the end of baking. • Verify doneness.
Cooling	**5** min	**3** hr **10**	• Immediately place the baked loaves in a wicker basket or on cooling racks.

Rye bread with a sponge starter

Introduction

Rye bread made with a sponge (semi-liquid starter) offers the same quality results as rye bread based on a mixed or fermented dough starter. Although making bread with a sponge saves time, the fermentation is more difficult to control and therefore requires expertise and professional experience.

Making the Sponge

Use a base temperature of 70°C (225°F), and blend the following ingredients in an electric mixer on low speed for 5 minutes:

1.1 kg rye flour (2 lb. 6.5 oz.)
50 g yeast (1.5 oz.), diluted in 1.1 L water (37 fl. oz.) at the calculated temperature

Cover the sponge with a sheet of plastic wrap and allow it to ferment for 1½ to 2 hours at 22° to 25°C (71.5° to 77°F). The sponge will nearly triple in volume. When the sponge begins to fall, it is ready to be kneaded.

Caution: If the sponge is overfermented, the dough will become too liquid when kneaded, making it unsuitable for bread making.

Yield

Approximately 5.35 kg (11 pounds 13 ounces) of dough will yield 15 loaves of bread, each 350 grams (12.5 ounces).

Recipe

sponge
800 g rye flour (28 oz.)
40 g gluten flour (1.5 oz.), optional
1.2 kg bread flour (1 lb. 9.5 oz.)
1.1 L water (37 fl. oz.)
10 g salt (2 tsp.)
70 g yeast (2.5 oz.)

Kneading the Final Dough

In the kneading machine, use a base temperature of 65° to 68°C (213° to 219°F) and knead for 10 minutes on low speed. In an electric mixer, use 62° to 64°C (208° to 211°F) as the base temperature and knead the dough for 10 minutes on low speed.

Combine the water and yeast. In a mixing bowl, pour the yeast/water mixture over the sponge. Add the rye flour, bread flour, gluten (if used), and salt. The dough should have a fairly supple consistency.

The dough should be no more than 23° to 24°C (73.5° to 75°F) after kneading. Cover the dough with a sheet of plastic wrap to prevent a crust from forming. The remaining procedure is the same as for the previous rye breads.

Rye Bread with a Sponge Starter			
Preparation	5 min	0 min	• Prepare and weigh the raw ingredients. • Thoroughly mix the ingredients with water.
Kneading the sponge Fermenting the sponge	5 min 1½ to 2 hr	2 hr 10	• The fermentation time will vary depending on the temperature of the work area, which should be free of drafts. • Cover the dough with plastic wrap.
Preparing and kneading the final dough	15 min	2 hr 25	• Prepare, weigh, and measure the raw ingredients. • Calculate the necessary temperatures. • Check the consistency and temperature of the dough.
Fermenting	30 min	2 hr 55	• The area for fermenting should be free of drafts.
Weighing	5 min	3 hr	• Dusting with a minimum of rye flour, weigh and round the sections of dough.
Resting	15 min	3 hr 15	• Cover the sections with plastic wrap.
Shaping	10 min	3 hr 25	• Shape the loaves, dusting with a minimum of flour.
Proofing	1 hr	4 hr 25	• The time for proofing depends on the temperature and humidity of the work area. • Avoid overproofing the dough.
Preparing for baking	5 min	4 hr 30	• Verify the temperature of the oven. • Fill the oven with steam.
Baking	35 min	5 hr 05	• Remove or turn off the steam toward the end • Verify doneness.
Cooling	5 min	5 hr 10	• Immediately place the baked loaves in wicker baskets or on cooling racks.

Light rye bread

Introduction

The rye bread presented in this section is based on a mixture of wheat and rye flours where the proportion of rye flour is no less than 10 percent.

The method for making this lighter rye bread based on a fermented dough starter is relatively simple and offers the same advantages as the other starters regarding appearance, taste, and shelf life.

The flavor of this type of rye bread varies depending on the percentage of rye flour used. As it has less rye flour than the rye breads previously discussed, this bread is easily distinguished by its lighter color, smoother crust, and light weight.

Yield

About 5 kilograms (11 pounds) of dough will yield 14 loaves, 350 grams (12.5 ounces) each.

Recipe

1 kg fermented dough (2 lb. 3 oz.), taken from a previous batch of dough and fermented for at least 3 to 4 hours
1.6 kg bread flour (3.5 lb.)
900 g rye flour (31.5 oz.)
1.5 L water (51.5 fl. oz.)
30 g yeast (1 oz.)
50 g salt (1.5 oz.)

Kneading

The base temperatures given for this recipe are for a work area with a temperature of 22° to 25°C (71.5° to 77°F).

With a kneading machine, use a base temperature of 65° to 68°C (213° to 219°F). Knead the dough for 10 minutes on low speed.

With an electric mixer, use a base temperature of 62° to 64°C (208° to 211°F). Knead the dough for 10 minutes on low speed or for 5 minutes on low speed and 3 minutes on medium speed.

Mix the yeast and the water in a mixing bowl or kneading machine. Add the flours, salt, and fermented dough in small pieces and knead as directed.

Check the consistency of the dough.

When the kneading is finished, check the temperature of the dough. It should be no more than 24°C (75°F). Place the dough in a container and cover with plastic wrap.

Note the time the kneading was finished.

Fermenting

Allow the dough to rise for 30 to 40 minutes, depending on the temperature and humidity of the work area.

Sectioning and Weighing

Section and weigh the dough into 350-gram (12.5-ounce) sections and round them. Allow the sections to rest, covered, for 10 to 15 minutes.

Shaping

Dusting with a minimum of flour, shape the sections of dough into rounds or short loaves or place them in bread molds.

Remember to place the seam on the bottom of the loaf. Score each loaf with decorative incisions, such as the sausage cut or whatever is appropriate to the shape of the loaf.

Proofing

Proof the shaped loaves for 40 to 60 minutes, depending on the temperature of the work area.

Baking

Fill the oven with steam before placing the loaves in the oven.

Bake the loaves at 230° to 240°C (450°F) for 25 to 30 minutes.

Remove or turn off the steam 5 minutes before taking the loaves out of the oven.

For verifying doneness, cooling, and storing, refer to page 62.

Light Rye Bread

Preparation	15 min	0 min	• Calculate the necessary temperatures. • Prepare, weigh, and measure the raw ingredients and fermented dough taken from a previous batch of bread dough.
Kneading	10 min	25 min	• Knead the ingredients on low speed. • Check the consistency and temperature of the dough.
Fermenting	40 min	1 hr 05	• The fermentation time depends on the work area.
Weighing	5 min	1 hr 10	• Divide, weigh, and round the dough,
Resting	10 min	1 hr 20	• Cover and rest the rounded sections.
Shaping	10 min	1 hr 30	• Dusting with minimal flour, shape the dough as desired.
Proofing	1 hr	2 hr 30	• Proofing time is determined by the temperature and humidity of the proofing area, which should be free of drafts.
Preparing for baking	5 min	2 hr 35	• Verify the temperature of the oven. • Fill the oven with steam.
Baking	30 min	3 hr 05	• Turn off the steam 5 minutes before removing. • Verify doneness.
Cooling	5 min	3 hr 10	• Immediately place the loaves in wicker baskets or on cooling racks.

Rye breads and rolls with raisins

Rye Bread with Raisins

Any of the recipes given for rye bread in the previous sections (page 60 to 65) can be used for rye bread with raisins.

Use 250 grams (9 ounces) of raisins for every kilogram (2 pounds 3 ounces) of flour in the recipe. Rinse, blanch, and drain the raisins. Add them to the final dough when kneading is almost complete.

Follow the procedure given for the type of rye bread recipe used to finish the loaves.

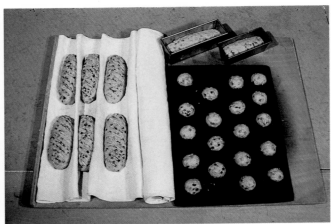

Short loaves are shaped with 350 grams (12.5 ounces) of dough.

The shaped dough should be proofed in molds or on canvas.

Bake the loaves for 35 for 45 minutes at 220°C (428°F) with steam.

Caution: This bread becomes very dark quickly, and so it should be covered toward the end of baking.

Raisin Rolls

These small rolls are made with 60 to 70 grams (2 to 2.5 ounces) of dough. Use the recipe and procedure for making rye bread with raisins. Shape small rolls and place them on a sheet pan.

Check the proofing frequently: avoid overproofing, which would cause a thick skin to form.

Start the steam before baking and bake at 230° to 240°C (450°F).

Score the top of each roll with a cross, using an appropriate sharp blade, just before placing them in the oven. Bake for 15 to 20 minutes.

Be careful not to overbake the rolls. They should be moist and tender in the center.

Whole-wheat breads

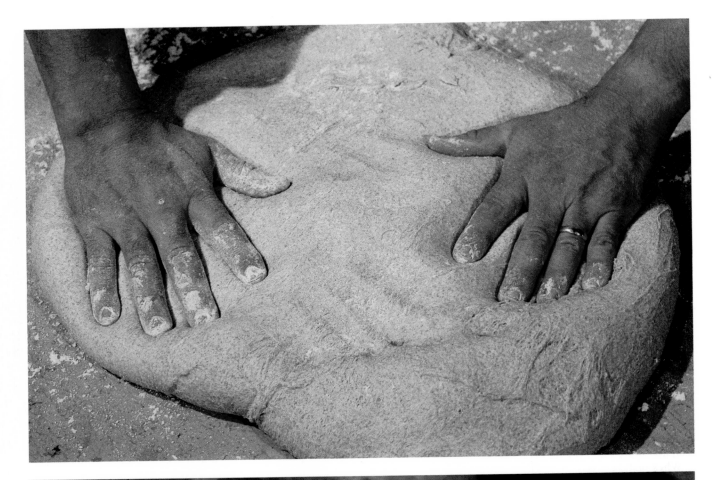

Whole-wheat bread with a mixed starter

Introduction

Whole-wheat bread is recommended by health professionals because of its high nutritional and high fiber content.

When making bread with whole-wheat flour, patent flour is added to raise the gluten level, and powdered milk is added to improve the flavor. The procedure for making whole-wheat bread presents no particular difficulties.

Shapes

Whole-wheat bread can be shaped into a variety of forms, including rounds or short loaves, or it can be baked in molds. Usually 300 to 400 grams (10.5 to 14 ounces) of dough is used per loaf.

Appearance

The crust should be deep golden brown, almost a caramel color. It should be burnished and smooth, without cracks.

The crumb should be supple, with a regular small honeycomb texture.

Uses

Whole-wheat bread goes well with all foods, especially delicate cheeses and seafood. It is even good simply sliced, toasted, and buttered.

A previous fermentation based on a mixed starter will yield a bread with a nicely rounded shape, good flavor, and long shelf life.

Yield

About 5 kilograms (11 pounds) of dough will yield 14 loaves, 350 grams (12.5 ounces) each.

Recipe

650 g mixed starter (23 oz.), made with patent flour
2.5 kg whole-wheat flour (5.5 lb.)
1.75 L water (59 fl. oz.)
55 g salt (2 oz.)
40 g yeast (1.5 oz.)
100 g butter (3.5 oz.) *or* 150 g powdered milk (5 oz.), optional

Storage

Whole-wheat bread has a good shelf life and does not go stale quickly.

It can be made a day ahead of being served.

Making the Mixed Starter

Prepare the yeast starter as for a country-style bread (pages 48 to 51).

Final Kneading

If the temperature of the work area is between 22° and 25°C (71.5° and 77°F), the base temperatures are as follows.

With a kneading machine, use a base

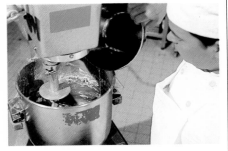

temperature of 65° to 68°C (213° to 219°F), and knead for 10 minutes on low speed.

With an electric mixer, use a base temperature of 62° to 64°C (208° to 211°F), and knead for 10 minutes on low speed.

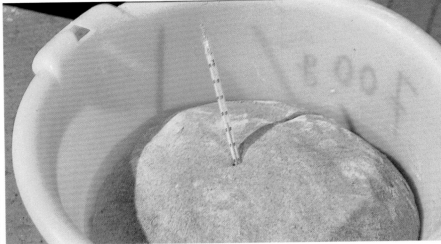

In the mixing bowl attachment, dilute the yeast in the water. Add the whole-wheat flour, salt, powdered milk or butter (previously softened), and finally the yeast starter.

Knead all ingredients. The dough should have a smooth, elastic consistency.

After kneading, check the temperature of the dough. It should be no more than 24° to 25°C (75° to 77°F)

Transfer the dough to a plastic container and cover with plastic wrap to prevent a crust from forming.

Note the time the kneading was stopped.

Fermenting

Depending on the temperature of the dough and the temperature and humidity of the work area, allow 80 to 90 minutes for fermentation.

Punch the dough down 40 minutes after the kneading was stopped.

Keep the dough covered.

Weighing

Weigh out 350-gram (12.5-ounce) sections of dough. Round the sections, being careful not to pull the dough too tightly. Allow the sections to rest for 5 minutes.

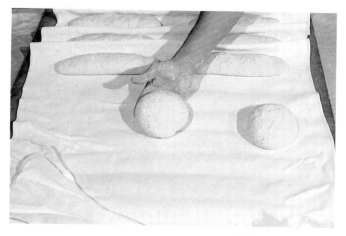

Shaping

Dust with a small amount of flour to prevent the dough from becoming too dry. Shape the sections into rounds or short loaves and lay them on canvas or place the dough in loaf pans.

Proofing

Allow approximately 1 hour for proofing, depending on the temperature and humidity of the work area. The dough should double in volume without drying out. Be careful not to overproof the dough. When using loaf pans, the dough can be proofed a little longer.

Preparing for Baking

Verify that the oven has been preheated to 230° to 240°C (450°F). Prick the loaves with a slender metal rod. A special tool is made for this purpose.

Start filling the oven with steam.

Baking

Allow 30 to 35 minutes for baking, depending on the shape of the loaf. Bread baked in a loaf pan usually takes about 40 to 45 minutes.

Turn the steam off 5 minutes before removing the bread from the oven.

When baking is done, the crust should be deep brown and sound hollow when tapped.

Cooling

Immediately place the loaves in a wicker basket or on a cooling rack after removing them from the oven.

Storage

Whole-wheat bread has a long shelf life if well baked, as the crumb holds moisture well because of the bran in the flour.

Whole-Wheat Bread with a Mixed Starter

1st DAY

Preparation Prepare the yeast starter Knead the starter	**5** min	**0** min **17** hrs (approx.)	• *Fermentation time of the starter varies, depending on the temperature of the work area, ranging from 13 to 17 hours.*

2nd DAY

Preparing the dough	**15** min	**0** min	• *Prepare, weigh, and measure the final raw ingredients.* • *Calculate the temperatures needed.*
Kneading	**10** min	**25** min	• *Check the consistency and the temperature of the dough, which should be no more than 24°C (75°F).*
Fermenting	**1** hr **30**	**1** hr **55**	• *Place the dough in an area free of drafts.* • *Punch the dough down after 40 minutes.*
Weighing	**5** min	**2** hr	• *Round the dough without pulling too tightly.*
Resting	**5** min	**2** hr **05**	• *Cover the sections of dough with plastic wrap.*
Shaping	**10** min	**2** hr **15**	• *Being careful not to tear the dough, shape as desired.*
Proofing	**1** hr to **1** hr **15**	**3** hr **30**	• *Proofing time is determined by the temperature of the work area. Avoid overproofing.*
Preparing for baking	**5** min	**3** hr **35**	• *Check the temperature of the oven.* • *Fill the oven with steam.*
Baking	**30** to **35** min	**4** hr **10**	• *Stop the steam 5 minutes before removing the bread.* • *Verify doneness.*
Cooling	**5** min	**4** hr **15**	• *Immediately place the loaves in a wicker basket or on a cooling rack.*

Whole-wheat bread with a sponge starter

Introduction

Using a sponge to make whole-wheat bread saves time but still results in flavorful bread with a good shelf life. It takes approximately 2 hours to prepare the sponge, compared to 17 hours for the mixed starter.

Yield

About 5 kilograms (11 pounds) of dough will yield 14 loaves, 350 grams (12.5 ounces) each.

Recipe

3 kg sponge (6 lb. 9.5 oz.)
1 kg whole-wheat flour (35 oz.)
500 g bread flour (17.5 oz.)
450 ml water (16 fl. oz.)
65 g salt (2 oz.)
20 g yeast (0.7 oz.)
100 g butter (3.5 oz.) *or* 150 g powdered milk (5.5 oz.), optional

Making the Sponge

Calculate the temperature of the water using a base temperature at 70°C (225°F).

Knead the ingredients for 5 minutes on low speed.

Whisk together 1.5 kilograms (53 ounces) whole-wheat flour with 40 grams (1.5 ounces) yeast dissolved in 1.5 liters (50.5 fluid ounces) water.

Cover the sponge with a sheet of plastic wrap, and allow it to ferment for 1½ to 2 hours at 22° to 25°C (71.5° to 77°F). The sponge should double in volume.

Final Kneading

The following base temperatures are calculated for a work area with a temperature between 22° and 25°C (71.5° and 77°F).

With a kneading machine, the base temperature is 65 to 68°C (213 to 219°F). Knead the dough for 10 minutes on low speed.

With an electric mixer, the base temperature is 62° to 64°C (208° to 211°F). Knead the dough for 10 minutes on low speed.

Put the sponge in the bowl of the kneading machine or mixer. Over it pour the yeast diluted in the water, the whole-wheat flour, bread flour, salt, and butter (softened) or powdered milk if used.

When the kneading is complete, the temperature of the dough should be no more than 23° to 24°C (73.5° to 75°F).

Note the time the kneading was stopped.

Fermenting

Depending on the temperature of the work area, allow 60 to 80 minutes for the fermentation.

Thirty minutes after the kneading was stopped, punch down the dough. Keep the dough covered to prevent a crust from forming.

Weighing

Weigh out sections of dough, 350 grams (12.5 ounces) each. Round the sections, being careful not to pull too tightly on the dough. Allow the sections to rest covered for 5 minutes.

Shaping

Dust with a minimum of flour to prevent the dough from becoming dry. Shape the sections into rounds or short loaves, or place in open loaf pans, keeping the seams on the bottoms.

Proofing

Depending on the temperature and humidity of the work area, allow 50 to 60 minutes for proofing the loaves. The loaves should double in volume without becoming dry. Be careful not to overproof the dough. Dough placed in loaf pans can be proofed slightly longer than shaped loaves.

Preparing for Baking

The oven should be preheated to 230° to 240°C (450°F).

Prick the rounded loaves and short loaves with a slender metal rod.

It is best to bake loaf pans on hot baking sheets.

Baking, Cooling, and Storing

Follow the procedures for whole-wheat bread with a mixed starter (see page 71).

Whole-Wheat Bread with a Sponge Starter

Preparation	**5** min	**0** min	• Prepare and weigh the raw ingredients.
Knead the sponge	**5** min		• Carefully dissolve the yeast in the water.
Ferment the sponge	**1** hr **30** to **2** hr	**2** hr **10**	• The fermentation time of the sponge depends on the temperature of the work area. • Cover the sponge.
Preparing and kneading the final dough	**15** min	**2** hr **25**	• Prepare, weigh, and measure the raw ingredients. • Calculate the necessary temperatures. • Check the consistency and temperature of the dough, which should be 23° to 24°C (73.5° to 75°F).
Fermenting	**1** hr to **1** hr **20**	**3** hr **45**	• Place the dough in an area free of drafts. • Punch down the dough after 40 minutes.
Weighing	**5** min	**3** hr **50**	• Weigh and round the dough, dusting with a minimum of flour. Do not pull tightly when rounding.
Resting	**5** min	**3** hr **55**	• Cover the rounded sections of dough.
Shaping	**10** min	**4** hr **05**	• Be careful not to tear the dough. • Shape as desired.
Proofing	**50** to **60** min	**5** hr **05**	• Proofing will be determined by the temperature and humidity of the work area. • Avoid overproofing the dough.
Preparing for baking	**5** min	**5** hr **10**	• Check the temperature of the oven. • Fill the oven with steam.
Baking	**30** to **35** min	**5** hr **45**	• Stop the steam 5 minutes before removing the bread. • Verify doneness.
Cooling	**5** min	**5** hr **50**	• Immediately place the loaves in a wicker basket or on a cooling rack.

Whole-wheat bread with a fermented dough starter

Introduction

Whole-wheat bread made with already fermented dough taken from a previous batch produces excellent results and is fairly easy to make. Using a fermented dough starter in the recipe will result in a lighter-textured bread that rises well.

Yield

About 5 kilograms (11 pounds) of dough will yield 14 loaves, 350 grams (12.5 ounces) each.

Recipe

600 g fermented dough starter (21 oz.), fermented 4 to 6 hours, from a previous batch of bread dough
2.5 kg whole-wheat flour (5.5 lb.)
1.7 L water (57.5 fl. oz.)
55 g salt (2 oz.)
40 g yeast (1.5 oz.)
100 g butter (3.5 oz.), softened, *or* 150 g powdered milk (5 oz.), optional

Kneading

For a work area with a temperature of 22° to 25°C (71.5° to 77°F), use the following base temperatures to calculate the temperature of the water.

In a kneading machine, the base temperature should be 65° to 68°C (213° to 219°F). Knead for 10 minutes on low speed.

In an electric mixer, the base temperature should be 62° to 64°C (208° to 211°F). Knead for 10 minutes on low speed.

Knead the fermented dough starter, the yeast previously dissolved in the water, the salt, and the softened butter or powdered milk as indicated for the machine used.

Check the consistency of the dough and add more water if it seems too dry.

The temperature of the dough should be 24° to 25°C (75° to 77°F) maximum when kneading is complete. The dough should be elastic and smooth. Place the dough in a plastic container, and cover the dough with plastic wrap to prevent a crust from forming.

Note the time at which the kneading was stopped.

Fermenting

Allow the dough to rise for approximately 80 to 90 minutes. Punch down the dough after 40 minutes of rising.

Weighing

Weigh and round the sections of dough, being careful not to round them too tightly. Allow the sections to rest for 5 minutes, covered, in an area free of drafts.

Shaping

Shape the sections in rounds or short baguettes or place them in loaf pans.

Proofing

Proof the dough for 80 to 90 minutes, depending on the temperature and humidity of the work area, which should be free of drafts.

The dough should double in volume.

Baking

The oven should be preheated to 230° to 240°C (450°F). Prick the loaves with a thin metal rod or score deeply before baking. Bake in the same way as other whole-wheat bread.

Whole-Wheat Bread with a Fermented Dough Starter			
Preparation	15 min	0 min	• Calculate the temperature of the water. • Prepare, weigh, and measure the raw ingredients and the dough from a previous batch that has fermented for 4 to 6 hours.
Kneading	10 min	25 min	• Knead the dough on low speed. • Check the consistency and temperature of the dough.
Fermenting	80 to 90 min	1 hr 55	• Cover the dough with plastic wrap during fermentation. • Punch down the dough after 40 minutes.
Weighing	5 min	2 hr	• Weigh and gently round the dough.
Resting	5 min	2 hr 05	• Cover the dough with plastic wrap while resting.
Shaping	10 min	2 hr 15	• Be careful not to tear the dough.
Proofing	1 hr	3 hr 15	• Proofing time is determined by the temperature and humidity of the work area, which should be free of drafts.
Preparing for baking	5 min	3 hr 35	• Check the temperature of the oven. • Fill the oven with steam.
Baking	30 min	4 hr 05	• Remove or stop the steam 5 minutes before the bread is finished baking • Verify doneness.
Cooling	5 min	4 hr 10	• Immediately place the loaves in a wicker basket or on cooling racks.

Apricot, apple, and prune breads

Introduction

Whole-wheat bread can be specially shaped and then filled with various dried or fresh fruits. These breads are not particularly difficult to make and add variety to any bakery.

Storage

Fruit-filled breads have a good shelf life.

Shapes

The dough is rolled out with a rolling pin using the same technique as for pommes chaussons (apple turnovers). Either large or individual serving sizes can be made.

Appearance

The crust should be dark and crisp. The fruit inside the bread keeps the interior soft and tender.

Uses

These breads can be eaten alone, for breakfast or at tea time. The apple-filled bread goes especially well with boudin noir (blood sausage).

Preparation

Prepare the dough for whole-wheat bread with a fermented dough starter.

Weigh out and round 300 grams (10.5 ounces) of dough for large breads. For individual-size breads weigh out 300 grams (10.5 ounces) of dough, divide each section into five equal pieces, 60 grams (2 ounces) each, and round.

Pit the prunes, peel, core, and slice, the apples, and prepare the other fruits to be used.

Filling the Breads

Using a rolling pin, roll out each round of dough into an oval shape. The ovals should be even in thickness except at the ends, which should be slightly thicker.

Place the fruit on half of the oval, leaving space at the edge of the oval so that it can be sealed. Moisten the entire border of the oval with water using a pastry brush.

Fold the empty half of the oval of dough over the fruit, pressing firmly on the edges to seal well.

Turn the piece upside down and place it on a baking sheet.

With an appropriate blade, decoratively score the dough, which will ensure even baking.

On top of the bread, place one or several pieces of the fruit used inside the bread. This will indicate the filling used and make the breads more attractive.

Proofing

Proof the breads in a proof box or in an area free of drafts for about 1½ hours.

Avoid overproofing the breads.

Baking

Bake the breads in an oven preheated to 220° to 230°C (425° to 450°F). Fill the oven with steam before adding the breads.

Bake for approximately 15 to 20 minutes, depending on the size of the bread. Carefully observe the baking.

Verifying Doneness

The breads are finished baking when they are golden brown and the crust sounds hollow when tapped.

Immediately place the breads on a cooling rack after removing them from the oven.

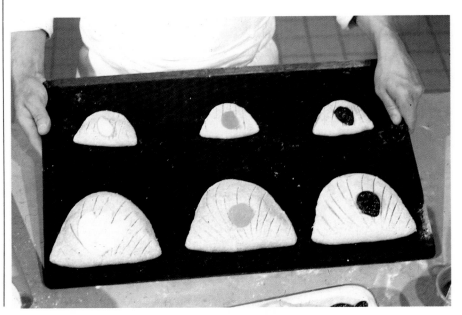

Seaweed bread

Introduction

Seaweed bread offers the nutrients found in seaweed and is not especially difficult to make. This bread has a unique flavor based on an infusion of *nori*, thin sheets of dried seaweed often used for making sushi.

Storage

Seaweed bread has a good shelf life because of the alginates, or salts, in the seaweed.

Shapes

Seaweed bread can be shaped into rounds, short loaves, or baked in loaf pans. Usually each loaf is based on 250 to 300 grams (9 to 10.5 ounces) of dough.

Appearance

The bread has a fine crisp, golden crust. It rises well and has a tender, light crumb.

Uses

Seaweed bread goes well with most foods, especially fish and seafood. It makes a good substitute for the more standard white breads because it is so nutritious.

Yield

Approximately 4.9 kilograms (10 pounds 13 ounces) of dough will yield 16 loaves, 300 grams (10.5 ounces) each.

Preparation

Use the base temperatures that follow in a work area with a temperature of 22° to 25°C (71.5° to 77°F). With an electric mixer, use a base temperature of 62°C (208°F). Knead the dough on low speed for 10 minutes. With a kneading machine, use a base temperature of 65° to 68°C (213° to 219°F). Knead the dough for 10 minutes on low speed.

With the given base temperatures, calculate the temperature needed for the water in the recipe. Prepare and weigh the raw ingredients.

Recipe

50 g *nori* seaweed (1.5 oz.)
2.4 kg bread flour (5 lb. 5 oz.)
1 kg fermented dough starter (2 lb. 3 oz.), fermented for at least 6 hours, *or* mixed starter
35 g salt (1 oz.)
35 g yeast (1 oz.)

Preparing the Infusion

Soak the *nori* in approximately 3 liters (101 fluid ounces) of cold water for 10 minutes.

Simmer the water and *nori* for 15 minutes over moderate heat. Cool the mixture, then drain the nori and place it on a dry towel. Save the infused water, and use about 1.4 liters (47.5 fluid ounces) of it in the recipe to moisten the dough.

Thinly slice the nori.

Final Kneading

Place all the ingredients, including the *nori*-infused liquid, in the bowl of the electric mixer or kneading machine and knead them. The consistency of the dough should be somewhat firm, as for regular bread.

The temperature of the dough should be 23° to 24°C (73.5° to 75°F) after kneading. Cover the dough and note the time the kneading was stopped.

Fermenting

Depending on the temperature of the dough and work area and the humidity of the work area, allow 1 hour for the dough to rise. The work area should be free of drafts. Thirty minutes after the kneading was stopped, punch down the dough and turn it over.

Weighing

Section and weigh the dough. Round the sections, and let them rest, covered with plastic wrap, for 5 minutes before shaping them.

Shaping

Shape the dough as desired. Place the loaves on canvas, seam side down, or in loaf pans in an area free of drafts for proofing.

Proofing

Allow approximately 1½ hours for proofing, depending on the temperature of the work area. Avoid overproofing the dough.

Preparing for Baking

Check that the oven is preheated to 230° to 240°C (about 450°F). Fill the oven with steam. Score decorative incisions in the loaves, such as sausage or polka incisions.

Baking

Verify doneness after 20 minutes of baking. Depending on the size of the bread, baking will take between 20 and 30 minutes. After removing the loaves from the oven, immediately place them in a wicker basket or on cooling racks.

Seaweed Bread			
Preparation	15 min	0 min	• Calculate the temperatures needed. • Prepare, weigh, and measure the raw ingredients. • Make the seaweed infusion.
Kneading	10 min	25 min	• Always knead on low speed.
Fermenting	1 hr	1 hr 25	• Place the dough in an area free of drafts to prevent a crust from forming.
Weighing	10 min	1 hr 35	• Section and weigh the dough, using as little flour as possible.
Resting	5 min	1 hr 40	• Round and cover the sections.
Shaping	10 min	1 hr 50	• Shape the rounds as desired.
Proofing	1 hr 30	3 hr 20	• Proof the dough in an area free of drafts. • Check the proofing after 1 hour.
Preparing for baking	5 min	3 hr 25	• Fill the oven with steam. • Verify the temperature of the oven.
Baking	30 min	3 hr 55	• Verify doneness after 20 minutes.
Cooling	5 min	4 hr	• Immediately place the loaves in a wicker basket or on cooling racks after removing them from the oven.

Brown bread

Introduction

In France brown bread is made with a light whole-wheat flour that shares qualities of bread flour and whole-wheat flour. It is possible to substitute for this flour a mixture based on 125 grams (4.5 ounces) of whole-wheat flour and 875 grams (30.5 ounces) of bread flour for each kilogram (35 ounces) of flour in the recipe.

This rustic bread is sometimes called peasant bread in France. It is necessary to make a mixed starter or use a fermented dough starter. This bread is not particularly difficult to make.

Storage

Brown bread is based on a mixed starter or fermented dough starter and therefore has a good shelf life.

Shapes

Generally brown bread is shaped in rounds or in short loaves. The amount of dough used for each loaf can range from 350 grams to 1 kilogram (12.5 to 35 ounces)

Appearance

The crust of brown bread ranges from deep golden to dark brown and is often dusted with flour before baking. This bread rises only moderately, resulting in a somewhat heavy bread. The crumb has a fairly tight texture and light brown color.

Uses

Brown bread goes well with most foods prepared with or without sauces, charcuterie (delicatessen meats), and strong cheeses such as Roquefort, Munster, and Livarot. Brown bread can also be toasted and buttered for breakfast.

Yield

About 5 kilograms (11 pounds) of dough will yield 14 loaves of bread, 350 grams (12.5 ounces) each, or 5 loaves 1 kilogram (35 ounces) each.

Recipe

2.5 kg light whole-wheat flour (5.5 lb.), or substitute flour as indicated above
750 g fermented dough (26.5 oz.), minimum fermentation 6 hours *or* mixed starter
1,750 ml water (59 fl. oz.), approximately
50 g salt (1.5 oz.)
20 g yeast (0.7 oz.)

Preparation

In a work area with a temperature of 22° to 25°C (71.5° to 77°F), use a base temperature of 62°C (208°F) with an electric mixer and a base temperature of 65° to 68°C (213° to 219°F) with a kneading machine.

Calculate the temperature needed for the water using the appropriate base temperature. Prepare, weigh, and measure the raw ingredients.

Kneading

Place the mixed starter or the fermented dough in the bowl of the electric mixer or kneading machine. Add the salt, flour, and the yeast, which has previously been dissolved in the water. Knead the ingredients on low speed for 10 minutes. Check the temperature of the dough at the beginning of the kneading.

The temperature of the dough at the end of kneading should be 24°C (75°F). The texture of the dough should be somewhat firm yet malleable. Note the time the kneading was stopped.

Fermenting

The dough should be covered during fermentation and placed in an area free of drafts. Allow the dough to ferment for 80 to 90 minutes, depending on the temperature of the dough and the temperature and humidity of the work area. Forty minutes after the kneading was stopped, punch the dough down.

Weighing

Weigh out sections of dough. Round the sections, being careful not to tear them. Let them rest for 5 to 10 minutes, covered with plastic wrap.

Shaping

After resting, shape the rounds as desired, using a minimum of flour.

Proofing

Proof the loaves on canvas, seam side down, or place the rounded loaves in molds. Allow 1 to 1½ hours for proofing, depending on the temperature and humidity of the work area. Avoid overproofing, which could cause a crust to form on the loaves.

Preparing for Baking

Preheat the oven to 220° to 230°C (425° to 450°F). Score the loaves decoratively. Fill the oven with steam.

Baking

Bake the loaves for 25 to 35 minutes, depending on their weight. Turn the steam off 5 minutes before the breads are removed. When the breads are baked, remove them from the oven and immediately place them in a wicker basket or on cooling racks.

Brown Bread			
Preparation	**15** min	**0** min	• Calculate the necessary temperatures. • Prepare, weigh, and measure the raw ingredients.
Kneading	**10** min	**25** min	• Knead on low speed.
Fermenting	**80** to **90** min	**1** hr **55**	• Fermentation time depends on the temperature of the work area. • Punch the dough down after 40 minutes.
Weighing	**5** min	**2** hr	• Round the sections of dough, using a minimum of flour.
Resting	**10** min	**2** hr **10**	• Rest the dough in an area free of drafts.
Shaping	**5** min	**2** hr **15**	• Shape as desired.
Proofing	**1** hr to **1** hr **15**	**3** hr **30**	• Proofing time depends on the temperature of the work area, which should be free of drafts. • Check the loaves after 1 hour.
Preparing for baking	**5** min	**3** hr **35**	• Check the temperature of the oven. • Add steam, but not too much.
Baking	**25** to **40** min	**4** hr **15**	• Baking time depends on the size and shape of the loaves.
Cooling	**5** min	**4** hr **20**	• Immediately place the loaves in wicker baskets or on cooling racks.

Brié bread

Introduction

A rustic Norman specialty, brié bread is rather rustic and was developed centuries ago.

It is essential to use a mixed starter or a fermented starter when making brié bread. The characteristics unique to brié bread result from the kneading and from the low hydration (amount of water) in the recipe. This makes for a very firm dough that is best made in a kneading machine that can run in reverse.

Bread flour is used for brié bread. When making this bread, pay close attention to the kneading, and use high-quality equipment.

Storage

Brié bread has a good shelf life.

Shapes

Brié bread is shaped into rounds or short loaves, each of 300 and 600 grams (10.5 to 21 ounces) of dough or more.

Appearance

Pale golden in color, brié bread is fairly heavy, developing little during fermentation. The interior has a very tight crumb and is creamy white in color.

Yield

Approximately 4.9 kilograms (10 pounds 11 ounces) of dough will yield 16 loaves of bread, 300 grams (10.5 ounces) each.

Recipe

1 kg bread flour (35 oz.)
3.5 kg mixed starter or fermented dough starter (7 lb. 11 oz.), fermented for a maximum of 6 hours
150 g butter (5 oz.)
150 ml water (5 fl. oz.)
20 g salt (1½ Tbsp.)
20 g yeast (0.7 oz.)

Preparation

In a work area ranging in temperature from 22° to 25°C (71.5° to 77°F), use a base temperature of 65°C (213°F) for a kneading machine.   Prepare, weigh, and measure all the raw ingredients.

Kneading

In the bowl of a kneading machine, place the flour and salt, and add the mixed starter or fermented dough. Turn the machine to low speed in reverse (if possible), add the butter, and slowly add the yeast, which has previously been dis-solved in the water. Knead the dough for 6 to 7 minutes. Sometimes it is necessary to hold onto the bowl during kneading to keep it in place, as this dough is very firm and may agitate the bowl.

The dough should have a firm texture and a temperature of 24°C (75°F) after kneading.

Fermenting

The dough will take approximately 40 minutes to rise and should be punched down after 20 minutes.

It is important to cover the dough during fermentation, as it easily develops a crust.

Weighing

Section and weigh the dough, dusting with a minimum of flour. Do not round the loaves.

Shaping

Dusting with a minimum of flour, shape the sections of dough as desired (see the photograph above for examples).

Proofing

Proof the shaped dough on canvas, seam side down. Decorative scoring can be done at the beginning of proofing or just before baking.   Proofing takes between 1 and 1¼ hours. Do not overproof, or a crust may form.

Preparing for Baking

Check that the oven has been preheated to 230°C (450°F) and filled with steam.

Baking

Bake the loaves for 20 to 25 minutes. Remove or turn off the steam 5 minutes before removing the bread. When the bread is baked, immediately place the loaves in a wicker basket or on cooling racks after removing them from the oven.

Brié Bread (with fermented dough)

Preparation	10 min	0 min	• Calculate the necessary temperatures. • Prepare, weigh, and measure the raw ingredients.
Kneading	8 min	18 min	• Knead on low speed, in reverse, in a kneading machine.
Fermenting	40 min	58 min	• After 20 minutes, punch down the dough.
Weighing	5 min	1 hr 03	• Section the dough without rounding, dusting with a minimum of flour.
Resting	5 to 10 min	1 hr 10	• Cover the sections of dough with plastic wrap.
Shaping	5 min	1 hr 15	• Shape the dough as desired, dusting with a minimum of flour.
Proofing	1 hr to 1 hr 15	2 hr 30	• Avoid overproofing, to prevent a crust from forming. • Check the proofing after 1 hour.
Preparing for baking	5 min	2 hr 35	• Verify the temperature of the oven. • Fill the oven with steam.
Baking	20 to 30 min	3 hr 05	• Baking time depends on the shape and size of the loaves. • Check for doneness after 20 minutes.
Cooling	5 min	3 hr 10	• Immediately place the baked loaves in wicker baskets or on cooling racks.

Four-grain bread

Introduction

Four-grain bread is a very rustic bread made with four different flours in various amounts, with the proportions based on the characteristics of each flour. A fermented dough or mixed starter is used, which enriches the bread and adds to its nutritional value. This bread is not particularly difficult to make.

Storage

Because of its ingredients, particularly the mixed or fermented dough starter, this bread has a very good shelf life.

Shapes

Four-grain bread can be shaped into rounds or short loaves or baked in loaf pans.

Appearance

Four-grain bread is very rustic in appearance, with a deep brown crust. It is a nicely rounded bread that rises fairly well, producing a crumb with an even, tender texture.

Uses

Four-grain bread is a flavorful bread and is particularly appreciated by gourmets. It goes well with dishes with sauces, chicken, game birds, and cheeses.

Recipe

For 14 loaves, 350 g (12.5 oz.) each

1.2 kg bread flour (2 lb. 9.5 oz.)
800 g rye flour (28 oz.)
200 g barley flour (7 oz.)
200 g oat flour (7 oz.)
1 kg mixed starter (35 oz.) *or* fermented
  dough (minimum 4 hours)
50 g salt (1.5 oz.)
30 g yeast (1 oz.)
1.65 L water (55.5 fl. oz.)

Preparation

With a room temperature of 22° to 25°C (71.5° to 77°F), use a base temperature of 62° to 64°C (208° to 211°F) if using an electric mixer or 65° to 68°C (213° to 219°F) if using a kneading machine. With these figures, calculate the temperature needed for the water in the recipe.

Prepare, weigh, and measure the raw ingredients.

Kneading

In the mixing bowl or kneading machine, blend the four flours together well. This will prevent patches of one flour from appearing in the finished bread because of poor mixing. Add the salt and the mixed starter or fermented dough starter. Dissolve the yeast in the water and incorporate.

Regardless of the machine used, allow 10 minutes on low speed for kneading.

The temperature of the dough should be between 23° and 24°C (73.5° and 75°F) at the end of kneading; the texture, firm. Cover the dough to prevent a crust from

forming. Note the time the kneading was finished.

Fermenting

Allow 80 to 90 minutes for fermentation, in an area free of drafts. Punch down the dough 40 minutes after the kneading was stopped.

Weighing

Weigh out 350-gram (12.5-ounce) sections of dough, dusting with as little flour as possible. Round the sections, and allow them to rest for 15 minutes in an area free of drafts.

Shaping

Shape the sections as desired. Place the shaped loaves on canvas, seam side down, dusting with a minimum of flour.

Proofing

Proofing takes between 1 and 1¼ hours, depending on the temperature and humidity of the work area. Avoid over-proofing, which would cause a crust to form.

Preparing for Baking

Verify that the oven has been preheated to 220° to 230°C (425° to 450°F) maximum. Fill the oven with steam. With an appropriate blade, score sausage or polka cuts or score a single-line incision along the length of the loaves. For a large round, it is preferable to make polka incisions.

Baking

For 350-g (12.5-oz.) loaves, allow 25 to 30 minutes of baking. For a large 750-g to 1-kg (26.5- to 35-oz.) round, allow 40 to 45 minutes for baking. Remove or turn off the steam 5 minutes before baking is completed. Verify doneness. After removing the loaves from the oven, immediately place them in wicker baskets or on cooling racks.

Four-Grain Bread			
Preparation	10 min	0 min	• Calculate the necessary temperatures. • Prepare, weigh, and measure the raw ingredients.
Kneading	10 min	20 min	• Knead on low speed for 10 minutes.
Fermenting	80 to 90 min	1 hr 50	• Place in an area free of drafts to prevent a crust from forming. • Punch the dough down after 40 minutes of rising.
Weighing	5 min	1 hr 55	• Round the sections of dough, dusting with a minimum of flour.
Resting	15 min	2 hr 10	• Cover the sections with plastic wrap.
Shaping	10 min	2 hr 20	• Shape as desired, dusting with a minimum of flour.
Proofing	1 hr 15	3 hr 35	• Proof the dough in an area free of drafts. • Avoid overproofing.
Preparing for baking	5 min	3 hr 40	• Verify the temperature of the oven. • Fill the oven with steam.
Baking	25 to 40 min	4 hr 20	• Baking time depends on size and shape. • Remove or turn off the steam 5 minutes before removing the loaves from the oven.
Cooling	5 min	4 hr 25	• Immediately place the loaves in wicker baskets or on cooling racks.

Chorizo bread

Introduction

Chorizo bread adds to the variety of innovative and special breads. Chorizo is a piquant Spanish sausage that can range in spiciness. Chorizo bread is made with bread flour and a mixed starter or fermented dough starter. Making chorizo bread is not particularly difficult.

Storage

Chorizo bread has a good shelf life because of the type of starter used. The olive oil gives this bread a rich flavor.

Shapes

Chorizo bread can be shaped into rounds or short loaves or baked in open loaf pans. The size of each loaf usually ranges from 250 to 500 grams (9 to 17.5 ounces) of dough.

Appearance

The thin crust has an attractive, burnished, golden orange hue. The texture of the crumb is supple and tender, with even air pockets.

Uses

Chorizo bread goes particularly well with couscous, paella, pasta with sauce, and other piquant dishes. Chorizo bread can also be eaten alone as it is a hearty, flavorful bread.

Yield

About 4.8 kilograms (10.5 pounds) of dough will yield 16 loaves, 300 g (10.5 ounces) each.

Recipe

1.9 kg bread flour (4 lb. 3 oz.)
1.4 kg fermented dough (3 lb.), fermented
    for 4 hours minimum, *or* mixed starter
1.1 L water (37 fl. oz.)
400 to 500 g chorizo (14 to 17.5 oz.)
35 g salt (1 oz.)
20 g yeast (0.7 oz.)
100 ml olive oil (3.5 fl. oz.), optional

Preparation

In a work area with a temperature of 22° to 25°C (71.5° to 77°F), use a base temperature of 62°C (208°F) if using an electric mixer or 65° to 68°C (213° to 219°F) if using a kneading machine.

Calculate the necessary water temperature. Prepare, weigh, and measure the raw ingredients.

Final Kneading

In the mixing bowl of the machine used, place the flour, the fermented dough or mixed starter cut in small pieces, the salt, the yeast that has been previously dissolved in the water, and the olive oil if used.

Knead all the ingredients together on low speed for 10 minutes, regardless of the machine used.

Remove the casings of the chorizo sausages and dice them. Add the diced chorizo to the batter during the last 3 to 5 minutes of kneading.

Check the consistency of the dough throughout kneading. At the end of kneading, the temperature of the dough should be 24°C (75°F). The consistency of the dough should be firm. Cover the dough after kneading, and note the time the kneading was stopped.

Fermenting

Allow 1½ to 1¾ hours for fermentation, depending on the temperature of the dough and the temperature and humidity of the work area, which should be free of drafts. Punch down and turn over the dough 40 minutes after the kneading was stopped.

Weighing

Using a minimum of flour, weigh and section the dough.

Round the sections, and allow them to rest, covered with plastic wrap, for 5 minutes.

Shaping

The dough can be shaped into short loaves or in rounds and placed on a sheet of canvas, seam side down. Open loaf pans can also be used.

Proofing

Allow approximately 1 hour for proofing, depending on how the bread is shaped. When using loaf pans, allow about 1¼ hours for proofing.

Preparing for Baking

Check that the oven has been preheated to 220° to 230°C (425° to 450°F). Fill the oven with steam. With an appropriate blade, prick holes or score decorative incisions, such as the sausage cut, into the bread.

Baking

Allow approximately 20 minutes for baking shaped breads and 25 minutes for those baked in loaf pans. Check the bread for doneness by examining the color of the crust, tapping for resonance, and judging lightness. Immediately place the loaves in a wicker basket or on cooling racks after removing them from the oven.

Chorizo Bread

Preparation	15 min	0 min	• Calculate the necessary temperatures. • Prepare, weigh, and measure the raw ingredients. • Dice the chorizo.
Kneading	10 min	25 min	• Knead the dough on low speed.
Fermenting	1 hr 30	1 hr 55	• Place the dough in an area free of drafts to prevent a crust from forming. • Punch down the dough after 40 minutes.
Weighing	5 min	2 hr	• Weigh and round the sections using a minimum of flour.
Shaping	10 min	2 hr 10	• Shape as desired, using a minimum of flour.
Proofing	1 hr to 1¼ hr	3 hr 25	• Proof the dough in an area free of drafts.
Preparing for baking	5 min	3 hr 30	• Fill the oven with steam. • Check the temperature of the oven.
Baking	20 to 25 min	3 hr 55	• Observe the baking carefully, especially breads in loaf pans.
Cooling	5 min	4 hr	• Immediately place the baked loaves in wicker baskets or on cooling racks.

Cumin bread

Introduction

Cumin bread is a very aromatic bread with a pronounced flavor derived from cumin seeds. It is a simple though original bread, with a rustic appearance. Making this bread is not particularly difficult.

Storage

Cumin bread has an excellent shelf life, due to the fermented dough or mixed starter and the addition of rye flour.

Shapes

Cumin bread can be shaped in rounds or short loaves. The weight of a single loaf can range from 250 to 400 grams (9 to 14 ounces) of dough.

Appearance

Cumin bread develops nicely and has a deep golden brown crust. The crumb is light and airy in texture and has a light brown color because of the whole-wheat flour and cumin seeds in the bread.

Uses

Cumin bread goes particularly well with strong cheeses such as Munster, Livarot, and Pont-l'Evêque.

Yield

About 5.1 kilograms (11 pounds 3 ounces) of dough yields 17 loaves, 300 grams (10.5 ounces) each.

Recipe

1.4 kg whole-wheat flour (3 lb.)
1 kg rye flour (35 oz.)
800 g fermented dough or mixed starter (28 oz.)
50 g salt (1.5 oz.)
25 g yeast (1 oz.)
1,500 ml water (50.5 fl. oz.), approximately, depending on the flour
200 to 300 g cumin seeds (7 to 10.5 oz.)

Preparation

In a work area with a temperature of 22° to 25°C (71.5° to 77°F), use a base temperature of 62°C (208°C) for an electric mixer or 64° to 68°C (211° to 219°F) for a kneading machine. With the appropriate base temperature, calculate the temperature needed for the water in the recipe. Prepare, weigh, and measure the raw ingredients.

Final Kneading

Mix the two flours and cumin seeds in the bowl of the kneading machine or mixer. After these ingredients are well blended, add the fermented dough or the mixed starter cut in small pieces. Add the salt and finally the yeast dissolved in the water.

Knead all ingredients on low speed for 10 minutes.

At the end of kneading, the temperature of the dough should be 23° to 24°C (73.5° to 75°F). The dough should have a fairly firm texture. Cover the dough with plastic wrap after kneading.

Fermenting

Place the dough in an area free of drafts to rise for 1 to 1¼ hours. The fermentation time will vary according to the temperature of the dough and temperature and humidity of the work area. Punch down the dough after 30 minutes.

Weighing

Weigh out sections of dough, round the sections, and allow them to rest for 5 to 10 minutes, covered with plastic wrap.

Shaping

By hand, shape the dough into rounds or short loaves. Place the shaped loaves on canvas, seam side down.

Proofing

Allow 1 to 1¼ hours for proofing, depending on the temperature and humidity of the work area, which should be free of drafts. Avoid overproofing.

Preparing for Baking

Check that the oven has been preheated to 220° to 230°C (425° to 450°F). Fill the oven with steam before adding the breads.

With an appropriate blade, prick holes or make attractive sausage incisions in the bread. With a pastry brush, brush water on the top of each loaf and sprinkle on cumin seeds.

Baking

Bake the breads for 25 minutes. Turn off the steam 5 minutes before baking is complete.

Cumin Bread			
Preparation	15 min	0 min	• Calculate the necessary temperatures. • Prepare, weigh, and measure the raw ingredients.
Kneading	10 min	25 min	• Knead on low speed for 10 minutes. • Check the consistency of the dough.
Fermenting	1 hr to 1¼ hr	1 hr 40	• The rising is determined by the temperature of the work area. • The rising area should be free of drafts. • Punch down the dough after 30 minutes.
Weighing	5 min	1 hr 45	• Round the dough, using a minimum of flour.
Shaping	10 min	1 hr 55	• Shape the dough as desired.
Proofing	1 hr to 1¼ hr	3 hr 10	• Proof the dough in an area free of drafts. • Avoid overproofing.
Preparing for baking	5 min	3 hr 15	• Fill the oven with steam. • Verify the temperature of the oven.
Baking	25 min	3 hr 40	• Check doneness after 20 minutes. • Remove the steam 5 minutes before the loaves are finished.
Cooling	5 min	3 hr 45	• Immediately place the loaves in wicker baskets or on cooling racks.

Carrot bread

Introduction

Carrot bread is an attractive bread with a bright crust and colorful crumb. This appealing bread helps to expand the variety offered by a bakery specializing in assorted breads. Making carrot bread is not particularly difficult.

Storage

Carrot bread has an excellent shelf life because of the butter and milk in the recipe.

Shapes

Carrot bread can be shaped into short loaves, rounds, or carrot shapes, or it can be baked in open loaf pans.

Appearance

The crust has a very bright, warm appearance. The crumb is supple with even air pockets. Carrot bread rises well and has a distinctive, slightly sweet flavor.

Uses

Carrot bread goes particularly well with salads, meats with sauces, and game.

Yield

About 4.8 kilograms (10.5 pounds) of dough will yield approximately 19 loaves of 250 g (9 oz.) each, or 16 loaves of 300 g (10.5 oz.) each.

Recipe

2 kg bread flour (4 lb. 6.5 oz.)
500 g fermented dough (17.5 oz.), fermented for at least 3 hours
800 g carrot (28 oz.), grated
40 g salt (1.5 oz.)
20 g sugar (1½ Tbsp.)
100 g butter (3.5 oz.), softened
50 g powdered milk (1.5 oz.), optional
1,100 ml water (37 fl. oz.), approximately, depending on the flour used
20 g yeast (0.7 oz.)

Preparation

In a work area with a temperature of 22° to 25°C (71.5° to 77°F), use a base temperature of 62°C (208°F) for an electric mixer or a kneading machine.

Calculate the temperature needed for the water in the recipe.

Prepare, weigh, and measure the raw ingredients.

Final Kneading

In the mixing bowl of the machine used, place the flour, grated carrot, salt, sugar, powdered milk, butter, and the yeast, which has been previously dissolved in the water. Knead for 8 to 10 minutes on low speed. At the beginning of kneading, called the frasage stage, slowly add small pieces of the fermented dough starter bit by bit.

The temperature of the dough should be 24°C (75°F) at the end of kneading. It should have a somewhat firm texture. Cover the dough with plastic wrap after kneading.

Fermenting

Allow 50 to 60 minutes for the first rising, depending on the temperature of the dough and the humidity and temperature of the work area.

Punch down the dough after 30 minutes.

Weighing

Section, weigh, and round the dough. Rest the rounded sections for 5 to 10 minutes.

Shaping

Shape the dough into rounds, short loaves, or carrot shapes. Place the loaves, seam side down, on canvas. Lightly buttered loaf pans can also be used.

Proofing

Proof the loaves for 50 to 60 minutes in an area free of drafts to prevent a crust from forming. The dough should double in volume.

Preparing for Baking

The oven should be preheated to 210° to 220°C (400° to 425°F). Fill the oven with steam. Prick holes or cut sausage incisions into the loaves.

Baking

Bake for 20 minutes. Verify doneness. Immediately place the breads in a wicker basket or on cooling racks after removing them from the oven.

Carrot Bread			
Preparation	15 min	0 min	• Calculate the necessary temperatures. • Prepare, weigh, and measure the raw ingredients. • Grate the carrots.
Kneading	8 to 10 min	25 min	• Knead on low speed. • At the frasage stage, add the fermented dough starter. • Check the temperature of the dough.
Fermenting	1 hr	1 hr 25	• Ferment the dough in an area free of drafts. • Punch down the dough after 30 minutes.
Weighing	10 min	1 hr 35	• Weigh and round the sections.
Resting	5 to 10 min	1 hr 45	• Allow the dough to rest for 5 to 10 minutes.
Shaping	10 min	1 hr 55	• Place the shaped loaves, seam side down, on canvas.
Proofing	50 to 60 min	2 hr 55	• Proof the loaves in an area free of drafts to prevent a crust from forming.
Preparing for baking	5 min	3 hr	• Verify the temperature of the oven.
Baking	20 min	3 hr 20	• Verify doneness.
Cooling	5 min	3 hr 25	• Immediately place the baked bread in wicker baskets or on cooling racks.

Herb bread

Introduction

Herb bread is flavored with an assortment of fresh herbs, which vary depending upon the season. Many combinations of fresh herbs can be used, but no single herb should dominate the others. Making herb bread is not particularly difficult.

Storage

Herb bread has a very good shelf life because of the the oil and milk in it.

Shapes

Herb bread can be shaped into short loaves or rounds or baked in open loaf pans. Herbs can be costly, so it is preferable not to make large breads with this dough, to maintain a more moderate price per loaf.

Appearance

Herb bread has a thin, golden brown crust. This bread rises well, producing a fresh, supple, light crumb.

Uses

Herb bread goes well with hot or cold charcuterie (delicatessen meats), salads, cold fish dishes, and especially well with delicate cheeses. It is also delicious with omelets.

Yield

About 3.9 kilograms (8.5 pounds) of dough will yield 13 loaves, 300 g (10.5 oz.) each.

Recipe

1.5 kg bread flour (3 lb. 5 oz.)
500 g whole wheat flour (17.5 oz.)
500 g fermented dough (17.5 oz.), minimum 5 to 6 hours fermentation
150 to 200 g fresh parsley (5 to 7 oz.)
150 g fresh chives (5 oz.)
8 sprigs fresh marjoram, leaves only, *or* 5 g dry marjoram (1 tsp.)
100 g milk powder (3.5 oz.)
50 ml olive oil (1.5 fl. oz.)
1,200 ml water (40.5 fl. oz.)
45 g salt (1.5 oz.)
30 g yeast (1 oz.)

Preparation

In a work area with a temperature of 22° to 25°C (71.5 to 77°F), use a base temperature of 62°C (208°F) with an electric mixer. Calculate the temperature needed for the water. Prepare, weigh, and measure the raw ingredients.

Final Kneading

In the bowl of the electric mixer, blend the two flours on low speed. Add the chopped parsley, marjoram, and chives. Then add the salt, powdered milk, olive oil, and the yeast, previously dissolved in the water. Turn the machine on low speed and knead for 10 minutes. As the ingredients combine, slowly add the fermented dough starter, bit by bit.

The temperature of the dough at the end of kneading should be 24°C (75°F). The dough should have a somewhat firm texture. Cover the dough after kneading to prevent a crust from forming. Note the time the kneading was finished.

Fermenting

Allow 1 hour for the first rising, depending on the temperature of the dough and the humidity and temperature of the work area. Punch down the dough 30 minutes after the kneading was stopped.

Weighing

Section, weigh, and round the dough. Allow the dough to rest for 5 to 10 minutes, covered with plastic wrap.

Shaping

Shape the sections of dough as desired into rounds, short loaves, or braids, or bake in lightly greased open loaf pans. Place unmolded loaves on canvas, seam side down.

Proofing

Proof the dough for approximately 1 hour in an area free of drafts to prevent a crust from forming. The dough should double in volume.

Preparing for Baking

Check that the oven has been preheated to 210° to 220°C (400° to 425°F). Prick holes or score sausage incisions on the top of the bread. Fill the oven with steam.

Baking

Bake for 20 minutes. Verify doneness. Immediately place the baked loaves in a wicker basket or on cooling racks after removing them from the oven.

Herb Bread			
Preparation	15 min	0 min	• Calculate the necessary temperatures. • Prepare, weigh, and measure the raw ingredients.
Kneading	8 to 10 min	25 min	• Knead on low speed. • At the frasage stage, add the fermented dough. • Check the temperature of the dough.
Fermenting	1 hr	1 hr 25	• Place the dough in an area free of drafts. • Punch down after 30 minutes.
Weighing	5 min	1 hr 30	• Section, weigh, and round the dough.
Shaping	10 min	1 hr 40	• Shape the dough as desired. • Place the loaves on canvas, seam side down.
Proofing	1 hr	2 hr 40	• Proof in an area free of drafts. • The loaves should double in volume.
Preparing for baking	5 min	2 hr 45	• Check the temperature of the oven.
Baking	20 min	3 hr 05	• Verify doneness.
Cooling	5 min	3 hr 10	• Immediately place the loaves in wicker baskets or on cooling racks.

Carrot-herb bread

Introduction

Carrot-herb bread marries the breads discussed on the two previous pages, resulting in a colorful, attractive, and appetizing bread. Carrot-herb bread is rich and flavorful. It is not particularly difficult to make.

Storage

Carrot-herb bread has a very good shelf life because of the fermented dough starter used in it.

Shapes

Carrot-herb bread can be shaped in short loaves or rounds or baked in open loaf pans.

Appearance

The golden crust of this bread is delicate and thin. The crumb is exceptionally colorful and supple, with even air pockets.

Uses

Carrot-herb bread goes well with salads, fish terrines, cold meats, meats with sauces, game, omelets, and fresh cheeses.

Yield

About 4.8 kilograms (10.5 pounds) of dough yields 19 loaves, 250 grams (9 ounces) each.

Recipe

1.8 kg bread flour (3 lb. 14.5 oz.)
100 g whole-wheat flour (3.5 oz.)
500 g fermented dough starter (17.5 oz.), fermented for at least 3 hours
700 to 800 g carrots (24.5 to 28 oz.), grated
200 g fresh parsley (7 oz.), chopped
8 sprigs fresh marjoram, leaves only
40 g fresh chives (1.5 oz.)
60 g salt (2 oz.)
40 g sugar (1.5 oz.)
100 g butter (3.5 oz.), softened, *or* 100 ml olive oil (3.5 fl. oz.)
50 g powdered milk (1.5 oz.), optional
1,200 ml water (40.5 fl. oz.), approximately, depending on the flour
30 g yeast (1 oz.)

Procedures

With an electric mixer, use a base temperature of 62°C (208°F). Knead for 8 minutes on low speed. To make this bread, follow the procedures given for herb bread on page 85.

Three types of bread

1. Carrot bread

2. Herb bread

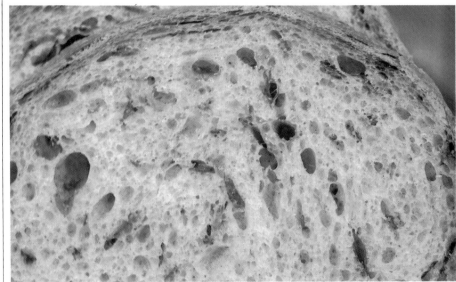

3. Carrot-herb bread

Whole-wheat bread with dried fruits

Introduction

Whole-wheat bread made with assorted dried fruits is both flavorful and attractive. The dried fruits add a tart, sweet flavor. This bread is not particularly difficult to make.

Storage

Whole-wheat bread with dried fruits has an excellent shelf life and can be made the day before it is to be sold or served.

Appearance

Whole-wheat bread with dried fruits has an attractive deep golden brown crust augmented by the dried fruits.

Uses

This is a hearty, filling bread, recommended for breakfast and tea time.

Yield

The recipe below yields approximately 16 loaves, 400 grams (14 ounces) each. The loaves are baked in either loaf pans or cake (génoise) pans.

Recipe

5 kg whole-wheat dough (11 pounds), see recipes, pages 69–74
400 g pitted prunes (14 oz.), quartered
400 g dried apricots (14 oz.), quartered
300 g hazelnuts (10.5 oz.), chopped
300 g raisins (10.5 oz.), blanched and drained

Making the Final Dough

Choose the recipe for the whole-wheat bread of preference. The dough must be somewhat firmer than usual, so use less water than the amount called for in the recipe. Add the dried fruits and hazelnuts at the end of kneading; mix on low speed for 2 minutes so they are well incorporated.

Checking the Dough

The temperature of the dough should be 24°C (75°F) after kneading. Remove the dough from the machine and cover it with plastic wrap. Note the time the kneading was stopped.

Fermenting

Allow 80 to 90 minutes for fermentation in an area free of drafts. Punch down the dough 40 minutes after the kneading was stopped.

Weighing

Divide and weigh 400-gram (14-ounce) sections of dough. Round the sections, and allow them to rest for 5 minutes.

With a pastry brush, butter the loaf pans or cake molds, if used.

Shaping

Shape the loaves as desired, dusting with a minimum of flour. Place the loaves in the molds, seam side down.

Proofing

Proof the loaves covered with plastic wrap in a slightly humid proof box at 25°C (75°F), or in a warm area free of drafts. The dough should rise 2 to 3 centimeters (¾ to 1⅛ inches) above the top of the mold.

Preparing for Baking

The oven temperature should be 210° to 220°C (400° to 425°F). Fill the oven with steam. Place the molds on hot sheet pans, leaving space between them.

Baking

Bake the breads for 30 to 40 minutes. Lower the temperature of the oven halfway through baking. Stop the steam 10 minutes before the breads are removed. Toward the end of baking, cover the loaves with parchment paper to prevent the crust from becoming too dark.

Cooling

Immediately place the breads on cooling racks as they come out of the oven.

This bread is best when eaten several hours after cooling.

Whole-Wheat Bread with Dried Fruits

Preparation	**15** min	**0** min	• *Calculate the necessary temperatures.* • *Prepare, weigh, and measure the raw ingredients.*
Kneading	**10** min	**25** min	• *Knead on low speed.*
Fermenting	**80 to 90** min	**1** hr **55**	• *Punch down the dough after 40 minutes.* • *Place in an area free of drafts.*
Weighing	**5** min	**2** hr	• *Weigh and round the sections, using a minimum of flour.*
Resting	**5** min	**2** hr **05**	• *Cover the rounds with plastic wrap.*
Shaping	**10** min	**2** hr **15**	• *Place the rounds in molds, seam side down.*
Proofing	**75 to 90** min	**3** hr **45**	• *Proof the loaves, covered, in a slightly humid proof box or in a warm area.*
Preparing for baking	**5** min	**3** hr **50**	• *Check the temperature of the oven.*
Baking	**30 to 40** min	**4** hr **30**	• *Do not supply excessive steam.* • *Observe the baking, and cover the loaves if necessary to avoid overbrowning.*
Cooling	**5** min	**4** hr **35**	• *Unmold and immediately place on cooling racks.*

Wheat-germ bread

Introduction
Wheat-germ bread is more common in Great Britain and the United States than it is in France, where it is only rarely made. Wheat-germ bread is made with wheat flour and 5 to 20 percent wheat germ, based on the amount of flour. This bread is recommended for its high nutritional value. Wheat-germ bread is not particularly difficult to make.

Storage
Wheat-germ bread has a good shelf life.

Shapes
Wheat-germ bread can be shaped into rounds or short loaves. Each loaf can consist of 200 to 400 grams (7 to 14 ounces) of dough.

Appearance
The crust has a reddish brown color with flecks of wheat germ throughout. The crumb is yellowish and light, with small air pockets.

Uses
This bread goes well with all food. It is especially recommended for those on a high-protein diet.

Yield
The recipe below yields approximately 15 loaves, using 350 grams (12.5 ounces) of dough for each.

Recipe
2.7 kg bread flour (5 lb. 14.5 oz.)
600 g fermented dough starter (21 oz.),
   fermented for a minimum of 3 hours
180 g wheat germ (6.5 oz.)
100 g powdered milk (3.5 oz.)
55 g salt (2 oz.)
45 g yeast (1.5 oz.)
1,700 ml water (57.5 fl. oz.)

Preparation
In a work area with a temperature of 22° to 25°C (71.5° to 77°F), use a base temperature of 62° to 64°C (208° to 211°F) for an electric mixer. Calculate the temperature needed for the water using the base temperature. Prepare, weigh, and measure the raw ingredients.

Final Kneading
Mix the wheat germ and flour in the bowl of the electric mixer until well blended. Dissolve the yeast in the water. Add the salt, powdered milk, and yeast/water to the flour and wheat germ.

Start the machine on low speed. When the ingredients begin to pull together (the frasage stage), slowly add the fermented dough starter in small pieces. Knead the dough for 10 minutes on low speed. The dough should take on body and elasticity throughout kneading.

The dough should have a temperature of 23° to 24°C (73.5° to 75°F) after kneading, with a rather firm consistency. Cover the dough with plastic wrap to prevent a crust from forming. Note the time kneading was stopped.

Fermenting
Allow the dough to rise for 80 to 90 minutes in an area free of drafts. Punch down the dough after 40 minutes.

Weighing
Divide and weigh out 350-gram (12.5-ounce) sections of dough. Round the sections and let them rest for 5 minutes, covered with plastic wrap.

Shaping
After resting the loaves, shape them as desired into short loaves or rounds, and place them on canvas, in rising molds or in open loaf pans to proof.

Proofing
Allow 1 to 1¼ hours for proofing, depending on the temperature and humidity of the work area. Avoid overproofing, which could cause a crust to form.

Preparing for Baking
Check that the oven is preheated to 220° to 230°C (425° to 450°F). Start filling the oven with steam.

Score the loaves with decorative sausage incisions and the rounds with crosses.

Baking
Bake the breads for approximately 30 to 35 minutes, depending on their shape. Breads baked in loaf pans tend to take longer than those baked freestanding.

After baking is complete, immediately place the bread in wicker baskets or on cooling racks after removing them from the oven.

Wheat-Germ Bread			
Preparation	10 min	0 min	• Calculate the temperatures needed. • Prepare, weigh, and measure the raw ingredients.
Kneading	10 min	20 min	• Knead the dough on low speed. • Add the fermented starter at the frasage stage. • Check the temperature of the dough.
Fermenting	90 min	1 hr 50	• Place the dough in an area free of drafts. • Punch down the dough after 40 minutes.
Weighing	5 min	1 hr 55	• Section, weigh, and round the dough.
Resting	5 min	2 hr	• Cover the sections with plastic wrap and allow them to rest.
Shaping	10 min	2 hr 10	• Shape the rounds as desired, placing them seam side down.
Proofing	1 hr 15	3 hr 25	• Place the loaves in an area free of drafts. • Avoid overproofing.
Preparing for baking	5 min	3 hr 30	• Verify the temperature of the oven.
Baking	30 min	4 hr	• Check the color and tap the crust to verify doneness.
Cooling	5 min	4 hr 05	• Immediately place the breads in a wicker basket or on cooling racks.

High-gluten bread

Introduction

High-gluten bread is considered good for those on a low-starch diet, as much of the starch is washed out of gluten flour. In France, regulations stipulate that a bread must contain a minimum of 20 percent gluten flour to be called low-gluten bread and a minimum of 60 percent gluten flour to be called gluten bread. No such regulations exist in the United States.

Both low- and high-gluten breads are made with wheat flour. Gluten breads are not particularly difficult to make.

Storage

Gluten bread has a good shelf life.

Shapes

Gluten bread can be shaped into straight or horseshoe-shaped loaves, baked in open loaf pans, or baked in sheet molds.

Appearance

Gluten bread has a thin, golden brown crust. The crumb has a creamy to yellowish color, depending on the amount of gluten used. The texture is airy and even.

Uses

Gluten bread is especially good for breakfast or at tea, toasted and untoasted.

Yield

About 4 kilograms (8 pounds 13 ounces) of dough will yield approximately 13 loaves, 300 grams (10.5 ounces) of dough each.

Recipe

400 g bread flour (14 oz.)
1.6 kg gluten flour (3.5 lb.)
60 g yeast (2 oz.)
60 g salt (2 oz.)
2 L water (67.5 fl. oz.)

Preparation

In a work area with a temperature of 22° to 25°C (71.5° to 77°F), use a base temperature of 56° to 58°C (197° to 201°F) for an electric mixer and 54°C (194°F) for a kneading machine.

Calculate the temperature needed for the water using the appropriate base temperature.

Prepare, weigh, and measure the raw ingredients.

Final Kneading

Sift together the flour and gluten flour, and place them in the bowl of the kneading machine or electric mixer. Add the salt, and then add the yeast, which has been previously dissolved in the water from the recipe. In an electric mixer, knead for 15 minutes on low speed. In a kneading machine, knead for 3 minutes on low speed, then for 12 minutes on medium speed.

The temperature of the dough after kneading should be 24°C (75°F).

Place the dough in a container, and cover with plastic wrap. Note the time kneading was stopped.

Fermenting

Place the dough in an area free of drafts and allow it to rise for 20 to 30 minutes. The length of time for fermentation will vary depending on the temperature of the dough and the temperature and humidity of the work area.

Weighing

Divide, weigh out, and round 300-gram (10.5-ounce) sections of dough.

Allow the dough to rest for 5 minutes, covered with plastic wrap.

Shaping

It may be necessary to shape the loaves in steps to prevent tearing the dough, as it is not very elastic. Dust the sections with a minimum of flour throughout this procedure.

Proofing

Place the shaped loaves, seam side down, on canvas to proof. Allow 1¼ to 1½ hours for proofing, depending on the temperature and humidity of the work area.

Be careful not to overproof the loaves, which could cause a crust to form.

Preparing for Baking

Verify that the oven has been preheated to 200° to 210°C (about 400°F). Start filling the oven with steam.

Score the loaves with decorative sausage incisions.

Baking

Bake the loaves for 40 to 45 minutes. Stop the steam 5 minutes before the breads have finished baking.

Verifying Doneness

When baked, the crusts will be golden and the loaves will sound hollow when tapped.

Cooling

Immediately place the baked breads in wicker baskets or on cooling racks after removing them from the oven.

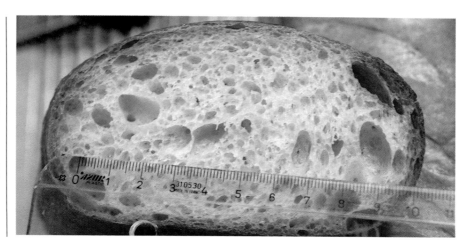

Low-gluten bread

This recipe produces approximately 12 loaves, 300 grams (10.5 ounces) of dough each.

Recipe

1.6 kg bread flour (3.5 lb.)
400 g gluten flour (14 oz.)
40 g yeast (1.5 oz.)
1,600 ml water (54 fl. oz.)

Final Kneading

Use a base temperature of 56° to 58°C (197° to 201°F) if using an electric mixer, or a base temperature of 54°C (194°F) if using a kneading machine. Calculate the temperature of the water in the recipe using the appropriate base temperature.

Blend the wheat flour and gluten flour in the bowl of the kneading machine or electric mixer. (The two flours can be sifted together before placing them in the machine.) Add the salt, and then the yeast, which has previously been dissolved in the water. In an electric mixer, knead for 15 minutes on low speed. In a kneading machine, knead for 3 minutes on low speed and for 12 minutes on medium speed.

The temperature of the dough should be 24°C (75°F) after kneading. The texture should be fairly firm, and the dough should have a good elasticity. Cover the dough with plastic wrap. Note the time kneading was stopped.

Fermenting

Allow 20 to 30 minutes for the dough to rise, depending on the temperature of the dough and the temperature and humidity of the work area.

Weighing

Divide and weigh the dough into 300-gram (10.5-ounce) sections. Round the sections carefully so as not to tear the dough. Allow the rounds to rest for 5 minutes, covered with plastic wrap.

Shaping

Shape the rounds of dough as desired, being careful not to tear the dough. The breads can be shaped into short loaves, rounds, or horseshoes, or they can be placed in loaf pans.

The loaves may be scored with decorative incisions before proofing.

Proofing

Place the loaves on canvas, seam side down. Allow 1¼ to 1½ hours to proof the loaves, depending on the temperature of the work area.

Be careful not to overproof the loaves, which could cause a crust to form.

Preparing for Baking

Check that the oven has been preheated to 200° to 210°C (about 400°F). Start filling the oven with steam. Score the loaves with decorative sausage incisions if they were not scored before proofing.

Baking

Bake the loaves for 35 to 40 minutes. Cool in wicker baskets or on cooling racks immediately after removing them from the oven.

Gruau bread

Introduction

In France regulations stipulate that the only flour to be used for making gruau bread is gruau flour. Gruau flour is most similar to patent flour in the United States. Adding 2 percent powdered milk and 1 percent malt, based on the amount of flour, will improve the taste and texture of the bread.

Storage

Gruau bread should be eaten when very fresh, within a day from when it was made.

Shapes

Gruau bread is often shaped into baguettes or loaves and baked on baking sheets or directly on the oven floor. The loaves can also be baked in open loaf pans, or the dough can be shaped into fanciful forms such as balloons, pouches, or split loaves.

Appearance

Gruau bread has a thin, crisp, golden crust with a supple, airy crumb.

Uses

Gruau bread can be eaten with all foods and is particularly good for breakfast and snacking.

Recipe

1 kg patent flour (35 oz.)
20 g salt (1½ Tbsp.)
10 g malt (2 tsp.)
20 g powdered milk (1½ Tbsp.)
30 g yeast (1 oz.)
700 ml water (23.5 fl. oz.)

Preparation

Use a base temperature of 60°C (204°F) to calculate the temperature needed for the water in the recipe.

Prepare, weigh, and measure the raw ingredients.

Final Kneading

In the bowl of an electric mixer, place the flour, salt, malt, powdered milk, and yeast, previously dissolved in the water.

Knead for 4 minutes on low speed, and then for 4 minutes on medium speed.

The temperature of the dough should be no more than 23° to 24°C (73.5° to 75°F) after kneading. It should have a somewhat firm texture.

Fermenting

Allow the dough to rise for 50 to 60 minutes, depending on the temperature of the work area, which should be free of drafts.

Weighing

Divide and weigh the dough as necessary for the shape to be made. Round the sections and allow them to rest for 10 minutes, covered with plastic wrap.

Shaping

Shape the sections of dough as desired. Place the shaped loaves on canvas or on lightly greased baking sheets.

Proofing

Cover the loaves with plastic wrap and proof for about 1½ hours, depending on the temperature of the work area, which should be free of drafts. Be careful not to overproof the dough.

Preparing for Baking

Check that the oven has been preheated to 230° to 240°C (about 450°F). Start filling the oven with steam. Make sausage incisions on tops of baguettes and loaves.

Baking

Bake the breads for 20 to 25 minutes. Turn the baking sheets halfway around toward the end of baking to ensure even baking.

Cooling

Immediately place the baked loaves in wicker baskets or on cooling racks after removing them from the oven.

Gruau Bread			
Preparation	15 min	0 min	• *Calculate the necessary temperatures.* • *Prepare, weigh, and measure the raw ingredients.*
Kneading	8 min	23 min	• *Knead on low speed for 4 minutes, then on medium speed for 4 minutes more.*
Fermenting	50 to 60 min	1 hr 20	• *Place the dough in an area free of drafts.*
Weighing	5 min	1 hr 25	• *Weigh and round the sections of dough.*
Resting	10 min	1 hr 35	• *Rest the sections, covered with plastic wrap, in an area free of drafts.*
Shaping	10 min	1 hr 45	• *Shape and cover the loaves to prevent a crust from forming.*
Proofing	1 hr 30	3 hr 15	• *Be careful not to overproof the dough.*
Preparing for baking	5 min	3 hr 20	• *Check the temperature of the oven.* • *Start filling the oven with steam.* • *Score decorative incisions in the loaves.*
Baking	20 to 25 min	3 hr 45	• *Check for doneness after 20 minutes.*
Cooling	5 min	3 hr 50	• *Immediately place the baked loaves in wicker baskets or on cooling racks.*

Oyster bread

Introduction

Oyster bread is very rustic and is not often made. It is based on a mixture of rye flour and whole-wheat flour or light whole-wheat flour. Either a mixed starter or fermented dough starter taken from a previously made batch of bread dough can be used. A flavorful and nourishing bread, oyster bread is not particularly difficult to make.

Storage

Oyster bread has a good shelf life. Bakeries often make oyster bread a day ahead, as it is easier to slice the day after baking.

Shapes

Oyster bread can be shaped into rounds or short loaves, or it can be baked in open or closed loaf pans or round molds. Each loaf usually consists of 350 to 400 grams (12.5 to 14 ounces) of dough.

Appearance

The crust is thin and golden brown. The crumb is light brown, airy, and supple.

Uses

Oyster bread goes particularly well with oysters, although it can also accompany other seafood. It is equally good toasted and buttered, with honey drizzled on top.

Yield

About 1.8 kilograms (3 pounds 14.5 ounces) of dough will yield approximately 16 loaves, 350 grams (12.5 ounces) of dough each.

Recipe

1 kg rye flour (35 oz.)
600 g mixed starter or fermented dough starter (21 oz.), fermented for a minimum of 4 hours
60 g salt (2 oz.)
40 g yeast (1.5 oz.)
2,100 ml water (71 fl. oz.)
100 g powdered milk (3.5 oz.)

Preparation

Use a base temperature of 62° to 64°C (208° to 211°F) for an electric mixer, and 65° to 68°C (213° to 219°F) for a kneading machine. Calculate the temperature for the water in the recipe using the appropriate base temperature. Prepare, weigh, and measure the raw ingredients.

Final Kneading

Blend the flour and powdered milk well, add the salt and the mixed starter or fermented dough starter, and the yeast, previously dissolved in the water. Knead for 10 minutes on low speed. The temperature of the dough after kneading should be 23° to 24°C (73.5° to 75°F). The dough should have a firm texture.

Fermenting

Allow the dough to rise for 1 hour, punching it down after 30 minutes.

Weighing

Divide and weigh out 350-gram (12.5-ounce) sections of dough. Round the sections, dusting with a minimum of flour. Allow the rounds to rest for 5 minutes, covered with plastic wrap.

Shaping

Being careful not to tear the dough, shape the dough as desired into loaves or rounds, or place it in round bread molds.

Proofing

Allow about 1 hour to proof the shaped dough, depending on the temperature of the dough and the temperature and humidity of the work area. The dough should be in a draft-free area to prevent a crust from forming. Avoid overproofing. The loaves should be nicely rounded.

Preparing for Baking

Check that the oven has been preheated to 220° to 230°C (425° to 450°F). Fill the oven with steam for loaves that are not in molds. No steam is needed for loaves baked in closed molds. Prick the loaves or score the loaves with shallow incisions.

Baking

Bake for 25 to 30 minutes. Stop the steam 5 minutes before the breads are removed from the oven. Immediately place the baked loaves in wicker baskets or on cooling racks after removing them from the oven.

Oyster Bread			
Preparation	15 min	0 min	• Calculate the temperatures needed. • Prepare, weigh, and measure the raw ingredients.
Kneading	10 min	25 min	• Knead on low speed for 10 minutes. • Check the consistency of the dough.
Fermenting	1 hr	1 hr 25	• Punch down the dough after 30 minutes.
Weighing	5 min	1 hr 30	• Dust with rye or light brown flour.
Resting	5 min	1 hr 35	• Cover the sections with plastic wrap.
Shaping	10 min	1 hr 45	• Dusting with a minimum of flour, shape the loaves as desired.
Proofing	1 hr	2 hr 45	• The length of time for proofing depends on the temperature of the work area (which should be draft free).
Preparing for baking	5 min	2 hr 50	• Check the temperature of the oven. • Use steam only for breads that are not in molds.
Baking	25 to 30 min	3 hr 20	• Stop the steam, if used, 5 minutes before the breads are removed from the oven.
Cooling	5 min	3 hr 25	• Unmold and immediately place the breads on cooling racks or in wicker baskets.

Italian bread

Introduction
A French version of Italian bread can be traced to southeastern France, where it is called "mains niçoises."

The procedure for making the dough for Italian bread is not particularly difficult, although shaping the loaves requires professional experience.

Storage
Because the crumb is very tight and small, Italian bread has an excellent shelf life.

Shapes
Italian bread can be shaped into large loaves, or the dough can be rolled out into a sheet with a rolling pin, cut into small pieces, and shaped as desired.

Appearance
The crust is thin and straw colored. Italian bread rises into a very round loaf and has a tight, even crumb.

Uses
Italian bread goes well with most foods, particularly salads. The olive oil used to prepare it contributes to the bread's distinctive, agreeable flavor.

Yield
About 5 kilograms (11 pounds) of dough will yield approximately 14 loaves, 350 grams (12.5 ounces) of dough each.

Recipe
2 kg fermented dough starter (4 lb. 6.5 oz.), fermented for 5 to 6 hours
2 kg bread flour (4 lb. 6.5 oz.)
200 ml olive oil (7 fl. oz.)
800 ml water (27 fl. oz.)
30 g salt (1 oz.)
30 g yeast (1 oz.)

Preparation
For a work area with a temperature of 22° to 25°C (71.5° to 77°F), use a base temperature of 60°C (240°F) for an electric mixer and 65° to 68°C (213° to 219°F) for a kneading machine. Calculate the temperature of the water used in the recipe with the appropriate base temperature. Prepare, weigh, and measure the raw ingredients.

Final Kneading
In the bowl of a kneading machine or an electric mixer, place the flour, olive oil, and salt. Add the yeast, which has been dissolved in the water.

Knead on low speed until the dough starts to come together (frasage stage), and then slowly add the fermented dough starter in small pieces. Knead for 8 minutes on low speed. Note the time kneading was stopped.

The temperature of the dough should be 24° to 25°C (75° to 77°F) after kneading. The dough should be firm and feel somewhat dry. Cover the dough with plastic wrap after kneading.

Fermenting
Allow 30 to 40 minutes for the first rising, depending on the temperature of the dough and the temperature and humidity of the work area. The dough should not be punched down during fermentation.

Weighing
Divide and weigh out 350-gram (12.5-ounce) sections of dough. Round the sections, dusting with a minimum of flour. Allow the rounds to rest for 5 minutes.

Shaping
Although breads of any shape can be formed with Italian bread dough, a specially shaped bread can be made by following the directions given here.

Shape the dough into loaves. Squeeze a section of dough at each end to create three sections of bread, all attached. The two equally sized ends should be smaller than the middle section. Score the loaves with straight lengthwise incisions in the larger, middle section. See, in photo above, the second bread from the left.

Proofing
Allow 1 to 1½ hours for proofing, depending on the temperature of the work area. The dough should double in volume. Cover the loaves with plastic wrap to prevent a crust from forming.

Preparing for Baking
Check that the oven has been preheated to 230° to 240°C (about 450°F). Start filling the oven with steam.

Baking
Bake for approximately 20 to 25 minutes. Check for doneness after 20 minutes; the loaves should sound hollow when tapped. Immediately place the loaves on cooling racks or in wicker baskets after removing them from the oven.

Italian Bread			
Preparation	15 min	0 min	• Calculate the temperatures needed. • Prepare, weigh, and measure the raw ingredients.
Kneading	8 min	23 min	• Knead on low speed. • At the frasage stage, add the fermented dough. • Check the temperature of the dough.
Fermenting	30 to 40 min	1 hr	• Allow the dough to rise in an area free of drafts.
Weighing	5 min	1 hr 05	• Dust with a minimum of flour.
Resting	5 min	1 hr 10	• Rest the dough for 5 minutes.
Shaping	10 min	1 hr 20	• Shape the dough as desired.
Proofing	1 hr to 1 hr 30	2 hr 30	• Avoid overproofing, which could cause a crust to form.
Preparing for baking	5 min	2 hr 35	• Start filling the oven with steam.
Baking	20 to 25 min	2 hr 55	• Verify doneness; the loaves should sound hollow when tapped.
Cooling	5 min	3 hr	• Immediately place the breads on cooling racks or in wicker baskets.

Corn bread

Introduction
The golden crust of corn bread makes this a particularly attractive bread. This bread is excellent for bakeries that specialize in assorted breads. The procedure for making corn bread poses no particular difficulties.

Storage
Corn bread has an excellent shelf life.

Shapes
Corn bread can be shaped into rounds or short loaves. Each bread is made with 300 to 500 grams (10.5 to 21 ounces) of dough.

Appearance
Corn bread has a smooth, shiny, thin, golden yellow crust. The crumb is pale yellow and quite tight.

Uses
Corn bread goes well with cold sliced meats such as salami, saucisson, mortadella, and ham. It is also delicious toasted and served with honey or preserves.

Yield
The following recipe yields approximately 14 loaves, 350 grams (12.5 ounces) of dough each.

Recipe
1 kg cornmeal (35 oz.)
1 kg bread flour (35 oz.)
1.8 kg fermented dough starter (3 lb. 14.5 oz.), fermented for a minimum of 6 hours
40 g salt (1.5 oz.)
25 g yeast (0.7 oz.)
1,200 ml water (40.5 fl. oz.)

Preparation
In a work area with a temperature of 22° to 25°C (71.5° to 77°F), use a base temperature of 62°C (208°F) for an electric mixer, and 65° to 68°C (213° to 219°F) for a kneading machine. Calculate the required temperature of the water. Prepare, weigh, and measure the raw ingredients.

Final Kneading
In the bowl of the kneading machine or mixer, blend the cornmeal, flour, and salt together. Dissolve the yeast in the water, and add to the flour mixture. Add the fermented dough starter, cut into small pieces. Knead for 10 minutes on low speed. Note the time kneading is completed.

The temperature of the dough should be 24°C (75°F) after kneading. The texture should be somewhat firm. Cover the dough with plastic wrap.

Fermenting
Allow the dough to rise for 80 to 90 minutes, depending on the temperature of the dough and the temperature and humidity of the work area. Punch down the dough after 40 minutes.

Weighing
Divide and weigh out 350-gram (12.5-ounce) sections of dough. Round the sections, and allow them to rest for 5 to 10 minutes, covered with plastic wrap.

Shaping
Shape the dough as desired into short loaves or rounds (see the photo above). Dust with a minimum of flour.

Proofing
Place the shaped loaves, which can be dusted with flour, onto canvas or in molds, seam side down. Allow approximately 1 hour for proofing, depending on the temperature of the work area. The loaves should double in volume. Be careful not to overproof the dough; the dough rises fairly quickly.

Preparing for Baking
Check that the oven has been preheated to 220° to 230°C (425° to 450°F). Place the breads on the peel. Score decorative incisions in the tops of the breads. Start filling the oven with steam; do not add too much.

Baking
Bake 350-gram (12.5-ounce) loaves for 25 to 30 minutes; 500-gram (17.5-ounce) loaves for 35 to 40 minutes. The breads will have an attractive golden yellow color when done.

Corn Rolls with Raisins
The dough for these rolls is the same as that for plain corn bread, with the addition of raisins. Halfway through kneading, add 250 grams (9 ounces) of previously blanched and strained raisins to the corn bread dough. The fermentation is identical to that for plain corn bread. Divide and weigh out 80-gram (3-ounce) sections of dough. Round the sections, cover with plastic wrap, and allow them to rest for 5 minutes. Shape the sections into small rounds or small loaves and place them on canvas or on baking sheets. Proof the breads carefully, as the dough rises quickly. Try to prevent a crust from forming. Prick the rounds, and score the small loaves with sausage incisions. Bake with steam at 240°C (450°F) for 15 to 20 minutes. Cool on cooling racks. These small breads should remain moist and tender.

Corn Bread			
Preparation	15 min	0 min	• Calculate the temperatures needed. • Prepare, weigh, and measure the raw ingredients.
Kneading	10 min	25 min	• Knead on low speed. • Check the consistency of the dough.
Fermenting	1 hr 30	1 hr 55	• After 40 minutes, punch down the dough.
Weighing	5 min	2 hr	• Round the sections fairly tightly, depending on the elasticity of the dough.
Resting	10 min	2 hr 10	• Cover the sections with plastic wrap.
Shaping	10 min	2 hr 20	• Shape the loaves as desired, dusting with a minimum of flour.
Proofing	1 hr	3 hr 20	• The length of proofing time is determined by the temperature of the work area. • Avoid overproofing.
Preparing for baking	5 min	3 hr 25	• Check the temperature of the oven. • Avoid using excessive steam.
Baking	25 to 40 min	4 hr 05	• Carefully watch the loaves while baking. Baking time is based on the size of the loaf.
Cooling	5 min	4 hr 10	• Immediately place the breads in wicker baskets or on cooling racks.

Méteil bread (Wheat/rye bread)

Introduction

Méteil bread is one of the traditional country-style breads. This bread differs greatly throughout the regions in France. In Brittany méteil bread is made from a mixture of wheat flour and buckwheat flour or barley flour in varying quantities. On the other hand, bread from central France is usually made with a mixture of wheat flour and rye flour in equal quantities. Originally, méteil flour was obtained by a special milling process that ground grains harvested from a field sown with equal quantities of wheat and rye. The most widely accepted definition for méteil bread today is bread made of· equal or varying quantities of rye and wheat flour. Wheat and rye flours are sometimes sold together under the name rye-blend flour in the United States.

Méteil bread is rustic and flavorful, with a pleasant, slightly acid taste. It is also highly nutritious.

Méteil bread is not particularly difficult to make.

Storage

Méteil bread has a very good shelf life because a mixed starter or fermented dough starter is used in the recipe.

Shapes

Méteil bread is usually shaped into exceptionally large rounds or ovals. A single loaf can be made with 500 grams to 1 kilogram (17.5 to 35 ounces) or more of dough.

Appearance

Méteil bread generally has a thick brown crust. It can be given a rustic look by dusting the shaped loaf with flour before baking. This bread rises fairly well and has a gray-colored crumb with a moderately tight texture.

Uses

Méteil bread goes well with all foods and is especially good for picnics and country buffets where hearty foods are served.

Yield

About 7 kilograms (15 pounds 6.5 ounces) of dough will yield 14 loaves, 500 grams (17.5 ounces) of dough each, or 7 loaves, 1 kilogram (35 ounces) of dough each.

Recipe

3.5 kg mixed starter or fermented dough starter (7 lb. 11 oz.) fermented for a minimum of 6 hours

2.16 kg rye flour (4 lb. 11 oz.)
1,300 ml water (44 fl. oz.)
45 g salt (1.5 oz.)
40 g yeast (1.5 oz.)

Preparation

In a work area with a temperature of 22° to 25°C (71.5° to 77°F), use a base temperature of 62°C (208°F) for an electric mixer and 65° to 68°C (213° to 219°F) for a kneading machine. Calculate the temperature needed for the water using the appropriate base temperature.

Final Kneading

In the bowl of an electric mixer or kneading machine, combine the rye flour and salt; add the yeast, which has previously been dissolved in the water. Start to knead on low speed.

At the frasage stage, slowly add small pieces of fermented dough starter.

The consistency of the dough should become more elastic while it is kneaded.

Knead for 10 minutes on low speed.

The dough should be 24°F (75°F) after kneading. Its texture should be firm.

Cover the dough with plastic wrap after kneading to prevent a crust from forming.

Fermenting

Allow 30 to 40 minutes for the dough to rise in a draft-free area, depending on the temperature of the dough and the temperature and humidity of the work area.

Weighing

Dusting with minimal flour, divide and weigh out 500-gram or 1-kilogram (17.5-

or 35-ounce) sections of dough.

Round the sections gently, dusting with very little flour. Let the sections rest for 5 minutes, covered with plastic wrap.

Shaping

Shape the breads as desired.

The placement of the seam will determine the thickness of the crust. For a thin crust, place the breads seam side down on canvas. For a thicker, more rustic crust, place the loaves on floured canvas or in rising molds with the seam on top.

Proofing

Proof the loaves for approximately 1 hour, depending on the temperature of the work area. Cover with plastic wrap, to prevent a crust from forming.

Avoid overproofing.

Preparing for Baking

Check that the oven has been preheated to 220° to 230°C (425° to 450°F), depending on the size of the loaves. The smaller loaves require a hotter oven. Start filling the oven with steam.

Score sausage incisions in long loaves and crisscross incisions on the tops of round loaves.

Baking

Bake 500-gram (17.5-ounce) loaves for 25 to 30 minutes, and 1-kilogram (35-ounce) loaves for 35 to 40 minutes. Stop the steam 5 minutes before removing the breads from the oven.

After verifying doneness by tapping for resonance and checking the color, remove the breads from the oven and immediately place them on cooling racks or in wicker baskets.

Méteil Bread			
Preparation	**15** min	**0** min	• Calculate the necessary temperatures. • Prepare, weigh, and measure the raw ingredients.
Kneading	**8** min	**23** min	• Knead on low speed.
Fermenting	**10** to **15** min	**38** min	• The area should be free of drafts to prevent a crust from forming.
Weighing	**5** min	**43** min	• Gently round the sections, dusting with a minimum of flour.
Resting	**5** min	**48** min	• Rest the sections, covered with plastic wrap.
Shaping	**7** min	**55** min	• Shape as desired.
Proofing	**1** hr	**1** hr **55**	• Proof in an area free of drafts. • Carefully watch the proofing.
Preparing for baking	**5** min	**2** hr	• Verify the temperature of the oven. • Start filling the oven with steam.
Baking	**25** to **40** min	**2** hr **35**	• Baking time is determined by the size of the loaves. • Stop the steam toward the end of baking.
Cooling	**5** min	**2** hr **40**	• Immediately place the loaves on cooling racks or in wicker baskets.

Pullman bread

Introduction

Pullman bread is of Anglo-Saxon origin. British tourists introduced this bread to France at the beginning of the twentieth century. It is known in France as pain de mie.

This bread's popularity is continually growing. It is used for toast at breakfast, canapés for aperitifs and at buffets, and for making sandwiches.

Storage

Pullman bread has a very good shelf life, keeping for several days after it is baked. It also freezes well if covered with plastic wrap.

Shapes

Shape by hand or machine and bake in open or closed square or round bread molds.

Appearance

Pullman bread has a straw-colored crust when baked in covered molds; it is darker when baked in open molds. The crust is very thin. The small white crumb and tight texture are the criteria for a well-made bread.

Uses

Pullman bread can be eaten toasted and buttered for breakfast, or plain at lunch or dinner.

This bread is commonly used in canapés, sandwiches, and in desserts such as apple charlottes.

Yield

The recipe below yields approximately 1.9 kilograms (4 pounds 1 ounce) of dough.

Recipe

1 kg bread flour (35 oz.)
25 g salt (2 Tbsp.)
40 g sugar (1.5 oz.)
40 g yeast (1.5 oz.)
50 g powdered milk (1.5 oz.)
600 ml water (20 fl. oz.)
150 g butter (5 oz.), softened

Preparation

In a work area with a temperature of 22° to 25°C (71.5° to 77°F), use a base temperature of 60°C (204°F) for an electric mixer and 58°C (201°F) for a kneading machine.

Prepare, weigh, and measure the raw ingredients.

Final Kneading

In the work bowl of an electric mixer or kneading machine, combine the flour, salt, powdered milk, sugar, and the yeast, which has been previously dissolved in the water.

Knead on low speed for 4 minutes in an electric mixer or 3 minutes in a kneading machine. Add the butter, and knead on medium speed for 4 minutes with an electric mixer or for 10 minutes with a kneading machine.

The temperature of the dough should be 25° to 26°C (77° to 79°F) after kneading.

The dough should be firm. Cover it with plastic wrap.

Note the time at which kneading was stopped.

Fermenting

Allow the dough to rise approximately 10 minutes, depending on the temperature of the dough and the temperature and humidity of the work area. Keep the dough covered while it rises.

Weighing

Divide and weigh the dough into sections, based on the final size of the loaf (see below). Round the sections.

Allow the sections to rest for 15 minutes in a draft-free area.

Shaping

Shape the dough by hand or use a machine that is made for this purpose.

Place the shaped sections in buttered molds, seam side down. The molds can then be covered, or they can be left uncovered.

For large breads to be baked in covered molds, it is recommended that each section of dough be divided into two equal parts. Shape each section to be long and tight, giving the dough several successive folds if shaping by hand. The two sections are then twisted around each other and placed in the mold. This technique prevents large air pockets from forming and keeps the crumb tight.

Examples of Loaf Sizes

- For an open mold 18 centimeters (7 inches) long by 8 centimeters (3 inches) wide and 8 centimeters (3 inches) high, use 300 grams (10.5 ounces) of dough.
- For a covered mold 38 centimeters (15 inches) long by 11 centimeters (4.5 inches) wide and 10 centimeters (4 inches) high, use 950 grams to 1 kilogram (33.5 to 35 ounces) of dough.
- For a covered mold 27 centimeters (10.5 inches) long by 10 centimeters (4 inches) wide and 9 centimeters (3.5 inches) high, use 750 to 800 grams (26.5 to 28 ounces) of dough.

Proofing

Allow about 1 hour for proofing, depending on the temperature of the work area.

Breads in open molds should rise just over the edge of the mold, approximately tripling in volume.

Breads in closed molds should rise three-quarters of the way up the side of the mold. As the dough rises, close the mold lid on each, or cover with a towel.

Carefully watch the proofing.

Preparing for Baking

Check that the oven has been preheated to 220°C (425°F) for breads in open molds and 230° to 240°C (about 450°F) for breads in closed molds, depending on the size of the mold. Smaller molds require a higher temperature than larger ones.

Baking

Breads in open molds require approximately 25 minutes of baking. Breads in closed molds require approximately 35 to 45 minutes of baking, depending on their size.

Immediately unmold and place the breads on cooling racks after removing them from the oven.

Pullman Bread			
Preparation	15 min	0 min	• *Calculate the temperatures needed.* • *Prepare, weigh, and measure the raw ingredients.* • *Butter the molds.*
Kneading	8 to 13 min	28 min	• *Knead for 3 minutes on low speed, then 10 minutes on medium speed.* • *Check the temperature of the dough.*
Fermenting	15 min	43 min	• *Place the dough in a draft-free area.*
Weighing	5 min	48 min	• *Weigh and round the sections of dough.*
Resting	15 min	1 hr 03	• *Cover the dough with plastic wrap to prevent a crust from forming.*
Shaping	5 min	1 hr 08	• *Shape the dough and immediately place it in the molds, seam side down.*
Proofing	1 hr to 1 hr 15	2 hr 05	• *Place the molded dough in a draft-free area.* • *Carefully watch the rising.*
Preparing for baking	5 min	2 hr 10	• *Check the temperature of the oven.*
Baking	40 to 45 min	2 hr 50	• *Check the breads for doneness after 40 minutes of baking.*
Cooling	5 min	2 hr 55	• *Immediately unmold the breads and place them on cooling racks.*

Normandy cider bread

Introduction

Normandy cider bread is a rather rustic country-style bread with an agreeable, slightly acid taste.

Normandy cider bread is not particularly difficult to make.

Storage

Due to its somewhat lengthy fermentation time and the acidity of the cider, Normandy cider bread has an excellent shelf life.

Shapes

Normandy cider bread is usually made with a minimum of 1 kilogram (35 ounces) of dough, shaped into large round or crown- or loaf-shaped breads.

Appearance

Normandy cider bread has a fairly thick brownish crust.

This bread rises fairly well. It has a gray-colored crumb that is supple and moist, with irregular air pockets.

Uses

Normandy cider bread goes well with foods from the Normandy region, such as fish, meat, vegetable salads, and rillettes. It can also be sliced, toasted, and spread with salted butter.

Yield

The recipe below yields approximately 6.9 kilograms (15 pounds 3 ounces) of dough.

Recipe

1 kg rye flour (35 oz.)
1 kg whole-wheat flour (35 oz.)
1 kg bread flour (35 oz.)
2 kg mixed starter (preferred) or fermented dough started (4 lb. 6.5 oz.), fermented for a minimum of 6 hours
Moisten with 62 to 63 percent of liquid based on the amount of flour; approximately 930 to 945 ml (31.5 to 32 fl. oz.) sparkling cider and 930 to 945 ml (31.5 to 32 fl. oz.) water; the water and cider are used in equal amounts
65 g salt (2 oz.)

Preparation

In a work area with a temperature of 22° to 25°C (71.5° to 77°F), use a base temperature of 62°C (208°F) for an electric mixer and 65° to 68°C (213° to 219°F) for a kneading machine.

Calculate the temperature for the

water using the appropriate base temperature.

Prepare, weigh, and measure the raw ingredients.

Final Kneading

Place the mixed starter or fermented dough starter in the bowl of the kneading machine or electric mixer. Add the flours and blend. Then add the salt, water, and cider. Knead for 10 minutes on low speed.

The temperature of the dough should be 24°C (75°F) after kneading.

The texture of the dough should be somewhat firm.

Cover the dough with plastic wrap after kneading to prevent a crust from forming.

Note the time kneading was stopped.

Fermenting

In a draft-free area, allow 2 to 2½ hours for the dough to rise, depending on the temperature of the dough and the humidity and temperature of the work area.

Punch down the dough twice, at 1-hour intervals.

Keep the dough covered with plastic wrap while it rises.

Weighing

Divide, weigh, and round the dough into 1-kilogram (35-ounce) sections (or larger). Allow the sections to rest for 10 to 15 minutes, covered with plastic wrap.

Shaping

Shape the sections by hand into the desired forms. Refer to the photo on the opposite page for possible shapes.

Place the sections on canvas or in floured rising molds, seam side up.

Proofing

Allow 1½ to 2 hours for the dough to rise, depending on the humidity and temperature of the work area, which should be free of drafts.

Preparing for Baking

Check that the oven has been preheated to 210° to 220°C (400° to 425°F), depending on the size of the loaves. The larger the loaf, the lower the oven temperature should be. Start filling the oven with steam, which should not be excessive.

Baking

Bake the loaves for 40 to 45 minutes, depending on size and shape.

Stop the steam 5 minutes before the loaves are removed from the oven.

Immediately place the loaves on cooling racks or in wicker baskets after removing them from the oven.

Normandy Cider Bread			
Preparation	**15** min	**0** min	• Calculate the necessary temperatures. • Prepare, weigh, and measure the raw ingredients.
Kneading	**10** min	**25** min	• Knead on low speed. • Check the consistency of the dough.
Fermenting	**2** hr to **2** hr **30**	**2** hr **55**	• Punch down the dough twice, at 1-hour intervals.
Weighing	**5** min	**3** hr	• Round the sections, dusting with a minimum of flour.
Resting	**15** min	**3** hr **15**	• Cover the rounds to prevent a crust from forming.
Shaping	**10** min	**3** hr **25**	• Shape as desired.
Proofing	**1** hr **30** to **2** hr	**5** hr **25**	• Proofing time depends on the temperature of the work area, which should be free of drafts. • Watch the proofing carefully.
Preparing for baking	**5** min	**5** hr **30**	• Verify the temperature of the oven. • Start filling the oven with steam, though not excessively.
Baking	**40** min	**6** hr **10**	• Verify doneness.
Cooling	**5** min	**6** hr **15**	• Immediately place the loaves on cooling racks or in wicker baskets.

Hazelnut, walnut, and almond breads

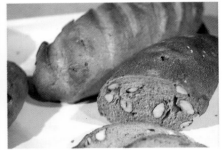

Introduction

Nut breads have a rustic-looking crust that is enhanced by the nuts dispersed throughout the bread.

Nut breads pose no particular difficulties in their preparation.

Storage

Nut breads are made with a fermented dough or mixed starter and rye and whole-wheat flours, all of which add to their excellent shelf life.

Shapes

Nut breads can be shaped into rounds or short loaves, or they can be baked in molds. Each loaf is usually made with 300 to 400 grams (10.5 to 14 ounces) of dough.

Appearance

The crust is deep brown in color. Nut breads rise well and have a supple, moist crumb, with nuts scattered throughout.

Uses

Nut breads go well with various salads, pâtés, terrines, and some fish dishes. They are especially good with cheeses.

Yield

About 4.8 kilograms (10.5 pounds) of dough will yield 12 breads, 400 grams (14 ounces) of dough each.

Recipe

2 kg fermented dough or mixed starter (4 lb. 6.5 oz.)
600 g rye flour (21 oz.)
600 g whole-wheat flour (21 oz.)
750 ml water (25.5 fl. oz.)
25 g salt (2 Tbsp.)
25 g yeast (1 oz.)
800 to 1,000 g nuts (28 to 35 oz.), walnuts, hazelnuts, or almonds

Walnut, Hazelnut, and Almond Breads

Preparation	15 min	0 min	• Calculate the necessary temperatures. • Prepare, weigh, and measure the raw ingredients.
Kneading	10 min	25 min	• Knead on low speed. • Check the consistency of the dough.
Fermenting	40 min	1 hr 05	• Fermentation time depends on the temperature of the work area, which should be draft-free to prevent a crust from forming.
Weighing	5 min	1 hr 10	• Round the sections, using a minimum of flour.
Resting	5 min	1 hr 15	• Rest the sections, covered with plastic wrap.
Shaping	10 min	1 hr 25	• Shape as desired, being careful not to tear the dough.
Proofing	45 min	2 hr 10	• Proof in a draft-free area. • Be careful not to overproof.
Preparing for baking	5 min	2 hr 15	• Check the temperature of the oven. • Start filling the oven with steam.
Baking	20 to 25 min	2 hr 40	• Check for doneness after 20 minutes. • Stop the steam toward the end of baking.
Cooling	5 min	2 hr 45	• Immediately place the loaves in wicker baskets or on cooling racks after baking.

Preparation

In a work area with a room temperature of 22° to 25°C (71.5° to 77°F), use a base temperature of 62°C (208°F) for an electric mixer and 65° to 68°C (213° to 219°F) for a kneading machine.

Calculate the temperature of the water using the appropriate base temperature.

Prepare, weigh, and measure the raw ingredients.

Final Kneading

Blend the two flours in the bowl of the kneading machine or electric mixer to ensure an evenly colored crumb. Add the fermented dough or mixed starter in small pieces, the salt, and the yeast, which has previously been dissolved in the water from the recipe.

Knead for 10 minutes on low speed.

With the machine on low speed, add the nuts. A short blending should be sufficient.

The temperature of the dough should be 23° to 24°C (73.4° to 75°F) after kneading.

The dough should have a firm texture.

Cover the dough with plastic wrap after kneading to prevent a crust from forming. Note the time kneading was stopped.

Fermenting

In a draft-free area, allow the dough to rise for 30 to 40 minutes, depending on the temperature of the dough and the temperature and humidity of the work area.

Weighing

Divide, weigh, and round 400-gram (14-ounce) sections of dough, using a minimum of flour. Allow the rounds to rest for 5 minutes, covered with plastic wrap.

Shaping

Shape the sections by hand as desired. Place the shaped loaves, seam side down, on canvas or in open molds or loaf pans.

Proofing

Allow 40 to 45 minutes for proofing, depending on the temperature and humidity of the work area. Molds or loaf pans tend to require more proofing than free-standing loaves do.

Preparing for Baking

Verify that the oven has been preheated to 230° to 240°C (about 450°F). Start filling the oven with steam.

With the appropriate blade, prick holes or score the loaves with decorative sausage incisions.

Baking

Bake for 20 to 25 minutes. When the breads are ready to come out of the oven, the crust will be golden brown and they will sound hollow when tapped.

Cooling

Immediately place the breads in wicker baskets or on cooling racks after removing them from the oven.

Onion, bacon, and onion/bacon breads

Introduction

Onion, bacon, and onion/bacon breads are very tasty, attractive breads. They are not particularly difficult to make. These breads are appreciated by many and can be made by the beginning baker as well as the experienced professional.

Storage

Onion and bacon breads have a good shelf life.

Appearance

Onion and bacon breads have a thin, dark brown crust. These breads rise well and have a supple airy crumb, flavored and garnished throughout with onion, bacon, or both.

Uses

Onion and bacon breads go well with sauced foods, poultry, and game birds. They are also delicious toasted and served with onion soup or omelets.

Yield

About 6 kilograms (13 pounds) of dough will yield 15 breads, 350 grams (12.5 ounces) of dough each.

Recipe

2 kg bread flour (4 lb. 6.5 oz.)
2 kg fermented dough or mixed starter (4 lb. 6.5 oz.)
45 g salt (1.5 oz.)
40 g yeast (1.5 oz.)
1,100 ml water (37 fl. oz.), approximately

Onion Bread
1 kg onions (35 oz.)
50 ml oil (1.5 fl. oz.)
salt and pepper to taste

Bacon Bread
1 kg bacon (35 oz.)

Onion/Bacon Bread
500 g onions (17.5 oz.)
25 ml oil (1 fl. oz.)
salt and pepper to taste
500 g bacon (17.5 oz.)

Preparing the Onions

Halve the onions and slice lengthwise. Sweat them in a covered sauté pan with the oil, salt, and pepper until golden. Cool without draining.

Preparing the Bacon

Dice the bacon (it is preferable to use smoked bacon) and render it in a sauté pan (without adding any oil). Be careful not to overcook the bacon, which would make it dry and tough. Cool the bacon without draining.

Preparation

In a work area with a room temperature of 22° to 25°C (71.5° to 77°F), use a base temperature of 62°C (208°F) for an electric mixer and 65° to 68°C (213° to 219°F) for a kneading machine. Calculate the temperature for the water using the appropriate base temperature. Prepare, weigh, and measure the raw ingredients.

Final Kneading

Place the mixed starter or fermented dough starter in the work bowl of the kneading machine or electric mixer. Add the flour, salt, and the yeast, which has been previously dissolved in the water. Knead for 10 minutes on low speed. Incorporate the onions, bacon, or both 5 minutes before the kneading is finished.

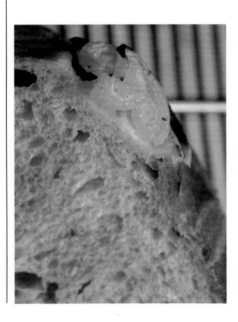

The temperature of the dough should be 24°C (75°F) after kneading. The texture should be somewhat firm. Cover the dough after kneading with plastic wrap. Note the time kneading was stopped.

Fermenting

In a draft-free area, allow the dough to rise for 1 hour and 45 minutes to 2 hours, depending on the temperature of the dough and the temperature and humidity of the work area. Punch the dough down and turn it over after 1 hour. Keep the dough covered with plastic wrap.

Weighing

Divide and weigh out 350-gram (12.5-ounce) sections of dough. Round the sections, and let them rest for 10 minutes, covered with plastic wrap.

Shaping

Shape the sections of dough by hand into rounds or short loaves (see photo on the opposite page for possibilities).

Proofing

Place the shaped loaves on canvas, seam side down. Proof the loaves for 1¼ to 1½ hours, depending on the temperature and humidity of the work area. Cover with plastic wrap to prevent a crust from forming.

Preparing for Baking

Check that the oven has been preheated to 230° to 240°C (about 450°F). Start filling the oven with steam.

Onion breads can be decorated by placing one thin round onion slice in the center of the bread or several round slices lengthwise down the center after moistening the dough with water. Either prick holes or score the tops of the loaves decoratively with an appropriate blade.

Baking

Bake for 25 minutes. Immediately place the baked loaves in wicker baskets or on cooling racks after removing them from the oven.

Onion, Bacon, and Onion/Bacon Breads

Preparation	15 min	0 min	• Calculate the necessary temperatures. • Prepare, weigh, and measure the raw ingredients.
Kneading	10 min	25 min	• Knead on low speed. • Check the consistency of the dough.
Fermenting	1 hr 45 to 2 hr	2 hr 25	• Punch down the dough after 1 hour. • Place in an area free of drafts to prevent a crust from forming.
Weighing	5 min	2 hr 30	• Weigh and round the sections of dough, dusting with a minimum of flour.
Resting	10 min	2 hr 40	• Cover the rounds with plastic wrap.
Shaping	10 min	2 hr 50	• Shape as desired.
Proofing	75 to 90 min	4 hr 20	• Place in a draft-free area. • Watch the rising carefully.
Preparing for baking	5 min	4 hr 25	• Verify the temperature of the oven. • Start filling the oven with steam.
Baking	25 min	4 hr 50	• Observe the baking carefully.
Cooling	5 min	4 hr 55	• Immediately place the breads on cooling racks or in wicker baskets after baking.

Olive bread

Introduction
Olive bread is a moist and flavorful bread; the olives impart a salty tang. It is not particularly difficult to make.

Storage
Olive bread has a very good shelf life because of the mixed starter or fermented dough starter used in it.

Shapes
Olive bread can be shaped into rounds, short loaves, or individual-size breads, or it can be baked in loaf pans. Each loaf is made with 300 to 400 grams (10.5 to 14 ounces) of dough.

Appearance
Olive bread has a dark brown crust. This bread does not rise a great deal, and it has a moderately airy, supple crumb.

Uses
Olive bread goes very well with rustic or simple buffets, salade niçoise, meats, and poultry. It is also good for canapés, toasts, and for accompanying certain cheeses such as Roquefort, bleu d'Auvergne, and sheep-milk cheeses.

Yield
About 5.6 kilograms (12 pounds 5 ounces) of dough will yield 16 loaves, 350 grams (12.5 ounces) of dough each.

Recipe
1.8 kg bread flour (3 lb. 14.5 oz.)
300 g whole-wheat flour (10.5 oz.)
500 g rye flour (17.5 oz.)
300 g fermented dough or mixed starter
   (10.5 oz.)
60 g salt (2 oz.)
40 g yeast (1.5 oz.)
150 ml olive oil (5 fl. oz.)
1,650 ml water (55.5 fl. oz.)
800 g pitted black olives (28 oz.), preferably large Greek olives

Preparation
In a work area with a temperature of 22° to 25°C (71.5° to 77°F), use a base temperature of 62°C (208°F) for an electric mixer and 65° to 68°C (213° to 219°F) for a kneading machine. Calculate the temperature for the water using the appropriate base temperature. Prepare, weigh, and measure the raw ingredients.

Final Kneading
In the work bowl of the kneading machine or electric mixer, blend the flours well. Add the fermented dough or mixed starter, salt, olive oil, and the yeast, which has been previously dissolved in the water. Knead for 10 minutes on low speed. Five minutes before the kneading is complete, incorporate the pitted olives, preferably whole, although they can be cut in half.

At the end of kneading, the temperature of the dough should be 23° to 24°C (73.5° to 75°F). The dough should have a rather firm texture, important in obtaining an even crumb. Cover the dough after kneading with plastic wrap to prevent a crust from forming. Note the time at which kneading was stopped.

Fermenting
In a draft-free area, allow the dough to rise for about 1 hour, depending on the temperature of the dough and the temperature and humidity of the work area. Punch down the dough 30 minutes after kneading. Keep the dough covered with plastic wrap.

Weighing
Divide and weigh out 350-gram (12.5-ounce) sections of dough by hand. Round the sections, and let them rest for 5 minutes, covered with plastic wrap.

Shaping
Shape the sections of dough by hand as desired. Place the shaped loaves on canvas, in open molds, or in closed round molds, seam side down.

Proofing
Proof the loaves for 1 to 1½ hours, depending on their size and on if they are in molds. Breads in molds tend to take longer to proof.

Preparing for Baking
Check that the oven has been preheated to 220° to 230°C (425° to 450°F). Start filling the oven with steam.
Either prick holes or score the tops of the loaves with sausage incisions.

Baking
Bake free-standing loaves for 20 minutes, molded breads for 25 minutes. Verify doneness. Immediately place the loaves on cooling racks or in wicker baskets after removing them from the oven.

Olive Bread			
Preparation	15 min	0 min	• Calculate the required temperatures. • Prepare, weigh, and measure the raw ingredients.
Kneading	10 min	25 min	• Knead on low speed. • Incorporate the olives toward the end of kneading. • Check the temperature of the dough.
Fermenting	1 hr	1 hr 25	• Place in an area free of drafts to prevent a crust from forming.
Weighing	10 min	1 hr 35	• Section the dough, using a minimum of flour. • Allow the dough to rest for 5 minutes.
Shaping	10 min	1 hr 45	• Shape the sections into the desired forms.
Proofing	1 hr to 1 hr 30	3 hr	• Proof in a draft-free area. • Watch the proofing after 45 minutes.
Preparing for baking	5 min	3 hr 05	• Check the temperature of the oven. • Start filling the oven with steam.
Baking	20 min	3 hr 25	• Watch the baking carefully.
Cooling	5 min	3 hr 30	• Immediately place the breads on cooling racks or in wicker baskets after baking.

Barley bread

Introduction
Originally from Scandinavia, barley bread is an attractive, appetizing bread with a light chestnut-colored crust. Although not particularly difficult to make, it is important that each step be carefully followed.

Storage
Barley bread has a good shelf life because it is made with a fermented dough starter.

Shapes
Barley bread can be shaped into a variety of forms, such as short loaves or rounds.

Appearance
Barley bread has an attractive, soft, golden brown crust. This bread rises moderately well, producing a small crumb with a tight, even texture.

Uses
Barley bread goes well with all foods.

Yield
About 4.85 kilograms (10 pounds 9.5 ounces) of dough will yield 16 loaves, 300 grams (10.5 ounces) of dough each.

Recipe
1 kg bread flour (35 oz.)
1 kg barley flour (35 oz.)
1.5 kg fermented dough starter (53 oz.)
1,250 ml water (42 fl. oz.), approximately
45 g salt (1.5 oz.)
20 g yeast (0.7 oz.)
20 g gluten (0.7 oz.), optional

Preparation
In a work area with a temperature of 22° to 25°C (71.5° to 77°F), use a base temperature of 60°C (204°F) for an electric mixer and 58°C (201°F) for a kneading machine. Calculate the temperature for the water using the appropriate base temperature. Prepare, weigh, and measure the raw ingredients.

Final Kneading
Blend the flours well in the bowl of a kneading machine or electric mixer. Add the salt, gluten (if used), and the yeast, which has been previously dissolved in the water. Add the fermented dough starter in small quantities. Knead the dough for 5 minutes on low speed, then for 5 minutes on medium speed. The temperature of the dough should be 24°C (75°F) after kneading. The texture of the dough should be rather firm. Cover the dough with plastic wrap.

Fermenting
Allow the dough to rise for approximately 1 hour, depending on the temperature of the dough and the temperature and humidity of the work area. Punch down the dough 30 minutes after kneading. Keep the dough covered with plastic wrap while it is rising.

Weighing
Divide and weigh out 300-gram (10.5-ounce) sections of dough. Round the dough carefully to prevent tearing. Allow the dough to rest for 10 minutes, covered with plastic wrap.

Shaping
The sections of dough can be shaped into short loaves or rounds. Place them on canvas or in round or long proofing molds, seam side down.

Proofing
Proof the loaves for 1 to 1½ hours, depending on the temperature and humidity of the work area. Proof the loaves in a draft-free area to prevent a crust from forming.

Preparing for Baking
Check that the oven has been preheated to 220° to 230°C (425° to 450°F). Start filling the oven with steam, though not excessively. Score short loaves with sausage incisions and round loaves with polka incisions.

Baking
Bake the breads for 30 to 35 minutes. Verify doneness. Immediately place the baked loaves on cooling racks or in wicker baskets after removing them from the oven.

Barley Bread			
Preparation	15 min	0 min	• Calculate the necessary temperatures. • Prepare, weigh, and measure the raw ingredients.
Kneading	10 min	25 min	• Knead for 5 minutes on low speed. • Knead for 5 minutes on medium speed. • At the frasage stage, add the fermented dough or mixed starter. • Check the consistency of the dough.
Fermenting	1 hr 30	1 hr 55	• Place the dough in a draft-free area. • Punch down the dough after 30 minutes.
Weighing	5 min	2 hr	• Weigh, section, and round the dough.
Resting	10 min	2 hr 10	• Place the sections in a draft-free area, covered with plastic wrap.
Shaping	10 min	2 hr 20	• Shape the sections of dough as desired and place them on canvas or in proofing molds.
Proofing	1 hr 30	3 hr 50	• Proof the loaves in a draft-free area.
Preparing for baking	5 min	3 hr 55	• Check the temperature of the oven.
Baking	20 to 30 min	4 hr 25	• The steam should not be excessive. • Observe the baking closely.
Cooling	5 min	4 hr 30	• Immediately place the baked loaves on cooling racks or in wicker baskets.

Provençale fougasse

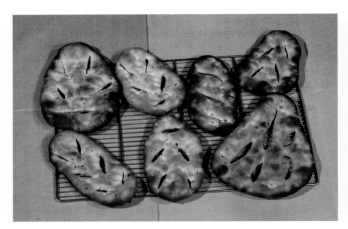

Introduction

As its name indicates, provençale fougasse originated in southern France. Its characteristic thin, flat shape forms a crispy bread consisting mostly of crust.

Provençale fougasse brings to mind the warmth of its native region and is a good addition to any bakery specializing in assorted breads.

Storage

Provençale fougasse has a limited shelf life because of its high proportion of crust and so should be eaten as soon after baking as possible.

Shape

Provençale fougasse is rolled out with a rolling pin into a flat oval and scored just before baking.

Appearance

Provençale fougasse has a very characteristic appearance, as the pictures show. It is ideal for those who love crusty breads.

Uses

Provençale fougasse can be served for breakfast or as a snack. Those who enjoy this bread think it goes well with all foods.

Yield

About 2 kilograms (4 pounds 6.5 ounces) of dough will yield approximately 12 fougasses using 80 grams (3 ounces) of dough for each, or 6 breads using 150 grams (5 ounces) of dough for each.

Recipe

1 kg bread flour (35 oz.)
550 ml water (18.5 fl. oz.), approximately

250 g mixed starter or fermented dough starter (9 oz.), fermented for a minimum of 6 hours.
20 g salt (1½ Tbsp.)
20 g yeast (0.7 oz.)
100 g butter (3.5 oz.), softened, or 100 ml olive oil (3.5 fl. oz.)
100 g bacon (3.5 oz.), thinly sliced, lightly browned

Preparation

In a work area with a temperature of 22° to 25°C (71.5° to 77°F), use a base temperature of 62°C (208°F) for an electric mixer and 65° to 68°C (213° to 219°F) for a kneading machine. Calculate the temperature for the water using the appropriate base temperature. Prepare, weigh, and measure the raw ingredients.

Final Kneading

In the work bowl of a kneading machine or electric mixer, combine the flour, salt, and the yeast, which has been previously dissolved in the water. Knead on low speed. At the frasage stage, incorporate the softened butter or olive oil. Then slowly add the starter or fermented dough starter in small pieces. Knead on low speed for 10 minutes. The dough

should have a supple consistency at this stage. Add the thinly sliced, lightly browned bacon 5 minutes before the end of kneading.

The dough should have a temperature of 24°C (75°F) at the end of kneading. Note the time the kneading is complete. Cover the dough with plastic wrap.

Fermenting

Allow the dough to rise for 50 to 60 minutes in a draft-free area. The temperature of the dough, the temperature and humidity of the work area, and the elasticity of the dough will all affect the fermentation time.

Weighing

Divide the dough into 80-gram (3-ounce) and/or 150-gram (3.5-ounce) sections and round them. Allow the sections to rest for 20 minutes, covered with plastic wrap.

Shaping

Using a rolling pin, roll out the 80-gram (3-ounce) sections into ovals about 10 centimeters (4 inches) long, 5 centimeters (2 inches) wide, and 5 millimeters (¼

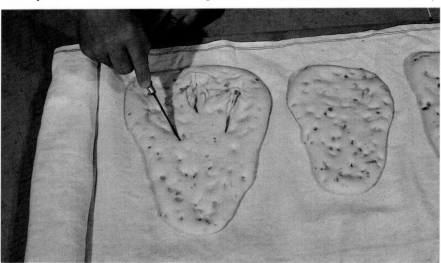

inch) thick. Roll 150-gram (3.5-ounce) sections of dough into ovals 20 centimeters (8 inches) long, 10 centimeters (4 inches) wide, and approximately 8 millimeters (⅓ inch) thick.

Proofing

Proof the dough for 40 to 60 minutes in a draft-free area. Avoid overproofing.

Preparing for Baking

Stretch the ovals of dough by hand until they are about half again as large. With a pastry cutter or paring knife, cut straight or angled incisions through the dough (see the photo on the opposite page). Start filling the oven with steam, but be careful not to add too much.

Baking

Bake the fougasses in a 250°C (475°F) oven. As the dough is rather thin, watch

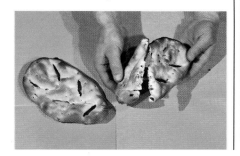

the baking carefully. Immediately place the fougasses on cooling racks or in wicker baskets after removing them from the oven.

Provençale Fougasse			
Preparation	15 min	0 min	• Calculate the necessary temperatures. • Prepare, weigh, and measure the raw ingredients. • Slice and brown the bacon.
Kneading	10 min	25 min	• Knead on low speed. • Incorporate the fermented dough a bit at a time. • Add the bacon halfway through kneading. • Check the temperature of the dough.
Fermenting	50 to 60 min	1 hr 20	• Place the dough in a draft-free area.
Weighing	15 min	1 hr 35	• Weigh and round the sections of dough.
Resting	20 to 30 min	2 hr	• Rest the rounds in a draft-free area.
Shaping	10 min	2 hr 10	• Roll the rounds into ovals with a rolling pin, and place them on canvas.
Proofing	40 to 60 min	3 hr	• Avoid overproofing.
Preparing for baking	5 min	3 hr 05	• Cut incisions in the dough with a pastry cutter.
Baking	8 to 10 min	3 hr 15	• Bake quickly in a hot oven. • Observe the baking carefully.
Cooling	5 min	3 hr 20	• Immediately place the baked bread in wicker baskets or on cooling racks.

Sesame-seed bread

Introduction

Sesame seeds add an agreeable flavor and texture to bread. This type of bread is a good addition for bakeries specializing in assorted breads.

Sesame-seed bread is not particularly difficult to make.

Storage

Sesame-seed bread has a very good shelf life because it is made with fermented dough starter or mixed starter. The powdered milk and sugar in it also add to the richness of this bread.

Shapes

Sesame-seed bread can be shaped into rounds or short loaves. Each bread is usually made with 250 to 350 grams (9 to 12.5 ounces) of dough.

Appearance

This bread rises well. It has a golden brown crust topped with sesame seeds that supply a lighter contrasting color. The even crumb has a supple, soft texture.

Uses

Sesame-seed bread goes well with all foods.

Yield

About 4.8 kilograms (10.5 pounds) of dough will yield 16 loaves of bread, 300 grams (10.5 ounces) of dough each.

Recipe

700 g light or regular whole-wheat flour (4.5 oz.)
1.3 kg bread flour (2 lb. 13 oz.)
500 g fermented dough or mixed starter (17.5 oz.)
45 g salt (1.5 oz.)
35 g yeast (1 oz.)
100 g powdered milk (3.5 oz.)
50 g sugar (1.5 oz.)
250 to 300 g sesame seeds (9 to 10.5 oz.)
1,500 ml water (50.5 fl. oz.), approximately

Preparation

In a work area with a temperature of 22° to 25°C (71.5° to 77°F), use a base temperature of 62°C (208°F) for an electric mixer and 65° to 68°C (213° to 219°F) for a kneading machine.
Calculate the temperature of the water using the appropriate base temperature.
Prepare, weigh, and measure the raw ingredients.

Final Kneading

On low speed, blend the flours and sesame seeds in the work bowl of the kneading machine or electric mixer. Add the fermented dough or mixed starter in small pieces, the salt, powdered milk, sugar, and the yeast, which has been previously dissolved in the water. Knead for 10 minutes on low speed.
The temperature of the dough should be 23° to 24°C (73.5° to 75°F) after kneading is complete. The texture of the dough should be somewhat firm.
Note the time kneading is stopped.

Fermenting

Allow the dough to rise for 1 to 1¼ hours in a draft-free area. The time required for rising depends on the temperature of the dough and the temperature and humidity of the work area.
Punch the dough down after 30 minutes.

Weighing

Divide and weigh out 300-gram (10.5-ounce) sections of dough by hand. Round the sections, and let them rest for 5 to 10 minutes, covered with plastic wrap.

Shaping

Shape the sections of dough into rounds or short loaves. Place the shaped loaves on canvas, seam side down.

Proofing

Proof the dough for 1 to 1¼ hours, depending on the temperature and humidity of the work area. Avoid overproofing.

Preparing for Baking

Verify that the oven has been preheated to 220° to 230°C (425° to 450°F).

Start filling the oven with steam.
With an appropriate blade, prick holes or score the loaves with sausage incisions.
With a pastry brush, brush water or milk on the shaped dough, and sprinkle with sesame seeds.

Baking

Bake the loaves for 25 minutes. Turn off the steam toward the end of baking. Verify doneness, and immediately place the breads in wicker baskets or on cooling racks after removing them from the oven.

Sesame-seed Bread			
Preparation	15 min	0 min	• Calculate the necessary temperatures. • Prepare, weigh, and measure the raw ingredients.
Kneading	10 min	25 min	• Knead on low speed. • Check the consistency of the dough.
Fermenting	1 hr to 1 hr 15	1 hr 40	• Punch down the dough after 30 minutes. • Allow the dough to rise in a draft-free area to prevent a skin from forming.
Weighing	5 min	1 hr 45	• Round the sections, using a minimum of flour.
Resting	10 min	1 hr 55	• Cover the sections with plastic wrap.
Shaping	10 min	2 hr 05	• Shape the sections as desired.
Proofing	1 hr to 1 hr 15	3 hr 20	• Place in an area free of drafts. • Avoid overproofing.
Preparing for baking	5 min	3 hr 25	• Check the temperature of the oven. • Start filling the oven with steam.
Baking	25 min	3 hr 50	• Carefully watch the baking after 20 minutes. • Stop the steam toward the end of baking.
Cooling	5 min	3 hr 55	• Immediately place the baked loaves on cooling racks or in wicker baskets.

Soy bread

Introduction

Soy bread, with its attractive golden brown crust, is a relatively new addition to French bread making. This bread is high in protein because it contains soy flour.

Storage

Soy bread has an excellent shelf life, due to the fermented dough starter and butter or shortening used in it.

Shapes

Soy bread can be shaped into any number of forms.

Appearance

Soy bread has a moderately thick crust. Its cream-colored crumb is supple and tender.

Uses

Soy bread goes well with vegetable salads and rice salads.

Yield

About 5.5 kilograms (12 pounds) of dough will yield 13 loaves of bread, 400 grams (14 ounces) of dough each.

Recipe

2 kg bread flour (4 lb. 6.5 oz.)
600 g soy flour (21 oz.)
300 g rye flour (10.5 oz.)
150 g butter or shortening (5 oz.), softened
400 g mixed or fermented dough starter (14 oz.)
60 g salt (2 oz.)
40 g yeast (1.5 oz.)
2 L water (67.5 fl. oz.), approximately

Preparation

In a work area with a temperature of 22° to 25°C (71.5° to 77°), use a base temperature of 62°C (208°F) for an electric mixer and 65° to 68°C (213° to 219°F) for a kneading machine. Calculate the temperature for the water using the appropriate base temperature. Prepare, weigh, and measure the raw ingredients.

Final Kneading

In the bowl of an electric mixer or kneading machine, blend the flours on low speed. Add the salt, softened butter or shortening, and the yeast, which has been previously dissolved in the water. Slowly incorporate the mixed starter or fermented dough starter, a bit at a time, on low speed. Knead the dough for 10 minutes on low speed.

The temperature of the dough should be 24°C (75°F) after kneading. The texture of the dough should be firm. Cover the dough after kneading, and note the time kneading was stopped.

Fermenting

Allow the dough to rise for approximately 1 hour, depending on the temperature of the dough and the temperature and humidity of the work area. Keep the dough covered while it is rising. Punch down the dough after 30 minutes.

Weighing

Divide and weigh sections of dough to the desired size, based on the size of the final loaves. Round the sections, being careful not to tear the dough. Allow the sections to rest for 5 minutes, covered with plastic wrap.

Shaping

By hand, shape the sections of dough as desired, into rounds, crowns, or short loaves, or bake in loaf pans or other bread molds. Place the shaped sections on canvas or in long or round proofing molds.

Proofing

Allow approximately 1 hour to proof the dough, depending on the temperature of the work area. Place the dough in an area free of drafts to prevent the formation of a crust.

Preparing for Baking

Verify that the oven has been preheated to 230° to 240°C (425° to 450°F), depending on the size of the breads. Smaller loaves require a hotter oven. Start filling the oven with steam, but be careful not to add too much.

Score the loaves with decorative incisions that are appropriate to their shape, such as sausage incisions for loaf breads or polka incisions for round loaves. Lightly dust the loaves with flour before placing them directly on the oven floor.

Baking

Bake for 25 to 30 minutes. Verify doneness, and immediately place the baked loaves in wicker baskets or on cooling racks after removing them from the oven.

Soy Bread			
Preparation	15 min	0 min	• Calculate the necessary temperatures. • Prepare, weigh, and measure the raw ingredients.
Kneading	10 min	25 min	• Knead on low speed, adding the fermented dough or mixed starter a bit at a time. • Check the temperature of the dough after kneading.
Fermenting	1 hr	1 hr 25	• Place in a draft-free area. • Punch down the dough after 30 minutes.
Weighing	10 min	1 hr 35	• Weigh and round sections of dough, being careful not to tear it.
Resting	5 min	1 hr 40	• Cover the sections to prevent a crust from forming.
Shaping	10 min	1 hr 50	• Place the shaped sections on canvas, seam side down, or in bread molds.
Proofing	1 hr	2 hr 50	• Proof in a draft-free area.
Preparing for baking	5 min	2 hr 55	• Check the temperature of the oven. • Start filling the oven with steam.
Baking	25 to 30 min	3 hr 25	• After 25 minutes, check carefully for doneness.
Cooling	5 min	3 hr 30	• Immediately place the baked breads on cooling racks or in wicker baskets.

Bran bread

Introduction
Bran bread is often eaten for its nutritional value and high fiber content. Bran contains protein, salts, minerals, and fiber. It is becoming increasingly popular because of growing interest in nutrition. Bran bread is not particularly difficult to make.

Storage
Bran bread tastes best if not too fresh. It has a very good shelf life and can be made the day before it is served.

Shapes
Bran bread can be shaped into rounds or short loaves and can be baked in loaf pans. Each loaf is made with 300 to 400 grams (10.5 to 14 ounces) of dough.

Appearance
Bran bread has a deep brown crust sprinkled throughout with bran. The crumb has an airy, supple, even texture.

Uses
Bran bread goes well with all foods. It is delicious sliced and toasted for breakfast.

Using a Mixed Starter
Although a fermented dough starter is recommended for bran bread, a mixed starter can be used. Simply replace the fermented dough starter with an equal amount of mixed starter. All procedures for making the bread remain unchanged.

Yield
About 5.6 kilograms (12 pounds 5 ounces) of dough will yield approximately 16 loaves, 350 grams (12.5 ounces) of dough each.

Recipe
600 g fermented dough starter (21 oz.), fermented for a minimum of 4 to 6 hours
450 g bran (16 oz.), preferably finely ground
2,550 g bread flour (5 lb. 9.5 oz.)
1,950 to 2,000 ml water (66 to 67.5 fl. oz.)
60 g salt (2 oz.)
40 g yeast (1.5 oz.)

Preparation
In a work area with a temperature of 22° to 25°C (71.5° to 77°F), use a base temperature of 62° to 64°C (208° to 211°F) for an electric mixer and 65° to 68°C (213° to 219°F) for a kneading machine. Calculate the temperature for the water using the appropriate base temperature.

Final Kneading
In the bowl of a kneading machine or an electric mixer, place the yeast, which has been previously dissolved in the water. Add the bread flour, bran, salt, and fermented dough starter. If using an electric mixer, knead for 10 minutes on low speed and then for 3 minutes on medium speed. If using a kneading machine, knead for 10 minutes on low speed and then for 5 minutes on medium speed.

The temperature of the dough should be 24° to 25°C (75° to 77°F) after kneading. The texture of the dough should be rather firm. Cover the dough with plastic wrap.

Fermenting
Allow the dough to rise for 60 to 80 minutes in a draft-free area. After 30 minutes, punch down the dough.

Weighing
Divide and weigh out 350-gram (12.5-ounce) sections of dough. Round the sections, being careful not to tear the dough. Allow the dough to rest for 5 to 10 minutes, covered with plastic wrap.

Shaping
Shape the sections of dough into rounds or short loaves, and place them on canvas, seam side down. Again, be careful not to tear the dough. Dust with only a minimum of flour when shaping.

Proofing
Proof for about 1 hour, depending on the temperature and humidity of the work area. The breads should double in volume, and the dough should not tear during this second rising. Be careful not to overproof the dough. The dough should remain smooth and not form a skin during proofing. A skin would prevent it from rising properly during baking.

Preparing for Baking
Check that the oven has been pre-heated to 230° to 240°C (about 450°F). Start filling the oven with steam 5 minutes before baking the breads. Score the breads with decorative sausage incisions using an appropriate blade.

Baking
Bake for 25 to 30 minutes, depending on the shape of the bread. Stop the steam 5 minutes before removing the breads from the oven. When the baking is complete, the crust will be deep brown and show resistance when pressed. The finished bread will also have a hollow sound when tapped.

Immediately place the baked breads on cooling racks or in wicker baskets after removing them from the oven.

Bran Bread			
Preparation	15 min	0 min	• Calculate the necessary temperatures. • Prepare, weigh, and measure the raw ingredients.
Kneading	10 min	25 min	• Knead on low speed, and then on medium speed.
Fermenting	1 hr 20	1 hr 45	• Punch down the dough after 30 to 40 minutes. • Keep the dough covered with plastic wrap.
Weighing	5 min	1 hr 50	• Round the dough, being careful not to tear it.
Resting	5 min	1 hr 55	• Cover the rounded sections of dough with plastic wrap.
Shaping	10 min	2 hr 05	• Be careful not to tear the dough.
Proofing	1 hr to 1 hr 15	3 hr 20	• Proofing time depends on the temperature and humidity of the work area. • Proof the dough in a draft-free area.
Preparing for baking	5 min	3 hr 25	• Check the temperature of the oven. • Start filling the oven with steam.
Baking	25 to 30 min	3 hr 55	• Observe the baking carefully. • Stop the steam toward the end of baking.
Cooling	5 min	4 hr	• Immediately place the baked breads in wicker baskets or on cooling racks.

Surprise breads

Introduction

Surprise breads are used for buffets and can be shaped in a variety of ways. Surprise bread gets it name from the way it is presented. The top of the bread is cut off and the inside crumb removed carefully so as not to tear either the crust or the crumb. Sandwiches and canapés are made with the interior of the bread. The decorative canapés and sandwiches are then placed back into the crust, which now serves as a container, and the top of the bread is placed on top to cover its "surprise" or is tilted to reveal its contents.

Surprise breads can be made with rye bread dough, méteil bread dough, or pullman bread dough. The recipe given in this section is for a méteil bread. This bread should be made with great care, as its presentation is especially important.

Storage

Surprise bread should be made a minimum of 48 hours before being served as it will be easier to cut without crumbling when slightly dry. This bread freezes well if covered tightly with plastic wrap.

Shapes

Generally, surprise breads are given a round shape and are baked in génoise molds or metal cake rings. The amount of dough per loaf is determined by the size of the mold used.

It is also possible to bake the breads in a variety of molds, such as squares, ovals, or hearts.

Appearance

Regardless of the type of dough used, the presentation should always be very neat and the texture of the crumb should be even and tight.

Uses

Usually surprise breads are used for buffets, receptions, and cocktail parties. A variety of canapés and small sandwiches can be made using smoked meats, smoked fish, cheese, and compound butters, to name but a few possibilities.

Yield

About 6 kilograms (13 pounds 3 ounces) of dough will yield 4 loaves, 1.5 kilograms (3 pounds 5 ounces) of dough each.

Recipe

1,250 g rye flour (44 oz.)
750 ml water (25.5 fl. oz.)
60 g yeast (2 oz.)
25 g salt (1 oz.)
4 kg fermented dough starter (8 lb. 13 oz.), fermented for a minimum of 6 hours

Preparation

In a work area with a temperature of 22° to 25°C (71.5° to 77°F), use a base

temperature of 62° (208°F) for an electric mixer and 65° to 68°C (213° to 219°F) for a kneading machine. Calculate the temperature for the water using the appropriate base temperature. Prepare, weigh, and measure the raw ingredients.

Final Kneading

In the bowl of a kneading machine or an electric mixer, blend the rye flour, salt, and the yeast, which has been previously dissolved in the water. At the frasage stage, slowly incorporate the fermented dough starter a bit at a time. Check to be sure the dough is not too dry. Knead on low speed for 8 minutes.

The temperature of the dough should be 24°C (75°F) and the texture should be firm after kneading. Cover the dough with plastic wrap, and note the time kneading was completed.

Fermenting

Allow the dough to rise for 10 to 15 minutes, covered with plastic wrap.

Weighing and Shaping

If using a round génoise mold that is 22 centimeters (8.5 inches) in diameter, divide and weigh the dough into 1.5-kilogram (3-pound 5-ounce) sections. The sections can be rounded or shaped into the same form as the mold used.

Place the shaped or rounded sections of dough into buttered molds, seam side down. Moisten the top of the dough with water, using a pastry brush, to prevent a crust from forming, which could cause the dough to dry and perhaps crack during proofing.

Proofing

Proof the molded dough for 45 to 60 minutes, depending on the temperature of the work area. The work area should be free of drafts.

Do not overproof the dough. Overproofing could result in a less tightly textured crumb and may cause an overabundance of air pockets to form, which would make the bread more difficult to cut after baking.

Preparing for Baking

Verify that the oven has been preheated to 220° to 230°C (425° to 450°F). Start filling the oven with steam. With an appropriate blade, score decorative crisscross incisions in the tops of the breads. The breads can also be lightly dusted with flour, using a drum sieve, before scoring.

Baking

Stop the steam in the oven 10 minutes before the breads are finished baking. Allow 35 to 40 minutes for baking, but check the breads for doneness after 35 minutes. Immediately place the breads on cooling racks or in wicker baskets after removing them from the oven.

Surprise Méteil Bread			
Preparation	15 min	0 min	• Calculate the necessary temperatures. • Prepare, weigh, and measure the raw ingredients. • Butter the molds.
Kneading	8 min	23 min	• Knead on low speed. • Check the temperature of the dough.
Fermenting	10 min	33 min	• Allow the dough to rise in a draft-free area.
Weighing	5 min	38 min	• Dust with a minimum of flour.
Shaping	7 min	45 min	• Round or shape the sections immediately after weighing. • Moisten the tops of the loaves with water.
Proofing	45 to 60 min	1 hr 45	• Proof in a draft-free area. • Watch the proofing carefully.
Preparing for baking	5 min	1 hr 50	• Start filling the oven with steam.
Baking	35 to 40 min	2 hr 30	• Stop the steam toward the end of baking. • Verify doneness.
Cooling	5 min	2 hr 35	• Immediately place the baked breads on cooling racks or in wicker baskets.

Viennese breads

Introduction

Viennese bread dough is similar in composition to pullman bread dough (page 98). The most characteristic quality of Viennese bread is its presentation; it has perhaps the most distinctive and attractive scoring of all breads. It is important that the scoring be made immediately after the dough is shaped.

Storage

Viennese bread has a good shelf life.

Shapes

Viennese breads can be shaped into baguettes and baked in long molds, or they can be given a variety of shapes, some of which can be seen in the photograph above.

Appearance

Viennese bread rises well and has a supple golden brown crust that shows scoring beautifully.

This bread has a supple, delicate, airy, and flavorful crumb.

Uses

Viennese bread is often served for breakfast and is a good snack for children.

Yield

About 1,850 grams (4 pounds) of dough will yield 6 baguettes, 300 grams (10.5 ounces) of dough each.

Recipe

1 kg bread or patent flour (35 oz.), or
    equal amounts of the two flours
600 ml water (20 fl. oz.), approximately
20 g salt (1½ Tbsp.)
50 g powdered milk (1.5 oz.)
40 g sugar (1.5 oz.)
50 g yeast (1.5 oz.)
80 g butter or shortening (3 oz.), softened

Preparation

In a work area with a temperature of 22° to 25°C (71.5° to 77°F), use a base temperature of 62°C (208°F) for an electric mixer. Calculate the temperature of the water using the base temperature.

Final Kneading

In the work bowl of an electric mixer, blend the flour(s), salt, powdered milk, sugar, and the yeast, which has been previously dissolved in the water from the recipe. After the frasage stage, knead for 5 minutes on low speed. Add the butter, still mixing on low speed. Increase the speed to medium, and knead for 3 minutes more.

The temperature of the dough should be 25° to 26°C (77° to 79°F) at the end of kneading. The dough should have a firm texture.

Note the time the kneading was completed, and cover the dough with plastic wrap.

Fermenting

Allow the dough to rise for 40 minutes in a draft-free area.

Punch down the dough after 20 minutes.

Weighing and Shaping

Divide and weigh out the sections of dough. Gently round the sections, and let them rest in a draft-free area for 10 minutes.

By hand or machine, shape the dough, dusting with a minimum of flour. Place the shaped dough on lightly buttered sheet pans or molds. Score deep, even sausage incisions in the tops of the shaped dough with a blade or scissors.

Proofing

Proof the loaves for approximately 1½ hours, depending on the temperature of the dough and the temperature and humidity of the work area. Be careful not to overproof.

Preparing for Baking

Check that the oven has been preheated to 210° to 220°C (400° to 425°F).

Egg wash can be brushed on the tops of the loaves with a pastry brush.

Do not use steam in the oven if the breads are brushed with egg wash. Do use steam if they are not—in which case, start filling the oven with steam before the breads are put in the oven.

Baking

Bake the breads for 15 to 20 minutes.

Verify doneness, and immediately place the baked breads on cooling racks or in wicker baskets after removing them from the oven.

Viennese Bread			
Preparation	**15** min	**0** min	• Calculate the necessary temperatures. • Prepare, weigh, and measure the raw ingredients. • Butter the baking sheets.
Kneading	**8** min	**23** min	• Knead for 5 minutes on low speed, and then for 3 minutes on medium speed. • Check the temperature of the dough.
Fermenting	**40** min	**1** hr **05**	• Place in an area free of drafts. • Punch down the dough after 40 minutes.
Weighing	**5** min	**1** hr **10**	• Weigh and gently round the sections of dough.
Resting	**10** min	**1** hr **20**	• Rest the rounds in a draft-free area.
Shaping	**5** min	**1** hr **25**	• Shape by hand or machine. • Score the breads deeply and evenly just after shaping with a blade or scissors.
Proofing	**1** hr **30**	**2** hr **55**	• Do not overproof.
Preparing for baking	**5** min	**3** hr	• Verify the temperature of the oven.
Baking	**15** to **20** min	**3** hr **15**	• Check for doneness after 15 minutes.
Cooling	**5** min	**3** hr **20**	• Immediately place the baked breads on cooling racks or in wicker baskets.

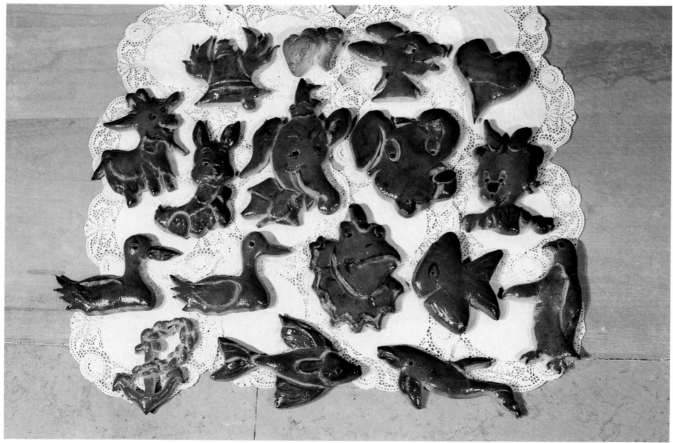

Chapter 3
Elaborate breads and Viennese breads

~~~~~~~~~~~~~~~~~

Definition

Elaborate breads and Viennese breads are prepared in a wide variety of shapes and sizes. This is accomplished with special shaping techniques or with templates.

Recipes and techniques for these breads are categorized as "elaborate breads" and "Viennese breads"; neither is baked in standard shapes or loaves. Because these breads can be sold at higher prices than breads shaped into traditional loaves, they can provide additional profit to a small bakery.

Elaborate Breads Using Special Molds

Elaborate breads are usually prepared with standard bread dough but are worked into decorative and fanciful shapes. The bread-making methods used are the same for these breads as with standard breads; only the final shaping is different.

Elaborate breads can be made in any size, from individual rolls to large loaves of 1 kilogram (2 pounds) or more. Typically, however, these breads are based on from 350 to 500 grams (12.5 to 17.5 ounces) of dough.

Preparation of elaborate breads does not require any special equipment, but it is helpful to have enough baking sheets and standard bread-baking equipment on hand.

Useful Equipment

Rising molds, elongated and circular shaped (canvas lined)

Canvas for lining rising molds (clean)

Standard rolling pin or thin rolling pin (cut-off broom handle)

Medium-size scissors, 20 to 24 centimeters (8 to 10 inches), with pointed tips

Pastry cutter (metal or plastic)

Appropriate blade for making incisions in loaves

Medium-size pastry brush, 30 to 40 millimeters (1.5 to 2 inches)

Medium-size drum sieve

Flour bin

Dusting Flours

Bakers often use a special mixture of flours that works particularly well for dusting the loaves and the canvas molds used for rising. The purpose of this mixture is to keep the bread from adhering to the rising canvas.

Sample Mixtures: "Gray" Flour

- two parts rye flour and one part white wheat flour or
- one part rye flour, one part rice or corn flour, and one part white wheat flour

These "gray" flours should be dehydrated before use by spreading them in a 1-centimeter (½-inch) layer on a baking sheet and leaving them in a proof box at 45° to 50°C (113° to 122°F) for 12 to 24 hours.

When flour has been dried in this way it tends to stick less and works very well for dusting loaves and molds.

Colored Glazes

These glazes usually contain coffee or caramel extract and give an appealing brown hue to the surface of the bread. The depth of color can be adjusted as needed.

Very dark colored glazes tend to be quite thick. They can be thinned with a small amount of milk.

Viennese Breads

These breads are usually baked on the same type of heavy metal sheet pans used for baking pastry.

The only special equipment needed to bake these breads is templates and stencils, both of which can be made of stiff cardboard. The templates can be used several times.

Other equipment used for Viennese breads is standard and found in most bakeries.

Glaze

Glaze is extremely important for baking Viennese breads. It not only gives the surface of the breads an appealing sheen, but can also be used to color designs that have been cut in the dough.

Equipment Needed

Heavy-bottomed baking sheets, 40 by 60 centimeters (16 x 24 inches)
Rolling pin
Flour brush
Small paring knife
Chef's knife
Medium-size pastry brush, 3 to 4 centimeters (1 to 1.5 inches) wide
Small pastry brush for shaping the dough
Pointed scissors

Recipe for Egg Glaze

10 eggs (500 g/17.5 oz.)
5 g fine salt (1 tsp.)

Beat the eggs with the salt. The salt is important for three reasons:

1. It helps give a liquid consistency to the glaze and thus allows it to be spread more evenly over the surface being coated.
2. It contributes a warm, reddish brown color to the surface of the bread.
3. It acts as a preservative.

Elaborate Breads

Elaborate breads can be made using regular bread dough, country-style bread dough, or special bread dough such as bran, whole wheat, or onion and bacon.

The different types of elaborate breads are categorized herein according to shape.

1. Round Breads

Auvergne style (auvergnat)
Pouches (tabatière)
Tricorns (tricorne)
Caps (casquette)
Braids (boule tressée)
Ropes (pain cordon)
Spirals (pain spiral)
Pithiviers (pain pithiviers)
Bear claws (patte d'ours)
Tulips (pain tulipe)

2. Elongated Breads

Split loaves (fendu)
Twists (tordu)
Braids (pain tressé)
Horseshoes (fer à cheval)
Crowns (les couronnes)
Lyons-style crowns (couronnes lyonnaise)

3. Rolled Breads

Folded loaves (pain plié)
Rolled loaves (pain roulé)
Crescents (pain croissant)
Country-style flat bread (fougasse)

4. Cut Breads

Sawtooth loaves (pain scie)
Wheat stalks (pain épis)
Flowering crown loaves (couronne épis)
Stars (étoiles)

Viennese Breads

These breads are prepared with bread dough that has been slightly sweetened with sugar (fougasse dough, Viennese bread dough, and milk-based bread dough are usually used).

Viennese breads are categorized herein into two groups.

1. Cutout Breads

Duck (canard)
Elephant (éléphant)
Doe (biche)
Bell (cloche)
Heart (coeur)

2. Shaped Breads

Turtle (tortue)
Crocodile (crocodile)
Rabbit (lapin)
Grapes (grappe de raisins)

Auvergne-style loaves (L'auvergnat)

Type of Dough Used

Standard bread dough.

Preparation

Remove a small piece of dough (about 10 percent) from each of the loaves; for example, remove 60 grams (1.5 ounces) of dough from a ball of 500 grams (17.5 ounces).

Roll both the large and small sections of dough into tight balls between the palms of the hands.

As soon as the balls of dough begin to rise, quickly roll them until they return to their original size.

Let the rolled sections of dough rise for 20 to 30 minutes.

Shaping

The large section of dough should be completely flattened to eliminate carbon dioxide that has accumulated during the resting period. The dough is then rolled

once more into its original spherical shape. Make sure the ball of dough is perfectly round and has no tears on its surface. The seam should be well centered on the bottom of the loaf.

The small section of dough should be flattened on the work surface with a rolling pin. Be sure to dust the work surface well with "gray" flour. Roll the dough into a disk having the same diameter as the large ball of dough.

Gently brush the surface of the disk to remove excess flour, being sure to leave a small amount of flour on the edges. Brush the edges of the disk with oil using a pastry brush.

Place the disk of dough atop the large ball. Gently pull on the edges of the disk. Attach the disk to the top of the large ball of dough by pushing a fingertip into the center. This also gives a novel appearance to the loaves.

Proofing/Final Rising

Place the finished loaves in the rising area and let them double in volume.

Baking

Place the Auvergne-style loaves on the oven-loading conveyor or on the peel. Remember that the flattened disk of dough is the top of the loaf.

Dust the top of each loaf with flour. Use more or less flour as desired. The flouring of the loaves may be done by hand or with a drum sieve.

Brush the edge of each disk with water using the tip of the finger or a pastry brush. This prevents the edge of the disk from adhering to the surface of the loaf.

Place the loaves in a medium oven. Avoid using too much steam for this type of loaf. Be sure to bake the loaves thoroughly, or they will sag or become soggy when removed from the oven.

Pouches (La tabatière)

Type of Dough Used

Standard bread dough, country-style bread dough, whole-wheat bread dough are just some of the choices.

Preparation

Roll the dough into round loaves.

Let the balls of dough rest. As soon as they begin to expand, quickly roll them to eliminate accumulated carbon dioxide. Let rest again for 10 to 15 minutes.

Shaping

Thoroughly dust the work surface with white or "gray" flour.

With a rolling pin, roll the end of the dough that is opposite you into a small flap. The flap should constitute about one-quarter the total amount of dough.

Be sure to use enough flour to prevent the dough from sticking to the rolling pin or work surface.

Roll the flap until it has a diameter equal to three-quarters of the remaining dough. The flap should be quite thin—2 to 3 millimeters (about ⅛ inch) is optimal.

During the baking of the pouch loaves, the flap (which will be folded back over the top of the original mound of dough before baking) must detach from around the edges. In order to facilitate this, brush a 3- to 4-centimeter (1- to 1.5-inch) ring around the top of the original mound with vegetable oil. The edges of the top flap should overlap this oiled ring.

Pull the flap back over the bread. Stretch it gently while folding it back to prevent creases.

Proofing/Final Rising

Place each shaped pouch in the rising area. Make sure that the rising area is dusted with flour. The tops of the loaves can also be dusted with white or "gray" flour.

Let the loaves double in volume.

Baking

Place the loaves either directly on the oven-loading conveyor or on the peel. The flap should be on top.

Brush off excess flour or add extra flour, depending on the desired appearance of the finished loaves. Additional flour can be dusted over the loaves by hand or by using a drum sieve.

To ensure that the flap detaches from the mounded base of each loaf, water can be brushed beneath the edges of the flap using a pastry brush.

Bake in a medium oven, avoiding an excess of steam. Be sure to bake thoroughly to prevent the loaves from collapsing while cooling.

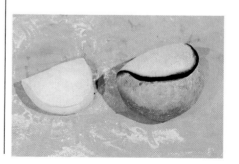

Tricorns (Le tricorne)

Type of Dough Used

Standard bread dough, country-style bread dough, and whole-wheat bread dough are some of the possible choices.

Preparation

Make sure that the sections of dough have been rolled into well-rounded spheres.

Give the balls of dough a quick second rolling as soon as they start to rise. Let them rest for 10 to 15 minutes.

Shaping

Place the balls of dough on a floured work surface (use either white or "gray" flour).

Use a rolling pin to create three equidistant flaps extending from the sides of each mound of dough. Each flap should be oval shaped and use about one-eighth of the total dough. The flaps should each have a length equal to the radius of the central mound of dough.

Brush the flaps with vegetable oil using a pastry brush.

Fold the flaps over the central mound of dough.

Proofing/Final Rising

Place the loaves in the rising area with the flaps facing down (to hold them in place during rising). Make sure that the work surface has been dusted with either white or "gray" flour.

Let the loaves double in volume.

Baking

When the loaves have doubled in volume, turn them over onto either the peel or directly onto the oven floor (if the oven is equipped with a loaidng conveyor). Make sure the flaps are now on top of the loaves.

Depending on the desired appearance of the finished loaves, the flour remaining on the surfaces of the loaves can be brushed off, or additional white or "gray" flour can be added either by hand or with a drum sieve.

In order to ensure that the edges of the flaps do not stay attached to the main body of the loaf during baking, use a pastry brush to brush the underside of the flaps with water.

Bake the loaves in a medium oven. Avoid an excess of steam during baking.

Make sure the loaves are thoroughly baked before removing them from the oven, or they may sag or remain excessively moist.

Caps (La casquette)

Type of Dough Used

Standard bread dough, country-style bread dough, and onion and bacon bread dough are some of the possibilities.

Preparation

After weighing the bread dough, remove one-quarter of the dough from each of the sections. Roll both the large and small sections by hand into even spheres. Allow both sections to rest for 15 to 20 minutes.

Shaping

With a rolling pin roll the smaller section of dough into an oval. The oval should be twice as long as it is wide and 2 to 4 millimeters (⅛ to ¼ inch) thick.

Brush the outer ring of this section with oil.

Gently press on the large mound of dough to flatten it slightly and give it a somewhat oval shape.

Place the large mound of dough over the rolled oval. Keep the larger mound to one side of the oval.

Make an indentation in the center of the mound with the elbow. Place a small ball of dough in this cavity to resemble a pom-pom or button in the center of the cap.

Proofing/Final Rising

Place the loaves in the rising area. The surface of the rising area should be very lightly floured. Keep the thin oval part of

the cap (which will eventually be the visor) on the bottom of the loaves during rising and baking.

Allow the loaves to double in volume.

Baking

Place the loaves either directly on the oven-loading conveyor or on the peel.

Brush the surfaces of the loaves to remove excess flour. At this point, the small ball in the center of the cap can be coated with poppy seeds.

Moisten the base of the large section of dough and the top of the visor with water, using a pastry brush.

Bake in a medium oven with plenty of steam.

Pay careful attention to the color of the loaves, particularly of the visors, during baking. If the loaves start to color too quickly, remove them from the oven and place them on baking sheets before returning them to the oven.

Be careful not to overcook these loaves.

Braids (La boule tressée)

Type of Dough Used

Standard bread dough, half rye/half wheat dough, and country-style bread dough are some possibilities.

Preparation

After weighing the bread dough into sections for the individual loaves, remove one-quarter of the dough from each of the sections. These smaller pieces of dough will be used for the braids. Roll both the larger and smaller sections into even balls. Let the rolled sections rest for 10 to 15 minutes.

Shaping

Gently press on the larger sections of dough to eliminate carbon dioxide.

To prepare the braid, divide the smaller sections of dough into three equal parts. Roll each of these three small sections into a thin rope. Make sure that all three ropes are of the same length and thickness; one or more of the sections may need some additional rolling.

Check the length of the ropes by comparing them to the large sections of dough. The desired length of the ropes obviously depends on the size of the finished loaves and their design.

Brush the larger section of dough with water using a pastry brush. Braid the three ropes and place them on the mound of dough.

After the braid is placed on the loaves, the ends should be pinched together to give the appearance of one continuous braid of dough. The ends of the braid can also be left overlapping each other.

Proofing/Final Rising

Place the finished loaves directly on the canvas surface of the rising area or in round molds.

Let the loaves double in volume.

Baking

Place the loaves either directly on the oven-loading conveyor or on the peel. Do not turn the loaves over at any point —the braid should remain on top.

Dust the tops of the loaves with additional flour using a drum sieve. Brush off any flour that falls on the braid with a pastry brush.

The surface of the braid can also be brushed with water using a pastry brush. This helps the individual ropes of dough to remain separate during baking and helps the braid stand out in greater relief.

Bake the loaves in a medium oven. Avoid an excess of steam. Both steam and oven temperature can be adjusted to give dry or moist loaves according to taste.

Ropes, Pithiviers, and spirals (Pain cordon, pain pithiviers, et pain spiral)

These three breads are all similar to braids and Auvergne-style loaves: they are round and are decorated with pieces of dough in various patterns. Standard bread dough or country-style bread dough can be used to prepare these breads. It is also possible to use special types of dough (such as soy or rye) to make these loaves.

Preparation

After weighing the dough into sections for individual loaves, remove the amount of dough needed for the decoration. Press down on each of these sections to eliminate carbon dixoide, but avoid over-working the dough.

Shaping

Ropes (Pain Cordon)

Take the small section of dough that has been removed from the loaf and roll it into two strands of equal length and thickness. Be sure to allow these strands to rest before applying them to the large mound of dough. This gives them time to shrink *before* they are placed on the loaf. Cross the two strands of dough over each other in an X pattern. Tuck the ends under the bottom of the loaf.

Pithiviers (Pain Pithiviers)

The base loaf for making Pithiviers bread is prepared using the same method as for Auvergne-style loaves. Only the pinwheel decoration on the surface is different.

To make the pinwheel decoration on the loaf's surface, use a paring knife to cut a series of arcs from the center to the outer edges of the loaf. This decoration should be applied to the bread immediately after the top disk is attached to the loaf and the loaf has been dusted with flour. Once the decorative arcs have been applied to the loaves, the loaves are ready for the final rising.

Spirals (Pain Spiral)

The strand of dough used for the decorative spirals on these loaves is sometimes prepared with special decorating dough (see page 179). In this case, the spiral of dough is attached to the moistened loaf just before baking, after the final rising.

If regular bread dough is being used for the decorative spiral, make sure that the strand of dough is given plenty of time to rest after rolling. It should be attached to the surface of the loaf midway during the final rising or near the end of the final rising.

Proofing/Final Rising

All three of these breads can be allowed to rise on a canvas work surface in the rising area or in round rising molds. The decorated surface should be on top at all times.

Allow the loaves to double in volume.

Baking

Bake the loaves in a medium oven. Avoid an excess of steam.

Before placing the bread in the oven, it is advisable to prick the tops and sides of the loaves with a trussing needle. This helps the loaves keep their shape during baking.

Be sure to bake the loaves until they are thoroughly cooked, or they may sag or remain soggy once cool.

Crowns (Les couronnes)

Type of Dough Used

A wide variety of bread dough can be used for crown-shaped loaves. Loaves baked in crown shapes have been popular for centuries, probably because the shape made the loaves easy to carry on long poles or on an outstretched arm.

Preparation

After sectioning and weighing the dough for individual loaves, gently press on each of the sections to eliminate carbon dioxide.

Let the dough rest for 10 to 15 minutes. When the mounds of dough begin to rise, press on them gently and then let them rest for another 10 to 15 minutes.

Shaping

Make a deep indentation in the center of each of the mounds of dough with the tips of all five fingers held tightly together or with the elbow. Make sure that the indentation is perfectly centered.

Pierce through the center of the dough with the fingertips and gradually work around the inside of the hole until it expands to the desired size. Be careful not to work the dough too quickly, or it may tear. It may be necessary to let the dough rest several times to allow it to relax before continuing to expand the center to the desired size.

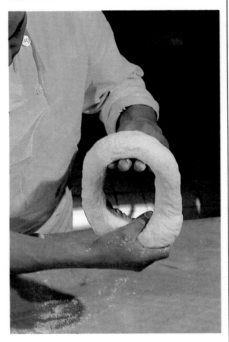

Proofing/Final Rising

Crown-shaped loaves are best allowed to rise upside down in appropriate-size rising molds. The molds can be floured if desired.

The time required for the final rising depends on the type of bread dough being used.

Baking

Just before baking, the dough should be turned out of the molds onto the oven-loading conveyor or onto the peel. When the loaves are in position, they can be given some final decoration with a scissors or a sharp blade. They can also be dusted with flour using a drum sieve. The flour can be applied to the tops of the loaves in decorative patterns using stencils cut from cardboard for this purpose.

The length of time required for baking depends on the size of the loaves, the type of dough used, and individual taste. Crown-shaped loaves are baked in the same way as elongated loaves.

Lyons-style crowns
(Les couronnes lyonnaises)

Type of Dough Used

Standard bread dough or country-style bread dough.

Preparation

After weighing the dough into sections for individual loaves, divide each section into smaller units. The number of units depends on the desired size of the loaves, but a typical example is 500 grams (17.5 ounces) of dough divided into eight equal units.

After making sure that the small pieces of dough all weigh the same, roll each into a tight ball.

Let the balls of dough rest for 20 to 30 minutes.

Shaping

Gently roll the balls of dough to eliminate accumulated carbon dioxide. Be careful not to tear the dough.

After a second resting period of 5 to 10 minutes, shape a flap on each of the small sections using a thin rolling pin. This technique is the same as that used for preparing pouches (see page 121). Be sure to flour the work surface with "gray" or white flour to prevent sticking.

Before folding the miniature flaps back over the mounds of dough, brush the top of each of the small sections of dough with oil. This will help the flaps to rise slightly during baking. Make sure the oil is evenly applied.

Constructing the Crowns

Lightly dust the inside of the crown-shaped rising mold with flour. Brush the sides of each of the small sections of dough with water so that they attach to each other during the final rising. Place the sections of dough, flap side down, next to each other in the mold.

Proofing/Final Rising

Cover the mold with plastic wrap to prevent a crust from forming during rising.

Allow the dough to double in volume.

Baking

Turn the dough out onto either the oven-loading conveyor or the peel. The small flaps should now be on the tops of the loaves.

At this point the loaves can be dusted with additional white or "gray" flour using a drum sieve.

Brush excess flour from the edges of the flaps. It is possible to dust every other flap with flour or to sprinkle alternate flaps with poppy or sesame seeds to create a decorative effect.

Brush the underside of each of the flaps with water to prevent them from melting into the loaf during baking.

Bake the loaves in a medium to hot oven. Avoid using too much steam.

These loaves should not be too brittle once baked, so be careful not to overbake them.

Bear claws (Les pattes d'ours)

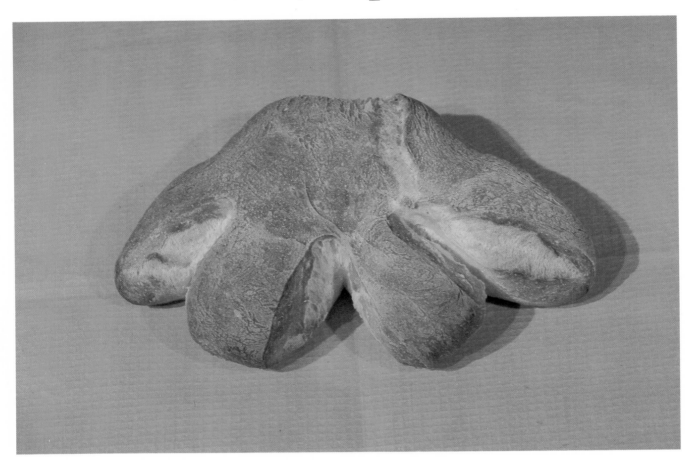

Type of Dough Used

Standard bread dough or country-style bread dough.

Preparation

After weighing the dough into sections for individual loaves, gently roll each section into even mounds and let rest for 15 to 20 minutes.

Shaping

Gently roll each of the sections of dough to eliminate carbon dioxide. Make sure that the surface of each mound of dough is smooth and even.

Let the loaves rest for 10 minutes.

Press down on the dough and gently work it into a fan shape. Place each of the fan-shaped sections on a work surface and make three equidistant cuts in each with a metal pastry cutter.

Pull each of the separate claws away from each other so they do not stick during the final rising.

Proofing/Final Rising

Usually bear claws are baked after a very short rising time. This results in a dense-textured dough and a thick, brittle crust.

Baking

Make sure that the individual claws have stayed separate during the final rising. Bake the bear claws in a medium oven until thoroughly cooked. Avoid using excess steam.

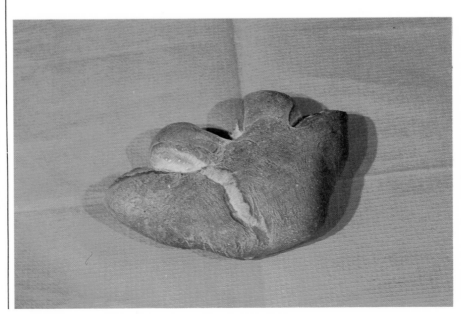

Split loaves (Les fendus)

Type of Dough Used

Standard bread dough or country-style bread dough.

Preparation

Gently roll and round the individual sections of dough after weighing.

Allow the sections of dough to rest for 20 to 30 minutes.

Shaping

On a lightly floured work surface, give the dough several successive folds and then roll the sections of dough into tight loaves of the length needed for the finished baked bread.

Place the loaves of dough parallel to the edge of the work surface and liberally dust the surface of the loaves with "gray" or white flour.

Use a thin rolling pin longer than the loaves (a section of broom handle works well for this) to form a well that runs down the center of each loaf. Press firmly on the rolling pin with both hands so that

it sinks into the loaf and divides it into two equal sections.

Roll the pin back and forth while press-

ing down firmly on the loaf. This rolling expands the well. The size of the center well depends on the size of the loaves. For a loaf of 350 grams (12.5 ounces), the

well should be about 4 centimeters (1.5 inches) wide. For a larger loaf of 500 grams (17.5 ounces), the well should be about 5 centimeters (2 inches) wide.

Note: While forming the center well, it is important to flour the loaf, the rolling pin, and the work surface continuously (preferably with "gray" flour) to prevent sticking. Once the well has been formed, it should be completely dry and well coated with flour. If this is not the case, be sure to flour the loaves liberally before the final rising.

Proofing/Final Rising

Roll the loaf so that each side folds in over the center well.

At this stage the two sides of the loaf should be touching but should not stick.

Turn the loaves over onto either a canvas rising surface or a lightly floured mold.

Allow the loaves to double in volume.

Baking

Turn the loaves out onto the oven-loading conveyor or onto the peel. The split between the two sides of the loaves should be on top.

Brush excess flour from the loaves.

Brush the opening that runs down the center of the loaves with a wet pastry brush to encourage it to open during baking. It can also be brushed with oil if the two sides appear to be sticking.

Bake the loaves in a medium oven until well cooked. Traditionally split loaves are baked until somewhat dry. Avoid using too much steam.

Horseshoes (Les fers à cheval)

Type of Dough Used

Standard bread dough or country-style bread dough.

Procedure

Prepare long, split loaves using the method for split loaves (page 129).

Place the loaves with the split facing down in a crown-shaped rising mold.

Twists (Les tordus)

Type of Dough Used

Standard bread dough or country-style bread dough.

Procedure

Prepare a long split loaf, as shown on page 129.

Twist each loaf so that the split makes two complete rotations over its entire length. Place each loaf in a lightly floured elongated rising mold.

Allow the loaves to double in volume.

Turn the loaves out onto the oven-loading conveyor or the peel.

Brush the twisted opening of each of the loaves with a wet pastry brush so that the split does not close in on itself during baking.

Bake the loaves in a medium oven. Avoid excess steam.

Bake the loaves in a medium oven. Avoid excess steam.

Allow the loaves to double in volume.

Turn the loaves out onto either the oven-loading conveyor or the peel. The loaves should be baked with the split facing up.

Brush the opening running along the top of the loaves with a wet pastry brush.

Folded loaves (Les pains pliés)

Type of Dough Used

Standard bread dough.

Preparation

After weighing the dough into sections for individual loaves, gently roll each loaf of dough to eliminate carbon dioxide. Allow the sections to rest for 20 to 30 minutes.

Shaping

Roll the sections of dough into rectangular shapes. Because the rectangles will

be folded over themselves, the width of the rectangles should correspond to the length of the finished loaves. The length of each rectangle should be approximately 45 centimeters (18 inches) for a 350-gram (12.5-ounce) loaf and 60 centimeters (24 inches) for a 500-gram (17.5-ounce) loaf.

Fold the base of the rectangle up to the center of the rectangle and the top of the rectangle down over the first fold as though folding a letter.

Do not worry if the folds do not seem to stick together—in fact, it is better if the folds are lightly coated with flour so they will separate while baking.

To further prevent the folds from melting into one another during baking, the flaps can be brushed with oil before making the final fold. In this way the loaves open slightly during baking.

Proofing/Final Rising

Place the loaves in the rising area. The canvas surface of the rising area should be lightly floured.

Allow the loaves to double in volume.

Baking

After they have risen, place the loaves either directly on the oven-loading conveyor or on the peel.

The tops of the loaves can be dusted with white flour using a drum sieve.

Brush the inner edges of the fold with a wet pastry brush to prevent it from sealing itself during baking.

Bake the loaves in a medium oven. Avoid using excess steam.

Do not overcook the loaves. They should be moist and soft and have a dense texture.

Variation

To vary the folded loaves, roll the dough into triangles rather than rectangles before folding. The triangular sections of pastry are then folded three to four times over themselves, starting at the base.

The points of the triangles should be brushed with oil before the final rising and brushed with water just before baking.

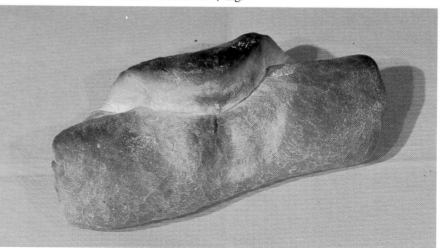

Crescents (Les pains croissants)

Type of Dough Used

Standard bread dough.

Preparation

Do not roll the individual sections into balls after weighing.

Allow the dough to rest for 10 to 15 minutes.

Shaping

Roll the dough into triangles about 5 to 7 millimeters (about ¼ inch) thick.

Brush a 2-centimeter (2-inch) strip along the borders of the triangles with vegetable oil and roll the triangles starting from the base in the same way as when preparing croissants.

Proofing/Final Rising

Place the crescent loaves in the rising area.

Baking

Do not let the loaves rise for too long before baking. They should be baked in a medium to hot oven. Use a moderate amount of steam during baking.

Make sure that the loaves are sufficiently cooked. They should have a fairly dense texture and a hard crust.

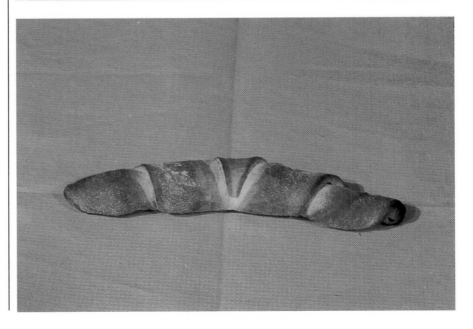

Country-style flat bread (La fougasse)

Type of Dough Used

Standard bread dough.

Preparation

After weighing the individual sections of dough, gently roll them into mounds. Do not overwork them.

Allow the mounds of dough to rest for 20 to 30 minutes.

Shaping

Press down on each of the mounds of dough with the hands held flat.

Roll the individual mounds of dough into oval or triangular shapes with a rolling pin.

Let the sections of rolled dough rest for 20 to 30 minutes to make sure they do not shrink during the proofing or baking.

Small slivers should be cut from the dough using an oval-shaped cookie cutter about 2 centimeters in length and 4 centimeters wide (1 by 1.5 inches) or a knife. Try to arrange the slivers as evenly as possible on the surface of the bread.

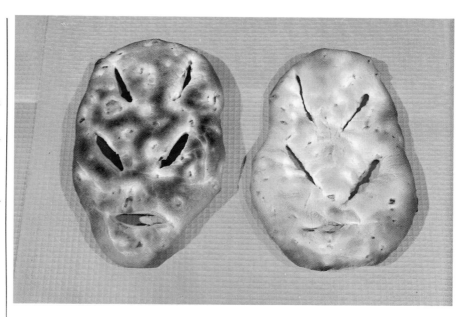

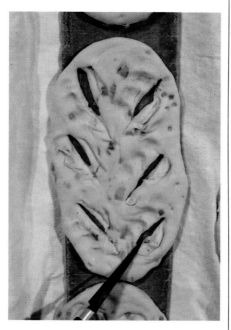

Proofing

The final proofing of the these breads has little importance. They should have a dense texture and so should not be allowed to rise excessively before baking. They are appreciated primarily for their crunchy crust.

Baking

After a short proofing, the loaves should be baked in a medium oven. Excess steam should be avoided.

Shaping loaves with scissors

Ears of Wheat (Pains Epis)

These breads undergo a final shaping by being cut with scissors.

Below are presented several of the more basic types of breads that are given a final shaping with scissors. The types of loaves most often found in French bread baking are wheat stalks (épis) and stars (étoiles). The shaping of these breads takes place in two stages: a preliminary hand shaping and a final shaping with sharp scissors just before the loaves are baked.

These breads are prepared with standard bread dough.

The preparation, first rising, and proofing of these loaves is the same as for standard French baguettes. Only the last stage of shaping, which takes place once the loaves have been transferred to the peel, differs. At this point, the bread is given its final shape with scissors.

These scissor-cut loaves can be prepared starting with standard baguette or French loaf shapes. The usual weight of the dough for these loaves ranges from 400 to 500 grams (14 to 17.5 ounces).

Preparation

When the loaves of raw dough have finished proofing, they should be transferred to the peel in the normal way. Be sure to leave at least a hand's width of space between each of the loaves so they do not touch each other while baking.

Medium-size scissors should be used to cut the loaves. They should be about 22 centimeters (8.5 inches) long.

Make sure that the scissors are perfectly clean before cutting the loaves. Otherwise they may stick and leave torn or uneven cuts on the surface of the loaves. If the bread dough is particularly loose or sticky, it is helpful to dip the scissors in cold water between each cut.

Cutting the Loaves

Hold the scissors at a 45-degree angle from the work surface.

Starting on the left side of the loaf at the end opposite you, make cuts three-quarters of the way through each loaf. Leave approximately 5 centimeters (2 inches) between each cut. As the sections of dough are cut with the scissors, every other piece of dough should be gently folded over to the opposite side of the loaf (see photo).

Be sure to cut the sections with short, quick movements of the scissors. This helps prevent sticking and gives the sections of dough a more natural appearance.

Continue in the same way until the entire loaf has been cut into sections. Usually a baguette should have ten cuts and standard French loaves should have six.

After the loaves have been cut with the scissors, the ends can be joined together to form crown shapes if desired.

Note

Because of the shape of these breads, baking is somewhat delicate and needs to be carefully controlled. They should be baked in an oven with considerable steam and must be cooked to an exact degree of doneness. If they are removed from the oven before being sufficiently baked, they become soggy and sag. If they are overcooked, they quickly become stale.

Because of the irregular shape of these loaves, they are fragile and must be handled carefully to avoid breaking.

When the breads come out of the oven, it is best to put them on cooling racks. Do not stack them more than three loaves high, or the loaves on the bottom may be flattened or crushed.

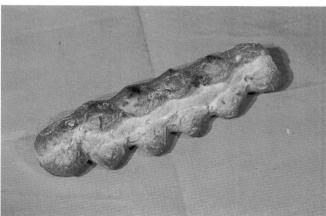

Stars

These loaves are formed by twisting elongated scissor-shaped loaves around themselves to form stars.

They are similar to wheat stalks because they are shaped with scissors in the same way. This includes the classic method for preliminary shaping of elongated loaves and cutting the elongated loaves with scissors after the proofing, just before they are baked.

Stars are usually prepared using standard bread dough.

The techniques used in the preparation of stars are also applicable to a variety of individual and innovatively shaped breads.

When preparing stars follow the same precautions used in preparing wheat stalks.

136

Preliminary Shaping

After the initial weighing of the dough into portions for individual loaves, gently roll the sections of dough into mounds.

Let the balls of dough rest for 15 to 20 minutes.

Once the sections of dough have rested, they can be rolled into elongated loaves or flattened disks. Be careful not to tear the dough during the rolling.

Avoid using excess flour.

Place the sections of dough in the rising area. Be careful not to let the dough rise too much before baking.

Final Shaping of the Dough

The elongated or round loaves should be placed either on the peel or the oven-loading conveyor before the final shaping with scissors. The loaves should then be cut into nine even sections with the scissors. In this case, be sure to cut completely through the loaves to form separate sections.

The sections of the loaf should then be set in place by arranging four of the pieces in a cross pattern and then inserting the remaining four pieces between the sections of the cross to form an evenly shaped star. One more piece of dough should be used to fill in the center of the star.

Note

Be sure that each of the nine pieces of dough sticks firmly to the others at the center, with no gaps in between. Otherwise the sections may separate during baking.

Round Loaves

When starting with sections of dough that have been flattened into round disks, the sides of the loaves are cut with scissors directly on the peel or the oven-loading conveyor.

When using this method, make sure that the cuts are perfectly even in relation to each other. This method allows the baker to improvise and invent different-shaped loaves.

Use the scissors to cut in from the sides of the loaves, halfway in toward the center. Hold the scissors at a 45-degree angle so the sections of dough that are formed resemble the blades of a fan. The dough can be cut in different directions to form a variety of shapes, as the baker desires.

Bake the loaves in a hot oven with a large quantity of steam. Be careful not to overcook these loaves, or the tips of the cut sections may harden, dry out, or even burn.

Milk bread dough
(La pâte à pain au lait)

History

Originally this bread was called *fouace* after the Latin word *focus,* meaning "hearth," because it was baked directly under the ashes. In the Middle Ages, it was a kind of unleavened cake made with flour. Over the centuries, it has gradually been improved and is of course now baked in the oven.

By the end of the Middle Ages, the *fouace* was made with yeast and became much appreciated and very popular. It was composed of butter, starter, eggs, milk, sugar, orange flower water, and flour. The *fouace* was prepared in all the provinces of France, and in certain regions it was called *fougasse.* The new name soon caught on and is often heard in France even today. By the beginning of the seventeenth century, *fougasses* were prepared with beer starters.

Today, in home cooking, the *fougasse* or *pain au lait* (milk bread) is usually prepared with commercial yeast. It is extremely popular.

Milk bread requires care and attention, especially with regard to fermentation of the dough. It takes about 35 minutes to prepare; including fermentation time, 3 hours 45 minutes. It can be prepared by hand or with an electric mixer; only the hand method is described here.

Uses

Plain

Plain milk bread dough can be used to make sandwiches, luncheon rolls, navettes, sweetened bread balls, mats or braids, crowns, and specially shaped breads such as turtles or crocodiles.

Flavored

Milk bread dough can be flavored in a variety of ways, to make such preparations as raisin, hazelnut, or walnut rolls, Lorraine-style cakes, apple cakes, brioche fruit tarts, candied fruit and raisin galettes, miniature raisin breads, and schnecks (snails).

Equipment

By Hand

A pastry cutter, brush, drum sieve, bowl for liquids, plastic tub, and wax paper or plastic wrap are all needed to prepare milk bread dough by hand.

By Machine

A mixer, mixing bowl attachment, dough hook, drum sieve, parchment paper, bowl for liquids, pastry scraper, plastic tub, and wax paper or plastic wrap are used to prepare it with an electric mixer.

Professional Recipe

For 2 kg (70.5 oz.) of dough

1 kg bread flour (35 oz.)
25 g salt (1 oz.)
100 g granulated sugar (3.5 oz.)
30 to 50 g yeast (1 to 1.5 oz.)
4 eggs plus milk to total 650 to 700 ml (22 to 23.5 fl. oz.)
250 g butter (9 oz.)
Liquid percentage: 65 to 70 percent, based on the flour

Alternative Recipe

1 kg bread flour (35 oz.)
15 to 30 g salt (½ to 1 oz.)
50 to 300 g granulated sugar (1.5 to 10.5 oz.)
20 to 80 g yeast (2 Tbsp. to 2.5 oz.)
1 to 8 eggs, plus water or milk to total 650 to 700 ml (22 to 23.5 fl. oz.)
100 to 300 g butter (3.5 to 10.5 oz.)
Liquid percentage: 65 to 70 percent based on the flour

Recipe for a Small Quantity

For 500 g (17.5 oz.) of dough; 10 miniature breads, 50 g (1.5 oz.) of dough each

250 g bread flour (9 oz.)
5 g salt (1 tsp.)
25 g sugar (1 oz.)
10 g yeast (2 tsp.)
1 egg plus approximately 120 ml milk (4 fl. oz.)
50 g butter (1.5 oz.)
Liquid percentage: 70 percent maximum, that is, 170 ml (5.5 fl. oz.) total liquid (eggs and milk)

Preparation

Make sure that the equipment and work area are perfectly clean. Both the equipment and the raw ingredients should be ready before the preparation of the dough begins. As for all leavened doughs, great care must be taken in the preparation. It is best to use a high-gluten flour. Weigh the salt, sugar, and the yeast separately. Break the eggs into a bowl, and soften the butter by tapping it with a rolling pin.

Procedure

Sift the flour onto an extremely clean work surface. Make two wells in the

flour. Put the salt and sugar into one well and the broken-up yeast in the other. This is to prevent the yeast from coming in contact with the salt, which kills it.

Moisten the yeast with a little milk, and work in a little of the flour to help

protect the yeast from the salt. Dissolve the salt and the sugar in the other half of the well with a little milk. Add the eggs. With the tips of the fingers, combine the

salt, sugar, yeast, eggs, and milk. Pour in the rest of the liquid. At this stage, the mixture should be worked with one hand only. The free hand is used to pour in the

liquid and eventually to bring all the ingredients together with the help of a pastry cutter.

With the tips of the fingers, bring the flour into the center of the well with the liquid ingredients. Work the mixture well at each stage so that the starch is moistened and the gluten is activated.

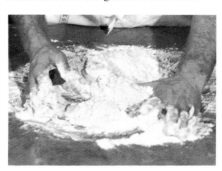

In order to obtain a malleable, elastic dough, it is necessary to work the ingredients together into a paste and to continue working them until they become elastic. At this stage use both hands to complete the incorporation of the flour. Always try to stretch the dough to activate the gluten. The result is a rough but already elastic dough.

If the dough is too runny, sprinkle it with flour and knead it rapidly to incorporate the flour without overheating it.

If the dough is too stiff, sprinkle some milk onto the dough to allow a rapid mixing without overheating the dough.

Dividing and Redividing the Dough

Once the dough has attained the desired consistency, it is necessary to smooth it out and to promote the development of elasticity. This involves repeatedly dividing and redividing the dough with the two hands. This is extremely important for developing the gluten in the dough.

Proceed as follows: hold the two hands under the dough with the palms facing upward. Bring the hands together while at the same time pinching the dough in half with the two thumbs. Bring the hands around in a half-circle. Rapidly slap the lifted half onto the first half. Repeat the process as many times as nec-

essary. This movement activates the gluten and smooths the dough without

overheating it. Stop the process as soon as the dough no longer sticks to either the hands or the marble.

Lifting and Dropping

Once the dough has developed elasticity, it should be lifted off the marble and allowed to fall back down onto the work surface. Repeat the operation. Finish by

smoothing out the dough, using a circular motion. This process works oxygen into the dough, which helps the yeast cells multiply and continues to activate the gluten so that the dough has the necessary elasticity. The process is completed when the dough no longer sticks to the fingers.

Working in the Butter

The butter must be worked in rapidly. To facilitate this procedure, work the softened butter with only a third of the dough. Continue as for dividing and redividing. Then spread the butter mixture over the unbuttered dough and continue again as for dividing and redividing and lifting and dropping. At this stage do not overwork the dough.

Working the Dough into a Ball

Once the dough is smooth and elastic, flour the work surface. With both hands, lift the dough and fold it over itself into a ball.

Fermenting

Place the finished dough in a plastic tub three times its size. Cover the dough with a sheet of wax paper or plastic wrap to keep a crust from forming. Put the

dough in a warm place to rise, 23° to 30°C (75° to 85°F), away from drafts. Avoid putting the dough near a heat source, as it might overheat, and some of the yeast could be killed. If the dough is over-heated, the gluten also loses some of its elasticity; 40°C (104°F) should be the maximum temperature.

If the dough is to be used immediately, let it rise until it has doubled in volume, then punch down the dough by pushing it down on the marble, and fold it over itself several times to push out the carbon dioxide. The dough should return to its original size. Let the dough rise a second time (about an hour), and again punch it down. This procedure works oxygen into the dough and enlivens the yeast cells, improving the quality of the dough.

Using the Dough

Before shaping the dough or placing it in molds, it is advisable to refrigerate it for at least one hour so that it is less sticky and easier to handle.

Storage

In most pastry kitchens, leavened dough is prepared the day before it is to be used. It is then easier to work with, being firmer because the butter has con-gealed, and it is much easier to roll out. When dough is prepared in this way, the kneaded dough is allowed to rise in the same way as above except that it is not necessary to wait until it has doubled in volume to refrigerate it. It will slowly

continue to ferment in the refrigerator, 5°C (40°F). It should be pushed down and covered with plastic wrap before refrig-eration.

When refrigerating dough, make sure that it is flattened to a thickness of no more than 5 centimeters (2 inches); oth-erwise it will take too long to cool and the fermentation will be too prolonged. Excessive fermentation leaves too much residual glucose in the dough, so that fla-vor is lost, and the pastries have an un-pleasant color when baked.

Freezing the Dough

The dough can be frozen for up to a week. In this case, the fermenting time must be limited to 10 minutes maximum. The dough must be taken out of the freezer 12 to 24 hours before baking and kept in the refrigerator, 5°C (40°F), so that it warms very gradually. It is also possible to cut the dough into 500-gram (17.5-ounce) sections before freezing so that only dough that is needed can be thawed.

Milk Bread Dough

PREPARATION	**0** min	
Assemble the equipment Prepare, weigh, and measure the raw ingredients		• Use bread flour and sift it directly onto the work surface. • Make two wells in the flour. • Put the salt and the sugar in one well, the broken-up yeast in the other. • Break the eggs into a bowl. • Soften the butter.
PROCEDURE	**5** min	
Fraise the dough		• Soften the yeast in a little milk. • Dissolve the salt and sugar in some milk. • Add the eggs. • Combine the raw ingredients with the fingertips; then pour in the rest of the liquid (at this stage, use only one hand). • Incorporate the flour a bit at a time into the liquids until a sticky, elastic dough is obtained. • At this stage use both hands to incorporate the flour.
Regulate the consistency	**15** min	• If necessary, add either additional flour or additional milk.
Divide and redivide the dough	**17** min	• This technique activates the gluten and makes the dough smooth and elastic. • Stop the process as soon as the dough no longer sticks to the hands or the marble.
Lift and drop the dough	**25** min	• Finish smoothing out the dough. • This procedure works oxygen into the dough and finishes activating the gluten.
Work in butter	**30** min	• The consistency of the butter should be the same as that of the dough. • The incorporation of the butter must be done quickly, without over-working the dough.
Perform second lifting and dropping	**33** min	• This procedure finishes smoothing out the dough. • Do not work the dough more than necessary, or it will be oily.
FERMENTATION	**35** min	
		• Place in a warm place, 25° to 30°C (75° to 85°F).
Check the rising	**1** hr	• Make sure the temperature of the rising area does not change. • Check the increase in volume.
Punch down the dough	**1** hr **30**	• The dough should have doubled in volume. • Refrigerate the dough to firm and relax it.
Punch down a second time	**2** hr **30**	• The dough should have doubled in volume a second time. • Put the dough back in the refrigerator for about 1 hour to relax and firm it.
READY TO USE	**3** hr **30**	• The baking time depends upon the amount of yeast used, the mois-ture content, the temperature, and the humidity.

STORAGE: Block the fermentation by refrigerating if the dough is to be used the next day.

Viennese breads

The Viennese bread dough presented on page 114 and the preceding milk bread dough can be used for a wide variety of breads such as individual rolls, sweetened rolls, round loaves, and raisin breads.

Because Viennese bread dough is malleable and relatively easy to work with, it is easy to prepare breads in a wide variety of shapes and sizes.

Viennese breads, cut into fanciful shapes and designs, are an attractive addition to a bakery's repertoire and help stimulate sales.

Two methods can be used to shape Viennese bread dough into the required shapes:

● with templates
● shaping by hand

Using templates to prepare Viennese breads

These breads are prepared by placing a template over a sheet of bread dough and then tracing around the perimeter with a sharp knife. The templates can be made in advance out of cardboard or from thin sheets of wood. If the templates are needed on a regular basis, wooden cutouts last far longer.

The shapes illustrated on the following pages serve only as examples. The number of designs that can be created is practically limitless.

Examples

Viennese breads can be cut into shapes for special events, such as pierced hearts for Valentine's Day, Christmas trees, pumpkins for Halloween, and miniature flags for the Fourth of July.

Preparation of Viennese Breads with Templates

Equipment

Heavy baking sheets, 40 by 60 centimeters (16 by 24 inches) with turned-up edges. (Note: This type of baking sheet is standard in France. The short turned-up edge serves as a guide for the thickness of the dough.)
Rolling pin
Flour brush
Paring knife
Medium-size knife
Large and small pastry brushes

Preparing the Dough

Prepare the Viennese bread dough shown on page 114.

The bread dough should be allowed to rise the day before baking. Let the dough rise at room temperature until it has doubled in volume. Press it down to eliminate carbon dioxide and spread it over a baking sheet. Cover it with a sheet of

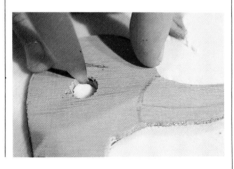

plastic wrap and refrigerate it at 5°C (40°F) overnight so it will be ready for baking the following day.

Rolling Out the Dough

To prepare a sheet of dough corresponding to the dimensions of the baking sheets, 40 by 60 centimeters (16 by 24 inches), use 1.5 to 1.8 kilograms (53 to 63 ounces) of dough.

Roll the dough into a sheet slightly thicker than the rims of the baking sheets—8 to 10 millimeters (¼ to ½ inch). Avoid using too much flour during the initial rolling. Place the sheets of dough on lightly buttered baking sheets.

After placing the sheet of dough on the baking sheet, roll the rolling pin over the surface of the dough. As the pin rolls along the upturned rims of the baking sheets, it will give the dough a smooth surface and even thickness. When using baking sheets that do not have turned-up rims, roll the dough as evenly as possible to a thickness of 8 to 10 millimeters (¼ to ½ inch).

Brush any excess flour from the sheets of dough and place the baking sheets in the freezer for 20 to 30 minutes. This gives the dough a firmer texture, making it easier to work with and cut into the desired shapes.

Cutting Designs from the Dough

Remove the baking sheets of raw dough from the freezer as they are needed. The dough should be very firm but not frozen.

Place the wooden or cardboard templates over the surface of the dough. Arrange the templates to avoid leaving too large a proportion of trimmings. Be sure

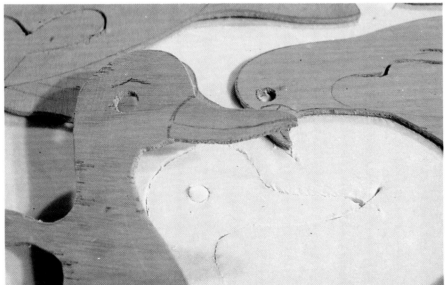

to leave at least 2 centimeters (1 inch) between each of the cutout designs. This spacing will prevent the breads from sticking to one another during baking or the final rising.

Cut around the edges of the templates with a very sharp paring knife. Hold the knife vertically with one hand while holding the template firmly against the surface of the dough with the other.

After the dough has been cut, decorative designs can then be cut into the surface of the dough cutouts, such as eyes on ducklings or fins on fish. The incisions for these designs should be quite deep, or they will be lost during the final rising and during baking.

After cutting out and making designs in the surface of the dough, carefully pull off the trimmings surrounding the cutouts. The trimmings should be saved for use in other breads.

After removing the trimmings from the baking sheets, brush the surface of the cutouts with plain (uncolored) egg wash. Place the baking sheets in a proof box at 30° to 35°C (86° to 95°F). Because the cutouts are relatively thin, they will warm up quickly in the proof box and so need to be watched carefully.

The cutouts should barely double in volume. They should have a soft texture, and no crust should have formed.

If the proof box appears to be too warm or too moist (the surface of the dough seems wet), remove the baking sheets from the proof box and let the cutouts sit at room temperature for 15 to 20 minutes before applying the final coating of egg wash.

Final Steps before Baking

When the cutouts of dough have doubled in volume, they should be brushed a second time with plain egg wash.

At this stage the surface of the breads can be decorated with egg wash tinted with coffee extract. Use a small pastry brush to accent or shade the designs cut into the surface of the dough.

Dried or candied fruits can also be used to decorate the surface of the breads:

- dried raisins for eyes
- kumquat halves for clowns' noses
- candied fruits cut into crescent or diamond shapes for mouths and eyes

Baking

Because Viennese breads are so thin, they should be baked in a hot oven, 230°C (450°F), to keep them from drying out. No steam should be used.

The baking time depends on the oven temperature, the recipe used for the dough, the consistency of the dough, and the exact thickness of the breads.

The breads should be baked until they have an appealing brown color.

As soon as the breads are removed from the oven, they should be taken off the baking sheets and transferred to cooling racks. This prevents the breads from reabsorbing moisture and becoming soggy.

Handle the breads carefully, using a metal spatula or a pastry cutter.

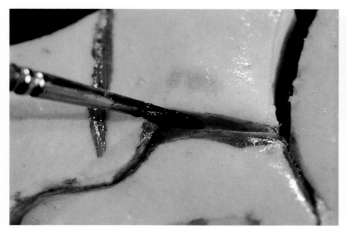

Examples of cutout breads

Examples of cutout breads

Examples of cutout breads

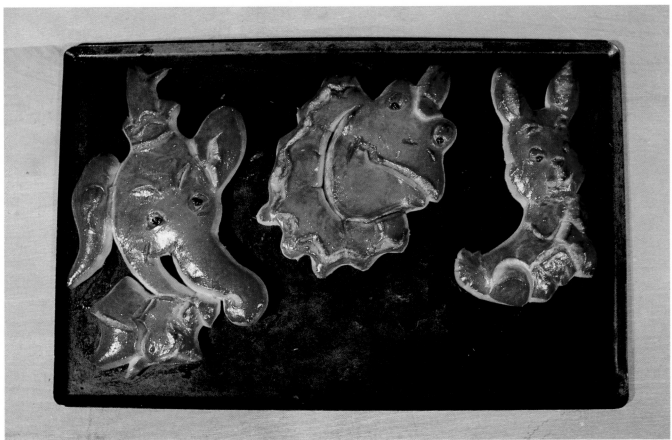

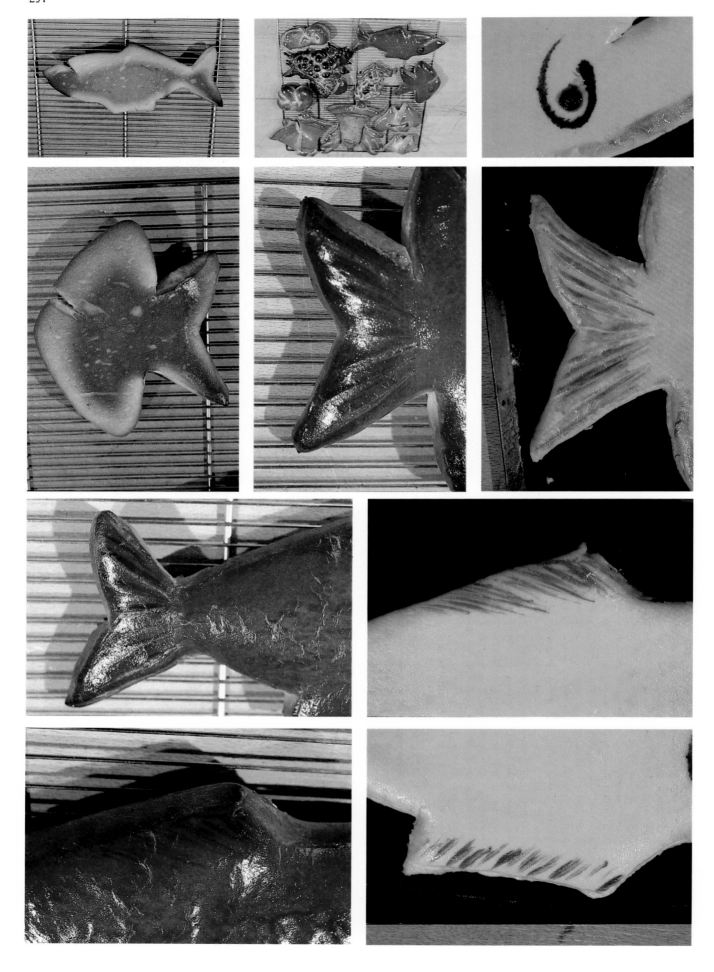

Hand-shaped breads

Introduction

Hand-shaped breads can be prepared with leftover trimmings from cutout breads or with freshly prepared Viennese bread dough and milk bread dough.

The breads can be shaped into large or individual-size loaves. The weight of the loaves can vary from 250 grams to 1 kilogram (9 to 17.5 ounces).

The examples given here are just a few of the possible designs for hand-shaped breads.

Equipment

No special equipment is required for hand-shaped breads, but the following standard baking equipment should be on hand:

Heavy baking sheets
Paring knife and medium-size knife
Scissors with pointed tips
Large and small pastry brushes
Rolling pin
Flour brush

Preparing the Dough

It is best to use dough that has been prepared the day before and allowed to rise slowly in the refrigerator, 5°C (40°F).

When using leftover trimmings from cutout Viennese breads, be sure to place them in the refrigerator and allow them to relax for 20 to 30 minutes before shaping them into loaves.

Weigh the dough into appropriate-size sections for shaping into loaves. Do not round the sections. Use as little flour as possible.

For miniature breads it is best to weigh a 500-gram (17.5-ounce) section of dough and then divide it into eight to twelve equal-size pieces. Each of these pieces is then shaped as desired.

Tips for Preparing Hand-shaped Breads

Use as little flour as possible.

Never tear the dough.

If the dough seems tough and lacks elasticity, be sure to let it rest.

Use chilled baking sheets that have been lightly buttered and sprinkled with water.

Keep the individual shapes as regular as possible. They should have the same weight and shape.

Brush off any excess flour.

Brush the breads twice with egg wash: once after the initial shaping and again after proofing.

Do not allow the dough to rise too quickly, or it may tear or become distorted.

If the breads are being decorated with fruits or if cuts are being made, finish this type of decoration at the last minute, just before baking.

Miniature breads should be baked in a hot oven so that they cook quickly and have an agreeable brown crust and the dough remains moist. It is also advantageous to use a large amount of steam during baking. Steam contributes to a thinner and shinier crust.

Transfer the breads to cooling racks as soon as they come out of the oven. This prevents them from reabsorbing moisture and becoming soggy.

For a dramatic effect, present miniature breads on racks or in baskets.

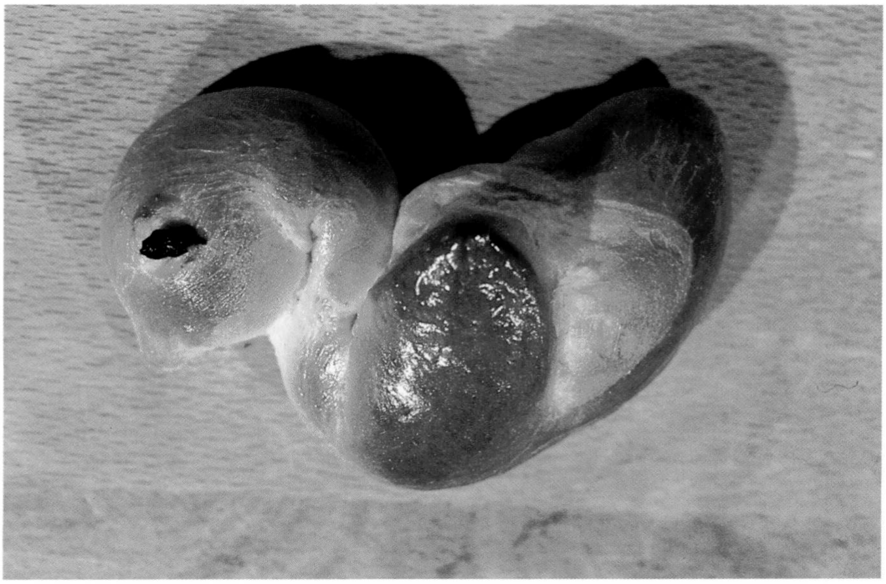

Examples of hand-shaped loaves

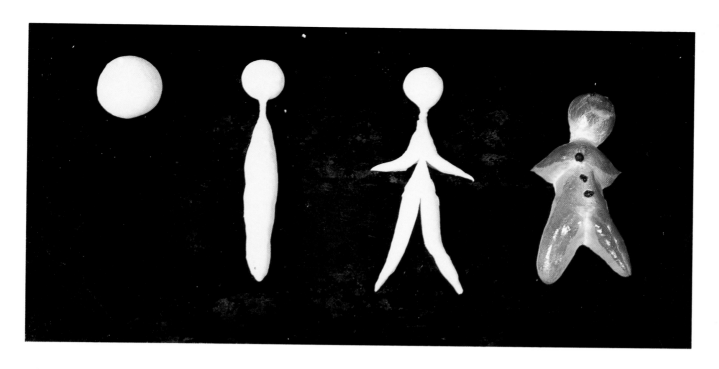

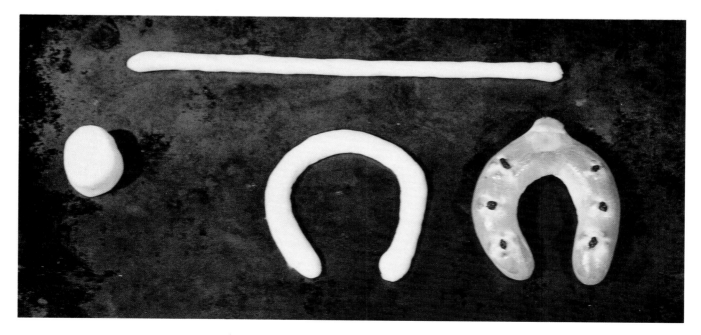

Examples of hand-shaped loaves

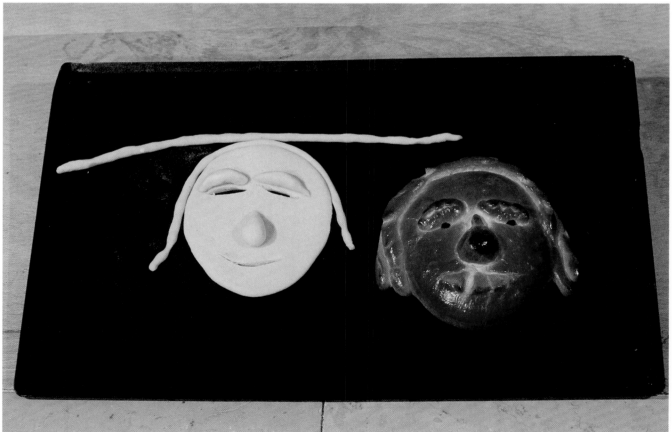

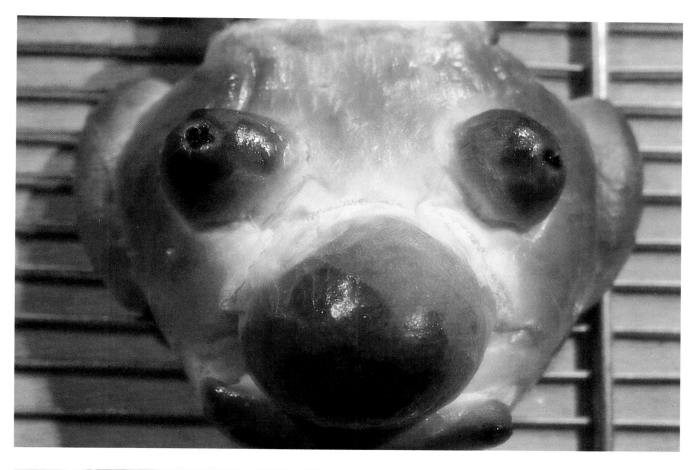

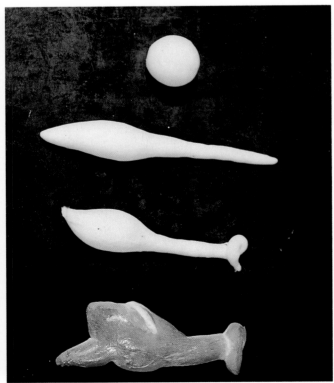

Examples of hand-shaped loaves

Examples of hand-shaped loaves

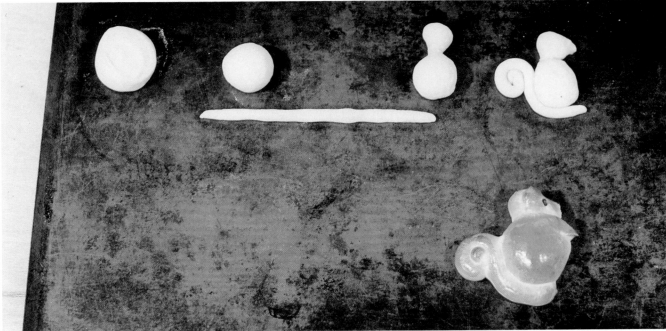

Displaying Viennese breads

Viennese cutout breads can be presented on cooling racks or on doilies.

If a large assortment of breads is to be presented, they can be arranged in baskets or cornucopias. A large number of different-shaped breads presented together gives a dramatic and festive effect.

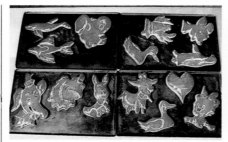

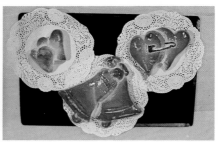

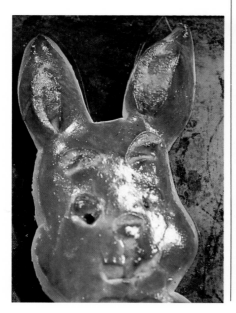

Braided loaves

Although it is possible to prepare braided loaves with as many as twelve separate strands of dough, most commercial bakeries limit themselves to loaves prepared with no more than four strands. Although complicated braided loaves make dramatic focal points for special presentations, they are too complicated and time consuming to be made practically on a regular basis. In the following pages, we have illustrated the preparation of braided loaves with both three and four strands of dough. To facilitate the illustrations, each of the strands has been colored differently. This is, of course, unnecessary in actual bread baking.

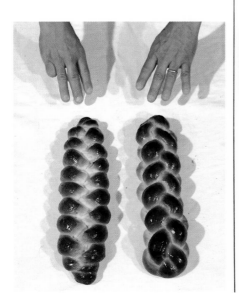

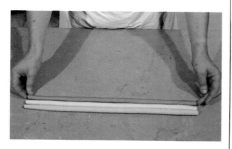

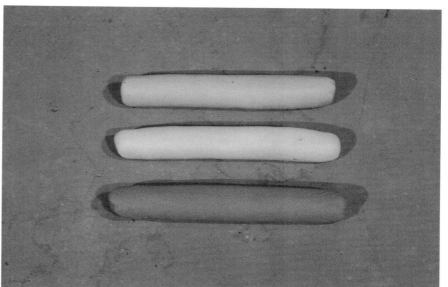

Types of Dough Used

Braided loaves are usually prepared with standard bread dough or Viennese bread dough.

Preparing the Dough

Weigh the dough into appropriate-size sections for each loaf. Braided loaves are usually prepared with sections of dough weighing from 250 to 1,300 grams (9 to 46 ounces).

Once the dough has been weighed into sections, divide each section into the number of strands to be used for the braiding (usually three or four).

Gently roll each of the pieces of dough to be used for the strands. Let them rest for 15 to 30 minutes, depending on the elasticity of the dough.

Shaping the Strands

Roll each of the sections into strands of equal length and thickness.

The individual strands of dough should taper very slightly at each end.

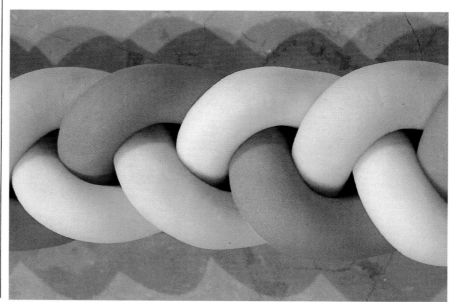

Braiding with three strands of dough

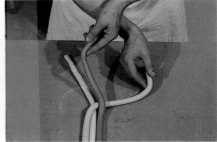

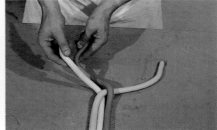

Place the three strands of dough next to one another. Make sure they are parallel and even at each end, perpendicular to the edge of the work surface. Begin braiding in the middle of the strands rather than at the ends. This helps ensure that the ends of the strands are even. Take one of the outside strands (left or right) and fold it over the center strand and then under the strand on the opposite side. Continue by alternating the outside strands, from right to left and then from left to right. Fold the strands first over another strand and then under the next strand (see photos). Continue in this way until all the strands have been used up. When one end of the strands is reached, press the ends together to form an oval shape.

When the first end of the strands has been reached, turn the strands around and repeat the process, working from the middle toward the other end.

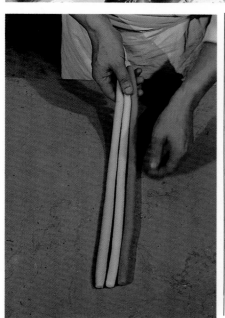

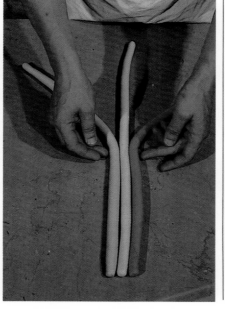

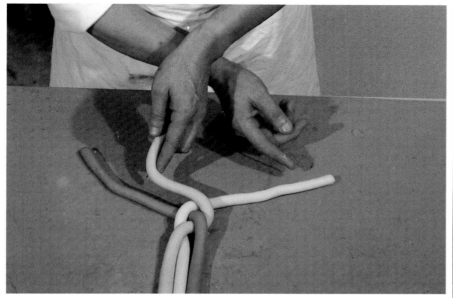
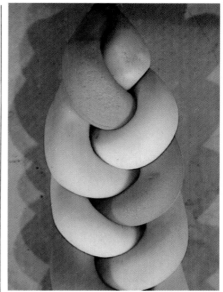
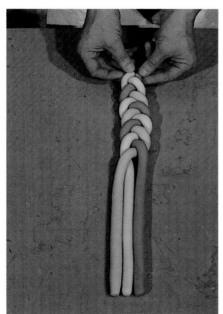
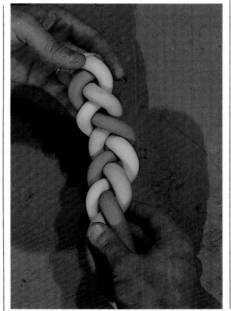
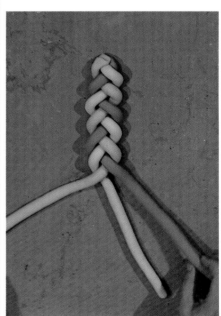

When the entire length has been braided, place the braid on a lightly buttered and moistened baking sheet. If necessary, press gently on the braid to correct any irregularities in its shape.

When using Viennese bread dough, brush the loaves with egg wash before proofing. Carefully watch the proofing.

Do not allow the braided loaves to rise too quickly in the proof box or rising area. Brush the loaves a second time with egg wash before baking.

Bake the loaves in a moderate oven (the exact temperature depends on the thickness of each of the strands). Use a large quantity of steam for loaves made with standard bread dough, but avoid using steam for loaves made with Viennese bread dough. Braided loaves are baked in the same way as other loaves made with the same types of dough.

Braiding with four strands of dough

Prepare the strands of dough in the same way as when braiding with three strands (page 172).

To braid with four strands of dough, place the ends of each of the four strands together to form a cross, as shown in the photos that follow. Cross two opposite ends, then cross the other pair of opposite ends. Continue crossing each pair until the entire length is braided. Let the loaves rise and bake as for three-strand braids.

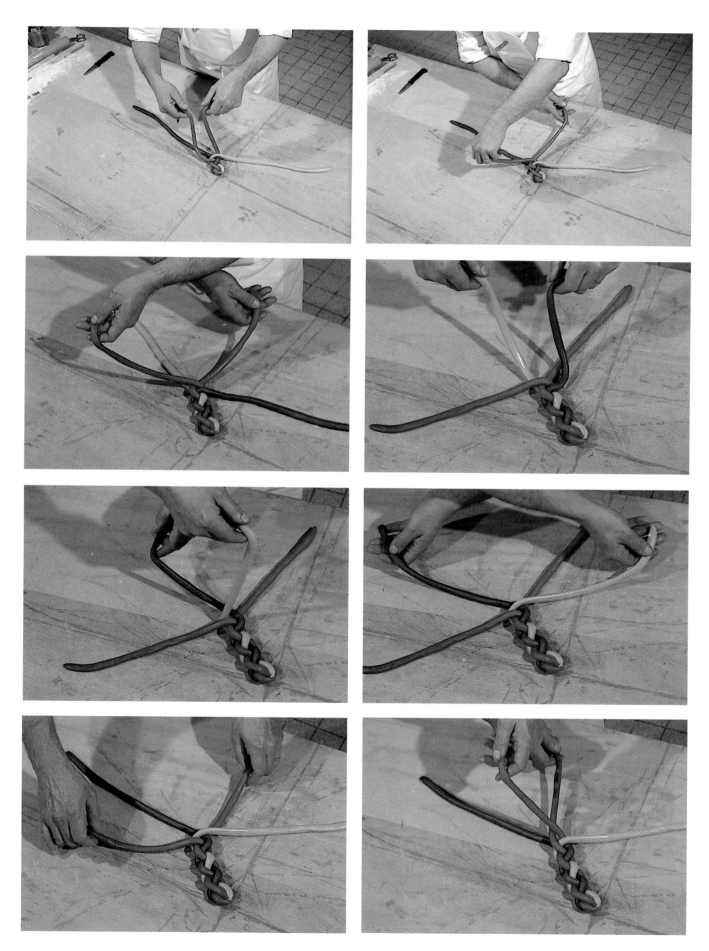

Chapter 4
Decorative breads

Bread has long been a source of nourishment for most of Western civilization. The sight of handmade breads strikes a fundamental chord in Europeans and Americans alike. Interest in handcrafted objects is on the rise as today's consumer reacts against the bland mediocrity of so many manufactured products. Bread exemplifies this trend, as people continue to demand carefully baked goods made by hand with quality ingredients.

It is up to the professional baker to revive the eating habits of the past, before the invention of mass-produced supermarket loaves. The professional baker should be aware that there are two approaches to any job: one that values the quantity to the detriment of quality, and its converse, which values quality while working with limited quantities. This book emphasizes the second approach.

This book also aims to describe to the baker who already knows how to make high-quality handcrafted bread, the techniques needed to decorate the loaves. These loaves are not only delicious, but appealing to the eye as well.

It is often advantageous to the baker to prepare several elaborately decorated loaves to be used as window displays. This not only helps attract customers but makes them aware that their baker is highly

skilled. Seeing these loaves may also encourage them to place special orders.

Breads with a Personal Touch

By decorating individual breads, the baker can give a personal touch to his or her products. Decorative breads also allow bakers to perfect their skills.

Decorative breads have an immediate appeal and make it easier for the baker to present more diverse products. Unfortunately, decorated breads are only rarely prepared—bakers have either forgotten the nec-essary skills or are unwilling to invest the time needed for this kind of work.

The pages that follow describe several straightforward techniques that will immediately allow bakers to improve the appearance of their products.

Basic decorating dough

A number of recipes exist for decorating dough. Unfortunately, many of these recipes are inconsistent and give unreliable results. Below are two recipes that have proven reliable and provide excellent results.

Preparation

Recipe 1
Basic Decorating Dough

1 kg bread flour (35 oz.)
15 g salt (½ oz. or 1 Tbsp.)
300 g butter or shortening (10.5 oz.)
100 g glucose (3.5 oz.)
100 ml warm water (3.5 fl. oz.)
3 egg yolks
100 ml cold water (3.5 fl. oz.)

Equipment

Measuring cups, scale, mixing bowl, plastic pastry scraper, plastic wrap, baking sheet, bowl and paddle attachment for electric mixer.

Procedure

Breaking Up the Butter or Shortening
(Sablage)
(about 10 minutes)

Cut the butter or shortening into cubes so that it can be easily broken up with the flour. If the butter is extremely hard, it can be softened by working it with the palm of the hand. Place the sifted flour, the salt, and the cubes of butter in the bowl attachment to the electric mixer. Attach the paddle blade to the electric mixer.

Turn the mixer to slow speed.

Dissolving the Glucose

While the flour, salt, and butter are being worked in the mixer, place the glucose and warm water in a mixing bowl.

Gently whisk the mixture to help dissolve the glucose.

Kneading

Add the glucose/water solution and the egg yolks to the ingredients in the mixer bowl. Gradually add the cold water to the mixture. It may not be necessary to add all the cold water; add only a little bit at a time.

Stop the mixer and check the consistency of the dough. If it seems too stiff, continue to add cold water. Basic decorating dough should have a firm yet supple consistency. It should not be overly dry or crumbly.

Continue adding the cold water until the dough has reached the right consistency. Knead the dough as little as possible.

As soon as the dough comes together into a solid mass, stop the mixer. The dough should not be kneaded beyond this point.

Transfer the dough from the mixer to a clean work surface. Do not use any flour at this point.

Flatten the dough into a rectangle on the work surface.

Cover the rectangle of dough with plastic wrap and transfer it to a baking sheet. Place it overnight in the refrigerator, 5°C (40°F). After it has rested overnight, it is ready to use.

Recipe 2
Basic Decorating Dough (Alternative Recipe)

Replace the 1 kilogram (35 ounces) of flour called for in recipe 1 with a mixture of 700 grams (24.5 ounces) bread flour and 300 grams (10.5 ounces) rye flour.

Note

The other ingredients are essentially the same as called for in recipe 1. The only difference is that recipe 2 requires more water. Measure out 150 to 200 milliliters (5 to 7 fluid ounces) cold water. The exact amount required will depend on the flour being used. The procedure is the same as for recipe 1.

Rye-flour-based Decorating Dough (without Butter or Shortening)

1 kg rye flour (35 oz.)
550 ml sugar syrup with glucose (18.5 fl. oz.), prepared by combining:
  1 L water (34 fl. oz.)
  1 kg sugar (35 oz.)
  500 g glucose (17.5 oz.)

Preparing the Dough

Sift the rye flour onto the work surface. Make a well in the center of the flour. Pour the syrup into the well.

Carefully combine the ingredients and "fraise" the dough by crushing it with the heel of the hand. Make sure that the ingredients are thoroughly combined.

This dough can be used immediately or covered with plastic wrap and refrigerated until needed. Because this dough contains no fat, it is particularly useful for decorated breads that will be kept for long periods.

Alternate Recipe (without Butter or Shortening)

The rye flour recipe described above can be prepared with regular wheat-based bread flour. The procedure is exactly the same.

Precautions for Use and Storage of Decorating Dough

Storing the Dough

Decorating dough can be stored in the refrigerator, 5°C (41°F), for up to 15 days if tightly wrapped in plastic wrap.

Decorating dough can also be frozen, but because it requires several hours to thaw, most bakers do not consider freezing worthwhile.

The recipes for decorating dough given on pages 179 and 180 are easy to use and extremely versatile. They can be stored for relatively long periods of time, provided certain precautions are taken.

Precautions

Make sure that decorating dough is always tightly wrapped in plastic wrap. This will prevent the formation of a crust on the surface of the dough, which usually makes it unusable. Decorating dough is particularly susceptible to rapid dehydration.

When using decorating dough, try to use only the amount needed for the project at hand; otherwise, the leftover pieces of dough may become too dried out to save.

Formation of a Crust

Advantages: In some cases it is desirable to let a crust form on the surfaces of handmade decorations so that they hold their shape during baking. It is best to place these decorations on cooling racks or sheets of cardboard, where the open air will quickly cause a crust to form.

Disadvantages: Because decorating dough is particularly susceptible to drying out in the open air, it is essential that any trimmings or leftover pieces of dough be quickly gathered and covered with plastic wrap if they are to be saved for later use.

Preparations for bread decoration

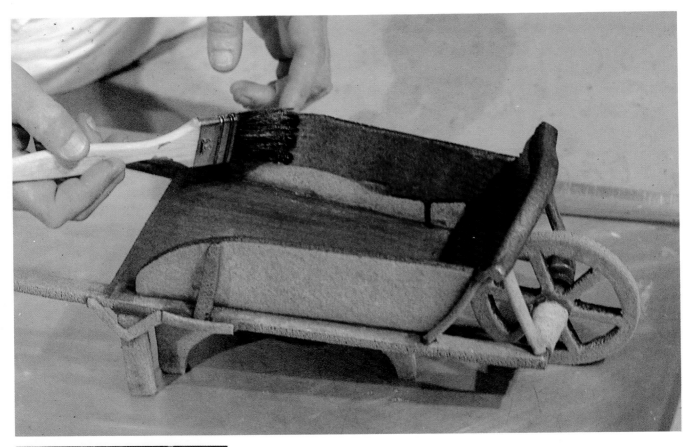

Basic Preparations for Bread Decoration

In order to assemble the various elements for decorating breads, certain basic preparations should be mastered so they can be quickly prepared as needed. Be sure to use only the best ingredients in their preparation.

1. Flour paste

2. Gelatin-based sealer

3. Using gelatin-based sealer on objects stained with coffee extract.

Flour Paste

Equipment

Saucepan
Whisk
Wooden spatula
Plastic pastry scraper
Mixing bowl
Drum sieve

Recipe

250 ml water (8.5 fl. oz.)
100 g bread flour (3.5 oz.)

Procedure

Sift the flour and combine it with the water in a saucepan. Whisk the mixture until it is smooth. Heat the mixture over medium heat, stirring constantly with a

wooden spatula. Continue to stir until the mixture thickens. Cook gently for 2 to 3 minutes more.

Transfer the paste to a mixing bowl.

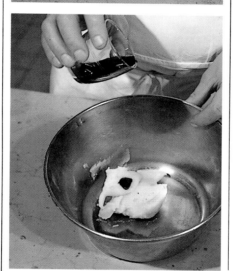

Note

1. When the flour and water are first combined, the mixture will have lumps. As the mixture heats, it thickens, and the lumps smooth out.

2. Flour paste must be used as soon as it is prepared.

3. Because flour paste liquefies soon after it is made, prepare only as much as will be needed right away.

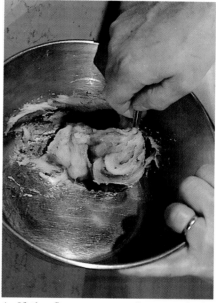

4. If the flour paste used to attach the decorating elements will be visible, tint it with coffee extract so that it has the same color as the surrounding sections of bread. Coffee extract can also be brushed on the paste after it has been applied to the decorated loaves.

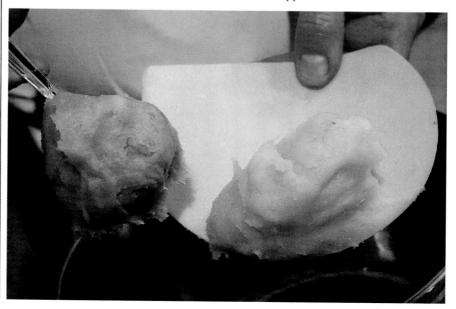

Gelatin-based Sealer

Equipment

Saucepan
Mixing bowl
Wooden spatula

Recipe

250 ml water (8.5 fl. oz.)
25 sheets (50 g) gelatin (1.5 oz.)
1 L cold water (34 fl. oz.), to soften the
sheets of gelatin

Procedure

Fill a mixing bowl halfway with cold water. Add the sheets of gelatin one by one, and let them soften for 5 to 10 minutes.

Lift the sheets of gelatin out of the cold water. Squeeze them to eliminate excess water. Place them in the saucepan with the water.

Pour the 250 milliliters (8.5 fluid ounces) of water into a saucepan.

Put the saucepan on the stove. Gently heat the mixture while stirring with a wooden spatula. Continue heating and stirring until the sheets of gelatin are completely dissolved.

Note

1. Be careful not to allow the gelatin mixture to boil. Boiling weakens the holding power of the gelatin.

2. The gelatin-based sealer should always be used hot. It can be applied to decorating dough with a pastry brush, or the dough can be immersed directly in the sealer.

3. Drain the pieces of decorating dough that have been coated with sealer on a cooling rack placed over a baking sheet.

Gelatin-based sealer is used to seal dough-based decorations with a film that protects them from moisture and therefore increases the shelf life of dough-based decorations.

It also helps improve the sheen and appearance of decorated breads.

Gelatin-based sealer can be used as a substitute for commercially available glazes.

Using Gelatin-based Sealer on Stained Objects

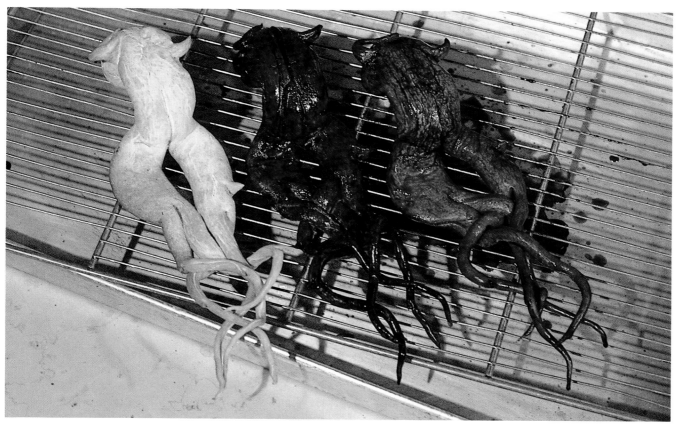

Gelatin-based sealer is used to coat decorative objects that are to look like wood. These objects are first stained with coffee extract. The stain is then lightened with clear gelatin-based sealer. Examples include grapevines, bakers' peels, miniature wine presses, and picture frames.

Equipment

Cooling rack
Baking sheets

Procedure

Illustrated below is a technique for coating a grapevine made with decorating dough. After the decorating dough is shaped, it is baked in a 180° C (350°F) oven.

1. As soon as the object to be coated comes out of the oven, brush it with coffee extract using a pastry brush.

2. Put the object back in the oven for about 2 minutes to dry the coffee extract. This preliminary drying also helps fix the stain. At this point the color will be extremely dark. This is normal.

3. Finish drying the object in a proof box or in a warm place. In any case, keep the object to be dried away from excess humidity.

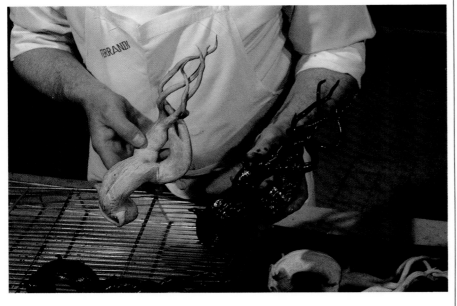

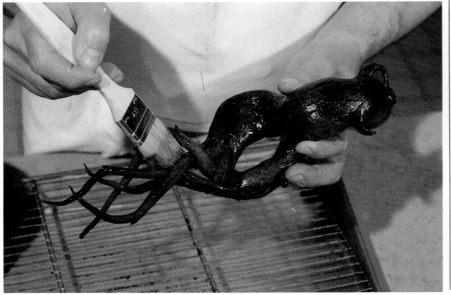

The Next Day: Lightening the Stain

4. Brush the stained and dried object with hot gelatin-based sealer using a pastry brush. The purpose of this step is not only to give an appealing sheen to the object but to remove some of the stain. As the excess stain is removed from the surface, the object takes on the warm appearance of natural wood.

Working with decorating dough

Molding Decorating Dough

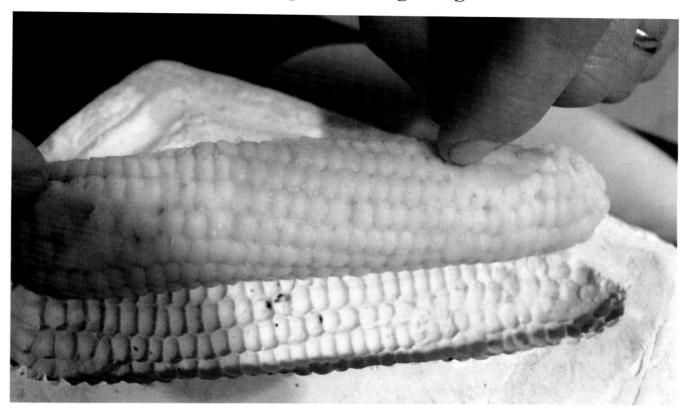

Making Molds

Introduction

Special molds made of plaster can be used to give a realistic appearance to certain decorative breads. This simple technique is used for a wide variety of presentations.

Illustrated below is a straightforward technique for preparing the plaster molds.

Materials

Plastic ice tray or other long plastic container (the bottom cut from a plastic water bottle can also be used)
Plaster of paris (quick setting)
Water
Salad oil
Object to be molded (such as an ear of corn)
Paper towels

Possible Shapes

Walnuts, chestnuts, ears of corn, or any firm object can be used as the basis of the mold.

Preparation of Plaster Molds (example: ear of corn)

1. Prepare the plaster so that it has a fairly firm consistency.
2. Pour the plaster into the plastic container and wait 1 to 2 minutes
3. Brush the surface of an ear of corn with salad oil. Use the side with the nicest appearance.
4. Hold the ear of corn firmly at each end and press it sideways into the plaster. Press firmly so that the corn is set halfway into the plaster. Hold it in this position for several seconds.
5. Carefully remove the ear of corn from the plaster using a back-and-forth motion. Check the imprint left in the plaster to make sure it is even and regular. If the imprint is unacceptable, repeat the process. Be sure to rinse the ear of corn and coat it with oil if the process is repeated.
6. Remove any excess salad oil remaining on the inside of the mold by gently dabbing the surface with paper towels.
7. Scrape the inside surface of the plaster mold with a knife to eliminate any rough edges. It should then be gently brushed with sandpaper.

8. Allow the mold to dry for at least 24 hours before using.

This method is used regardless of the object being molded.

Direct Molding

It is also possible to create decorative shapes by wrapping a thin sheet of decorating dough around objects such as carafes, vases, or wine bottles. The object used should be able to withstand a 200°C (400°F) oven temperature.

Preparation

Be sure to choose objects that have simple, even shapes. Avoid objects with irregularities or jutting edges. When molding sheets of decorating dough around solid objects, mold each half of the object separately. The two halves of shaped dough should then be allowed to dry. Once dry, they are attached with flour paste.

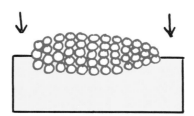

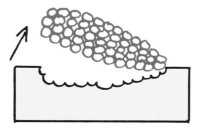

Wrap the object to be molded with aluminum foil before applying the decorating dough. Be sure that the foil adheres firmly to the surface of the object. There should be no wrinkles or irregularities in the foil.

Lightly brush the foil with melted butter and carefully smooth over the surface with the hands.

Use an egg carton to support the foil-coated object.

Roll out a thin sheet of rye-flour-based decorating dough and fit it over the surface of the foil-coated object. Press the dough over the entire surface of the object, making sure that the dough touches the aluminum foil at all points.

Cut the dough halfway down along the object with a paring knife. It is important to cut evenly so that the two halves of dough fit together.

Allow the object, half-coated with decorating dough, to dry for 2 hours in the open air. As the dough begins to form a crust, transfer the object with the dough still attached to a 200°C (400°F) oven for 30 to 40 minutes. If the oven is equipped with vents, they should be left open to facilitate drying of the dough.

Pull the molded decorating dough away from the object before it has completely cooled. Gently peel the aluminum foil away from the inside of the decorating dough.

When both sides of the dough are finished, carefully attach the two halves with flour paste. Dry the assembled dough in a low oven.

It may be necessary at some point to reinforce the seam where the two halves of dough are attached. Handles or other decorations should be attached at this point.

Go over the surface of the dough with a paring knife to scrape away irregularities. The dough should now be colored if desired.

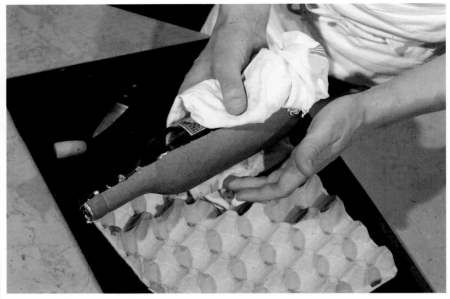

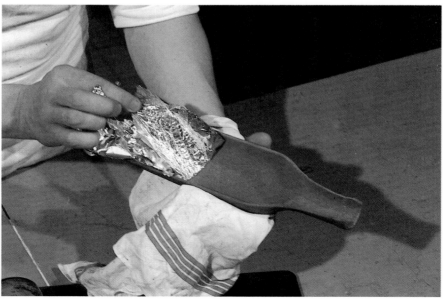

Hand-shaping Decorating Dough

Introduction

Decorating dough can be hand-shaped to form a wide variety of decorative objects. Rye-flour-based dough (without butter or shortening) works especially well for this.

Hand-shaped dough is molded directly by hand or with small tools such as scissors, paring knives, or miniature chisels.

Presented here are some of the simpler shapes, which lend themselves well to hand shaping. These shapes can be used to decorate loaves or can be assembled into presentation pieces:

1. Chestnuts
2. Pears, apples, lemons
3. Cherries
4. Hazelnuts
5. Olives

After the shapes have been formed, they are dried in a slow oven, 180°C (350°F), after an initial drying and resting period of several hours. They are colored with coffee extract while they are still hot, immediately after they come out of the oven. They are then assembled or attached to already prepared loaves with flour paste.

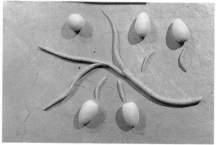

Hand-shaped Decorating Dough

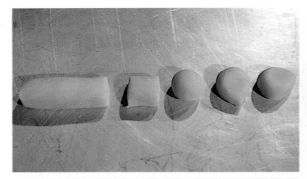

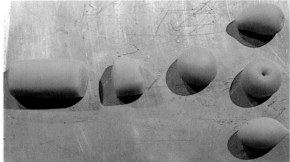

Cutting Out Decorating Dough

Miniature Cutouts

Miniature decorations can also be cut from sheets of decorating dough. One of two techniques can be used:

- The dough can be cut with a cookie cutter and then assembled into a variety of shapes such as flowers. These flowers are then attached to the loaves being decorated.
- Flat sheets of decorating dough can be cut directly with a paring knife. This free-form method allows the baker with an artistic bent to prepare personalized designs. This versatile technique can be used to prepare hearts for Valentine's Day, wedding bells, Christmas trees, and other special decorations.

Once the baker has mastered the more fundamental hand-cut shapes, he or she can then decorate breads with the same freedom as a pastry chef who decorates cakes and other pastries to order.

The variety of techniques available for shaping decorating dough allows the baker to custom-design breads for religious and civic holidays. Decorative breads also offer bakers the opportunity to be recognized as skilled artisans.

Cutting Decorating Dough with Templates

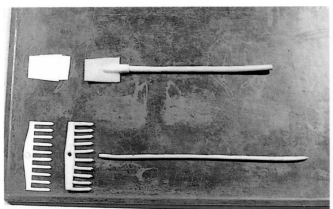

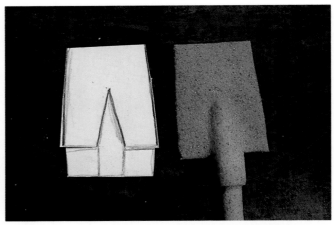

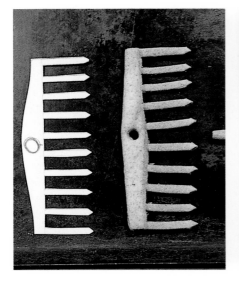

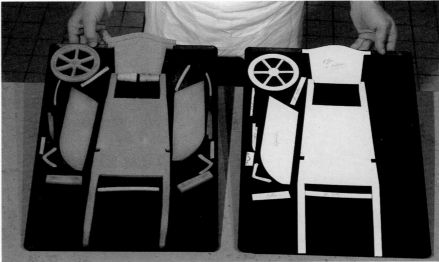

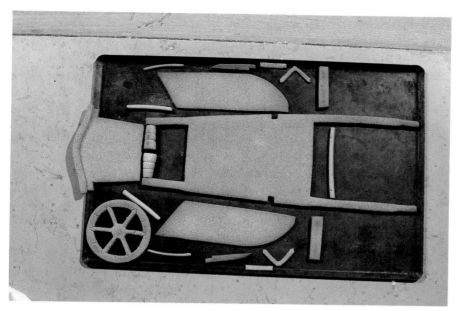
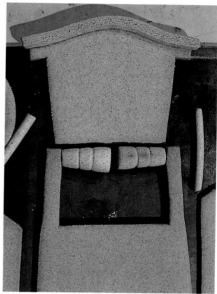

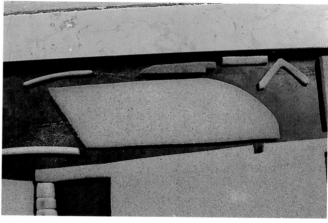

When decorating dough is being fashioned into relatively complicated objects, it is best to cut out the different pieces of dough with cardboard templates. The thickness of the decorating dough can be adjusted according to the requirements of the finished design.

It is possible to create virtually any shape or object with decorating dough. When preparing complicated objects, especially those that will be kept for relatively long periods, it is preferable to use rye-based decorating dough without butter or shortening. Because it contains no fat, this dough will not spoil or become rancid.

Preparing the Cardboard Templates

Successful assembly of the more complicated pieces depends on the accurate sizing and cutting of the cardboard templates. It is essential to draw each of the pieces carefully before cutting out the templates. Remember to calculate the thickness of each section of dough when determining the size of the various pieces. It is a good idea to make extra cutouts of the more fragile pieces of dough so it is not necessary to repeat the entire drying process if one small piece is broken.

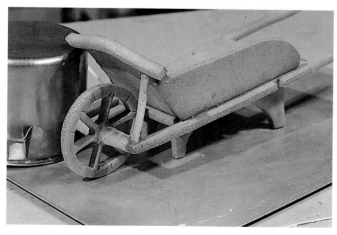

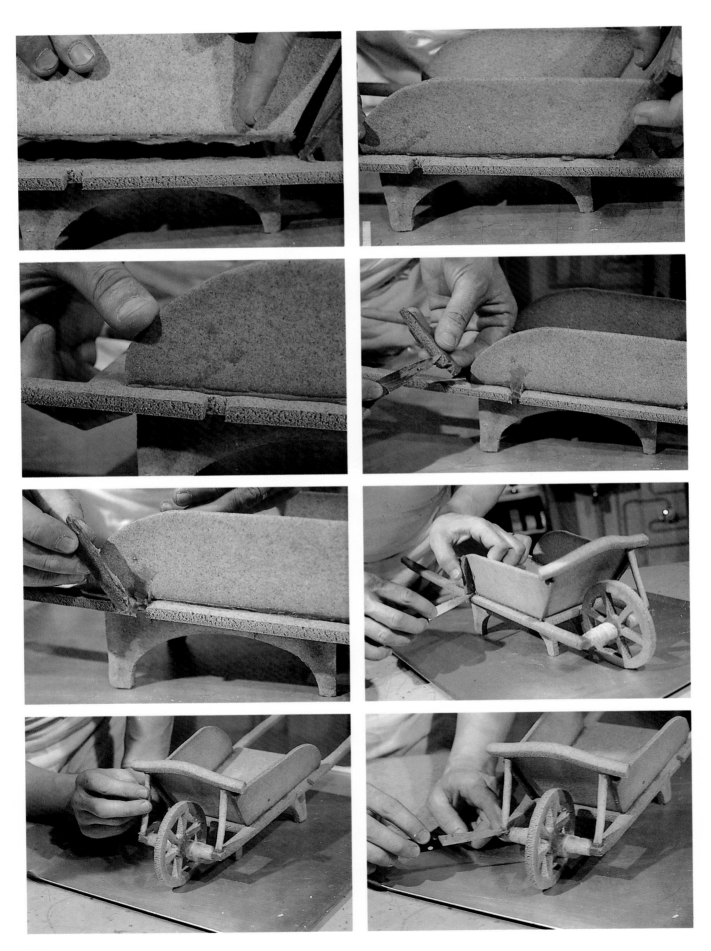

Decorating dough should be cut directly on the baking sheet used for the final baking. In this way, the dough does not need to be transferred from the work surface, which could alter its shape. Make sure that the baking sheets are thick and perfectly smooth, or the resulting shapes may end up twisted or warped.

The techniques for cutouts illustrated below demonstrate
- using thinly rolled decorating dough (rake and shovel)
- using thickly rolled decorating dough (wheelbarrow).

Summary of Techniques for Making a Wheelbarrow

Use rye-flour-based decorating dough without butter or shortening.

The base, wheels, and handles of the wheelbarrow should have a thickness of 1 centimeter (½ inch). The remaining pieces should be rolled out to a thickness of 5 millimeters (¼ inch).

The cutouts should be allowed to dry for 2 hours in the open air and then transferred to a slow oven, 180°C (350°F), with the vents open (if available) for final drying. The time needed for the final drying depends on the thickness of the individual pieces. Allow 35 minutes for the small support bars on the sides of the wheelbarrow, 50 minutes for the 5-millimeter-thick (¼-inch) sections, and 1 hour 15 minutes for the 1-centimeter-thick (½-inch) sections.

When all the sections have completely hardened and dried, they should be attached with freshly made flour paste. The paste should be colored with coffee extract so that it matches the other sections of dough.

The sections are glued twice. The sections of dough are attached by applying a fairly thick layer of flour paste to all the joints and junctures.

It is sometimes necessary to support the sections after they have been glued with molds or mixing bowls while the flour paste is drying. The glued pieces should be dried in a proof box at 90°C (200°F) for 1 hour.

After the wheelbarrow is removed from the proof box, any exposed flour paste should be smoothed off with a paring knife. Additional flour paste should then be applied to joints and edges where the pieces meet with the tip of a small knife to reinforce the first layer of paste. The wheelbarrow should then be returned to the proof box for another hour for the final drying.

When the wheelbarrow is removed from the proof box after the final drying, it should be brushed with coffee extract that has been lightly diluted with a strong liquor such as brandy or whiskey. If the wheelbarrow is left unvarnished and is protected from dust and moisture, it can be stored for several months.

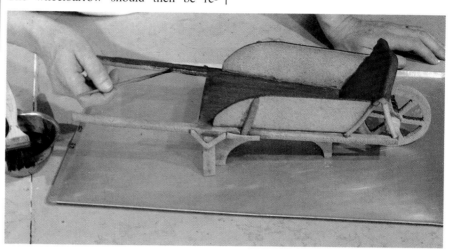

Below, another example: a sled with skis and poles

Grapevines

Individual Grapes and Grape Clusters

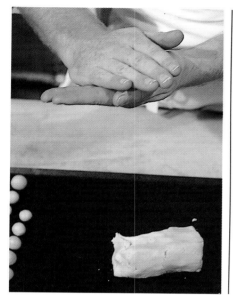

Materials

Baking sheet
Paring knife
Metal spatula
100 ml water (3.5 fl. oz.)
Flour paste
Egg cartons

Shaping the Dough

Divide the decorating dough into small pieces weighing from 10 to 20 grams (⅓ to ⅔ ounce) each. Roll the pieces of dough into little balls in the palms of the hands. Moisten the palms of the hands with a few drops of cold water before rolling the dough to lubricate the dough and make it easier to roll. Never use flour at this stage.

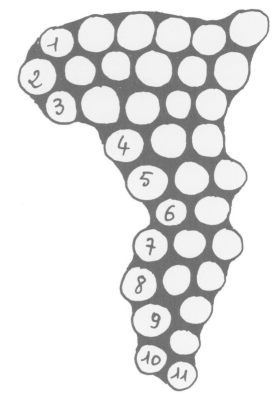

Make sure that each individual grape is perfectly smooth. Place the grapes on a baking sheet. Sometimes, after the grapes have been rolled, a seam forms on one side. Make sure that this is on the bottom when the grapes are being baked.

Bake the grapes in a 170°C (340°F) oven without steam for approximately 30 minutes. The grapes should have a pale beige hue at the end of baking.

Let the grapes cool. They can be stored in a covered mixing bowl or a cardboard box until needed.

Assembling Grape Clusters

First Day

Arrange the individual grapes so that a base for the grape cluster is formed. This base row will be the longest row. Attach the grapes to each other with flour paste using a paring knife.

Coat the top surface of the base row with flour paste using a metal spatula. Do not allow any of the flour paste to coat the surfaces of the last one or two grapes in the base row. These will be visible when the cluster is completed.

Attach a second layer of grapes to the surface of the base rows. Leave the last one or two grapes in the base row exposed (see diagrams).

Attach a third row of grapes to the base, again leaving a couple of grapes at the end of the previous row exposed.

This completes the construction of half a grape cluster. Gently slide this first cluster to one end of a baking sheet while working on other clusters.

Prepare five or six grape clusters following the same procedure. Make sure, however, to vary the shape of the clusters and the size of the grapes.

When the clusters are complete, carefully examine them to ensure that none of the flour paste has run down over the surface. Scrape off any irregularities with a sharp paring knife.

Place the clusters in a slow oven or proof box, 180°C (175°F), for 30 minutes to dry the flour paste.

Assembling the Grape Clusters

attached grapes

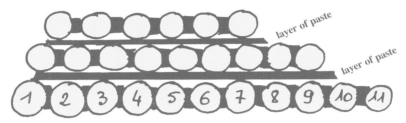

layer of paste

layer of paste

base row

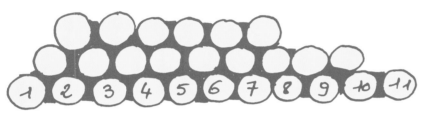

base row

Second Day

Place half a grape cluster flat side up on an egg carton. Make sure that the cluster rests firmly on the surface of the carton.

Spread the flat surface of the grape cluster with flour paste. Avoid getting any of the paste on the end grapes, which will be visible when the cluster is finished. Cover the flat surface with grapes, using the same technique as when con-structing the clusters on a baking sheet.

Continue constructing the cluster, add-ing a third layer of grapes. Remember, the second half is the inverse of the first and should be constructed in a similar way. When the cluster is finished, go over its surface checking for smudges of flour paste and other irregularities.

Carefully turn the cluster over and de-termine which side is the most attractive.

Add an additional grape or two if neces-sary to even out the appearance of the grape bunch.

When the bunches of grapes are con-structed, finish drying them in an 80°C (175°F) oven without steam for 30 min-utes.

When the grape clusters have cooled, store them in cardboard boxes overnight.

Second Day

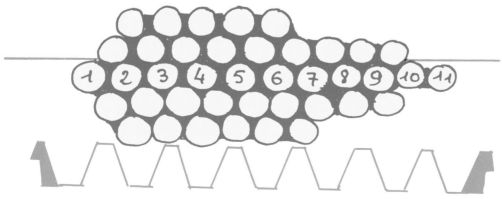

egg carton

Third Day

The grape clusters can be finished in one of three ways.

First, the grape bunches can be used as they are. Attach them at one or two points to a finished loaf or presentation piece with flour paste.

Or they can be dipped for 1 second in gelatin-based sealer.

Finally, if the grape bunches are to be used in a presentation piece that will not be eaten, they can be sprayed with a commercial lacquer. They will not be edible but will retain their sheen.

Grape Leaves

Equipment

Rolling pin
Paring knife
Plastic wrap
Cardboard egg cartons

Procedure

Work with 300 to 400 grams (10.5 to 14 ounces) decorating dough.

Roll the dough in a thin sheet, 1 millimeter (1/16 inch), on a pastry marble. It is best not to use flour to roll out the pastry, but if the pastry begins to stick, use as little flour as possible to prevent sticking.

Cut leaves from the dough with a cookie cutter or a cardboard template modeled after an actual grape leaf.

Immediately after cutting out the leaves, cover them with plastic wrap to prevent the formation of a crust on their surfaces.

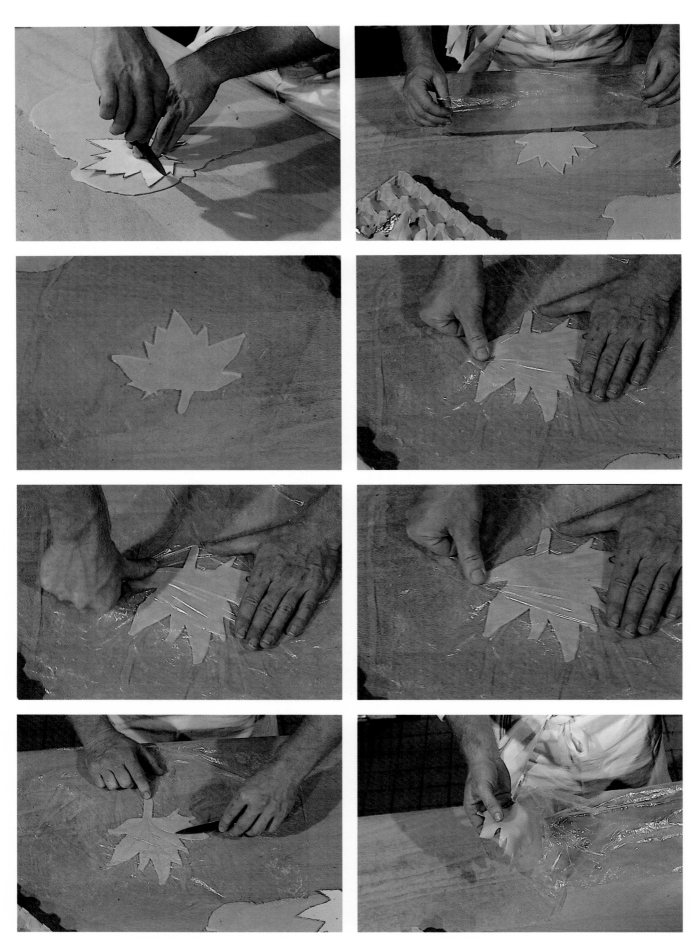

204

Working with one leaf at a time and keeping the plastic wrap in place, press the edges of the leaf with the thumb so that the edges are paper thin.

With the leaves still covered with plastic wrap, use a paring knife to incise veins into their surfaces. Make sure that the cuts are deep enough so the veins do not disappear during baking, but do not cut all the way through the leaves.

Remove the plastic wrap.

Carefully remove the leaves from the pastry marble by sliding the tip of a paring knife under the edges and gently lifting.

Rest the leaves on egg cartons so that they fall into natural undulating shapes. The leaves can be further shaped by wedging pieces of aluminum foil or egg carton under the leaves at different points.

Place the leaves, still on the egg cartons, on racks in the refrigerator, 5°C (40°F), for 48 hours to allow them to dry. Do not cover the leaves during this period.

Baking

Prebaking

Place the egg cartons with the leaves onto baking sheets and prebake in a 270°C (525°F) oven for 1 to 2 minutes.

The purpose of this preliminary stage is to brown the edges of the leaves. It is very easy to let them burn, however, so keep close watch on the leaves while they are in the oven.

The edges of the leaves should be dark brown, even a bit burned, but the centers of the leaves should be white or very pale brown. As soon as this is achieved, remove the leaves from the oven.

Carefully lift the leaves off the egg cartons and transfer them to baking sheets to cool and dry.

Baking

Transfer the leaves to the floor of a baker's oven preheated to 170°C (350°F). Bake for 3 to 4 minutes, until the centers are pale beige and the edges are dark brown.

Carefully remove the leaves from the oven, and place them on cardboard egg cartons on sheet pans to cool.

Finishing the Leaves

The leaves can be finished with any of the three techniques suggested for grape clusters.

Handmade flowers

The techniques used for making handmade flowers give the baker increased flexibility so that he or she can make varieties other than the classic rose or carnation. These techniques enable the baker to prepare tulips, a variety of orchids, lilies, and other species.

The method consists of preparing each flower petal separately. The individual petals are allowed to dry in the open air and are then baked. The flowers are then constructed by assembling the petals with flour paste.

Example: Tulips

Roll out a thin sheet of decorating dough without butter or shortening. Either rye-flour-based or wheat-flour-based dough can be used.

Cut elongated oval shapes from the sheet of dough. Doing this is easiest .f the sheet of dough is kept as close to the edge of the work surface as possible. A serving spoon or soup spoon is useful as a guide for cutting the oval shapes.

Press along the rim of each petal with the tip of the finger to thin the edges.

Shape the petals by placing them lengthwise on eggs. Turn up some of the edges of the petals to give them a natural shape. Each tulip requires six petals.

Prepare the stems, leaves, and pistils for the tulips (see photo, page 208).

Allow the petals (while still on the eggs) and other components to dry in the open air for 24 hours.

Gently remove the petals from the eggs and place them in the indentations of egg cartons.

Finish drying the components of the tulips in a 200°C (400°F) oven for 20 to 30 minutes. If the oven is equipped with vents, leave them open during the drying process. The petals should be left in the oven until the rims are lightly browned.

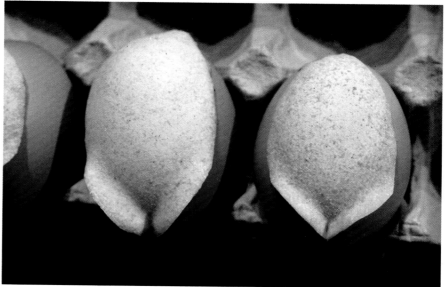

207

Keep close watch to avoid burning the petals.

The petals, stems, pistils, and leaves are then assembled with flour paste.

Assembling the Flowers

Start by assembling three of the smallest petals to form the inside of the flower. Attach the bases of the three petals together with flour paste. It is best to set the petals in a small mold or in an egg carton so that they hold their shape while the paste is setting.

The three petals can be more or less open, depending on the desired appearance of the finished flower. When preparing a bouquet of flowers, it is best to vary each one. Some of the flowers should be in full blossom while others should be barely open.

When the first three petals are attached, they should be gently dried in a low oven or proof box.

When the first group of petals has set, finish the flower by attaching three additional petals around the outside of the first group.

Color the pistil with coffee extract and attach it to the base of the flower with flour paste.

When the flower is attached to a bouquet or a finished loaf, the stems and leaves should be attached at several points with flour paste.

Note

The petals and leaves can be colored by applying coffee extract before assembling the flowers.

Handmade flowers can be prepared in advance and coated with gelatin-based sealer in the same way as roses and other cutout flowers.

This technique of assembling flowers is also used for other varieties such as the orchid petals shown below.

Ears of corn

The construction of decorations from molded decorating dough, as in these ears of corn, is a time-consuming process. Do not try to hurry the procedure.

Equipment

Container for flour
Chef's knife
Paring knife
Large cooling racks
Egg yolk and coffee extract for coloring
Plaster mold

Procedure

Depending on their exact size, each ear of corn requires approximately 100 grams (3.5 ounces) of dough.

First Day: Molding

Divide the dough into 100-gram (3.5-ounce) sections. Roll each section into an elongated cone shape. When molding, the seam that runs along one side of the dough should always face up.

Place the smooth (unseamed) side of the cone-shaped sections of dough in the container of flour so that the surface is thoroughly coated. This prevents the dough from sticking to the inside of the mold. Set the section of dough in the mold, floured side down, and press firmly.

Scrape the top surface of the dough with a back-and-forth motion to remove any excess dough that protrudes above the surface of the plaster mold.

Gently lift the dough out of the mold with a paring knife.

Transfer the molded dough to a cooling rack. Keep the molded side facing up. Allow the ears of corn to dry in the open air.

Remember that each molding results in *half* an ear of corn and that two moldings will be required for each ear.

Second Day: Hollowing Out the Dough

Make an incision around the flat edge of the molded ears of corn with a paring knife. While holding the section of dough firmly in the palm of the hand, remove excess dough from the inside of each ear.

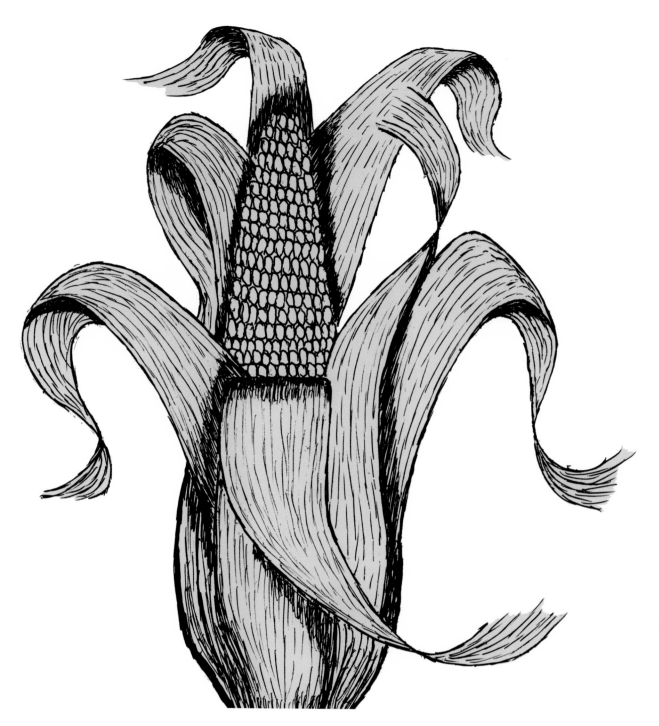

Return the hollowed-out ears to the drying rack for one more day.

Third Day

The ears can be further hollowed out in the same way as suggested above.

Fourth Day

Line the hollows of the molded dough with aluminum foil before baking. This is to prevent them from collapsing in the oven. Place the sections, molded side up, on baking sheets.

Bake the ears in a 170° to 180°C (about 350°F) oven with the vents open (if available) for 20 to 30 minutes. Do not allow the dough to brown. The sections should be pale beige when they come out of the oven.

When the ears come out of the oven, brush them with beaten egg yolk while they are still hot. Put them back in the oven for 1 to 2 minutes to dry the egg yolk coating. Remove the ears from the oven and let cool.

When the ears of corn have cooled, brush them with coffee extract that has been thinned with water or alcohol (two parts coffee extract and one part strong liquor, such as clear fruit brandy or whiskey).

Initially, the color will seem very dark. The next step is to lighten the color of the corn ears by brushing them with a fingertip dipped in cold water. Continue until the corn has a natural color.

Assembling the Ears

This step requires flour paste, a paring knife, and sandpaper.

Fifth Day

Carefully smooth off the inner surface and edges of the ears with coarse sandpaper. Continually slap the sandpaper to remove flour and bits of dough that accumulate on its surface.

Coat the inner edges of the ears with flour paste using a paring knife. Fit the two halves of each ear together. Gently remove any excess flour paste that seeps from the seams of the ears. Allow the assembled ears to dry overnight in the open air.

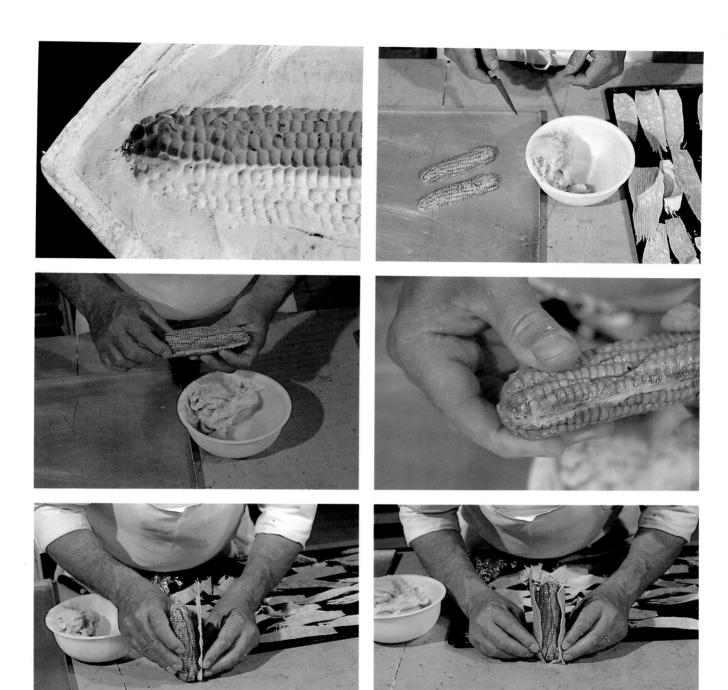

Sixth Day

The finished ears should be stored in a dry place until needed. The last stage consists of attaching the leaves (see pages 214 to 219).

The finished ears can be presented in two ways:

- unfinished, without additional sealer or lacquer
- lacquered, for presentation pieces

Corn leaves

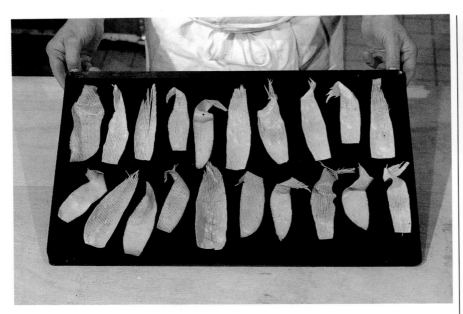

Equipment

Rolling pin
Grooved rolling pin
Container for flour
Paring knife
Baking sheet for baguette loaves or tuiles
Heavy-bottomed baking sheet

Procedure

Roll 200 grams (7 ounces) of decorating dough into a thin sheet, 1 millimeter (1/16 inch) thick. Both sides of the sheet of dough should be lightly coated with flour.

Cut the dough into long oval-shaped leaves with a paring knife.

Remove the trimmings of dough from around the leaves and cover the leaves with plastic wrap.

Work with one leaf at a time. Place a leaf directly in front of you. Firmly roll over the surface of the leaf with the grooved rolling pin. Move the pin from the base to the top of the leaf. While moving up the leaf with the rolling pin, press harder over the top part of the leaf so it is thinned out and elongated. The rolling pin should leave thin grooves on the surface of the leaves. This is an essential part of the decoration.

Place the leaves on the baking sheet used for baguettes or tuiles so they take on a rounded shape.

Let the leaves dry overnight in the baking sheets.

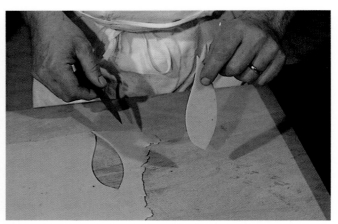

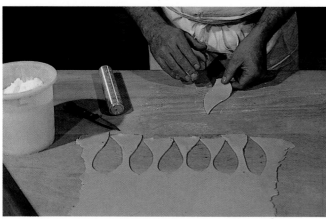

Corn

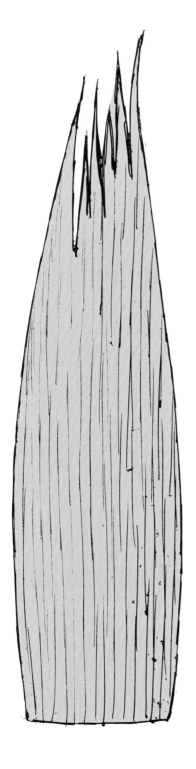

Examples of Shaped Corn Leaves

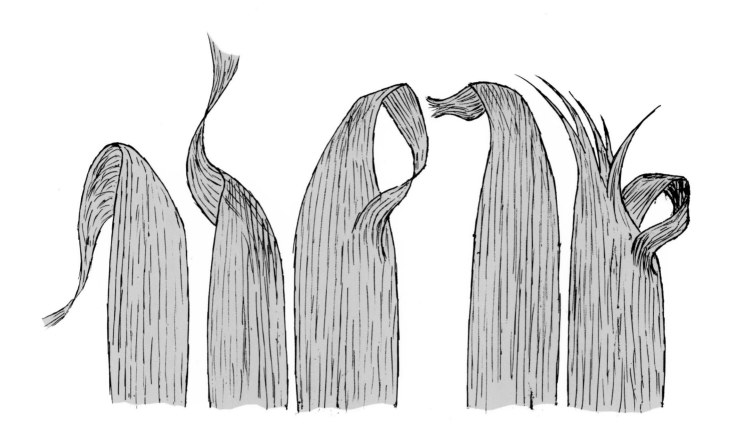

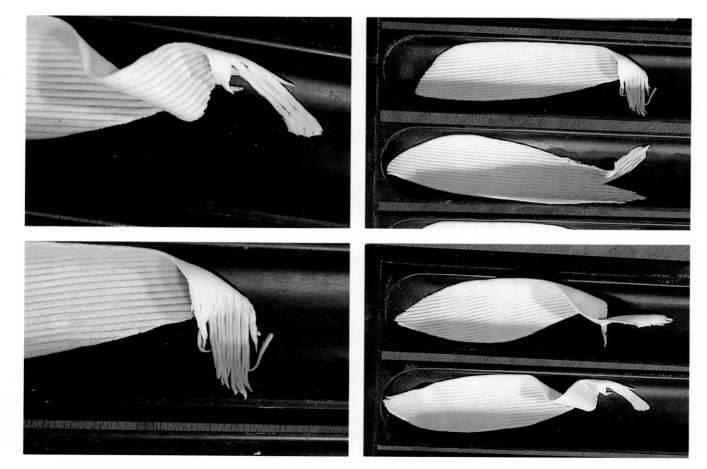

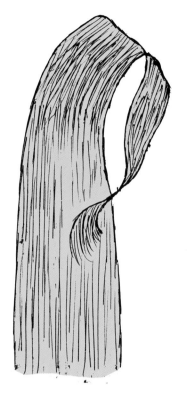

Baking

Bake the leaves in a 170°C (350°F) oven for about 10 minutes. No steam should be used. The leaves should not be allowed to brown but should be cream colored when removed from the oven. Keep a close watch on the leaves while they are in the oven—slight variations in thickness will cause them to brown differently.

Remove the leaves from the oven and allow them to cool. Gently transfer the leaves to a cardboard box. They should be stored in a dry place.

Note

During the initial drying of the leaves on the baking sheets, they sometimes take on a different shapes. This is caused by the irregular drying of the parts of the leaf that are exposed to air and those that are resting against the baking sheet. Avoid touching the leaves at this point, as they are very fragile. When they are baked, they will reassume their original shape.

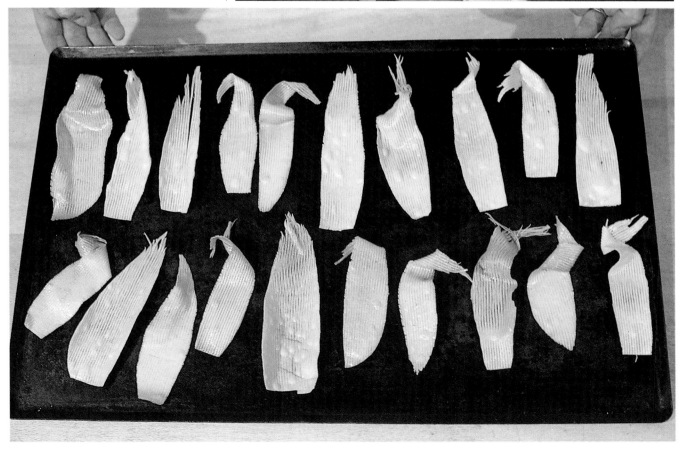

Ears of wheat

Single Ears

Equipment

Paring or chef's knife
Plastic wrap
Scissors
Rolling pin

Procedure

Roll 200 grams (7 ounces) of decorating dough into a long, even rope. The rope should be about the same thickness as your little finger. Cut the rope into sections 6 to 7 centimeters (3 to 4 inches) long. Gently roll each section to form a long strand with a thicker conical shape at one end. Cover them with plastic wrap to prevent a crust from forming on their surfaces.

Take one strand at a time and arrange it so the thick top is facing you. Sprinkle

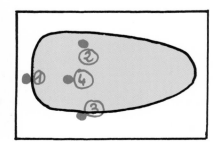

the surface of the marble with a few drops of water so that the dough stays in place.

Make staggered rows of small cuts in the thick end of the dough with scissors as follows:

1. Holding the scissors at a 45-degree angle to the dough, cut into the base end at the center, where the stem joins, forming a triangular piece, which is one grain of wheat.
2. Next cut into the left side of the ear.

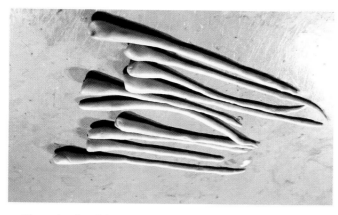
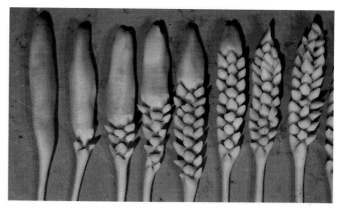

Keep the tip of the scissors against the marble, pointing toward the stem, to help make even cuts into the dough.

3. Cut into the right side of the ear, but reverse the angle of the scissors so that it again points toward the stem.
4. Cut in the center of the ear, above where the first cut was made. Continue to hold the scissors at a 45-degree angle.

Note

As the dough narrows near the tip of the ear, it will not be possible to continue in staggered rows. It is best to finish with two or three simple incisions at the tip.

Place the ears on baking sheets. Refrigerate them, 5°C (40°F), overnight. Do not cover them—it is important that they dry before baking.

Baking

Bake the ears in a 180°C (350°F) oven for approximately 20 minutes. If the oven is equipped with vents, they should be left open. The ears can be coated with egg wash before baking, but this is optional. When the ears have been removed from the oven, let them cool. Store them in cardboard boxes in a dry place.

219

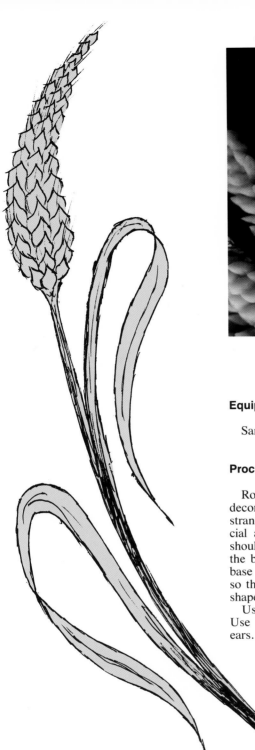

Entire Stalks of Wheat

Equipment

Same as for single ears.

Procedure

Roll 40 to 50 grams (1.5 to 2 ounces) of decorating dough into a long, even strand. When rolling the dough, pay special attention to the long stem, which should be thin and even until it runs into the base of the ear of kernels. Roll the base of the ear with the side of the hand so that the ear of kernels has a distinct shape.

Use scissors to make cuts in the ears. Use the same technique as for single ears.

Place the stalks on baking sheets. Store them overnight, uncovered, in the refrigerator.

Bake the stalks as described for single ears. The finished stalks should be stored in cardboard boxes in a dry place.

Sheaves of Wheat

Wheat sheaves are simple to prepare. Once single stalks have been made, they can be easily assembled into decorative sheaves.

Place raw, single stalks of wheat on baking sheets as they are prepared. Bunch the single stalks of wheat together on the baking sheet, and bend the bottoms of the stems in different directions while keeping the center of the sheaf together.

Keep layering the individual strands until the wheat sheaf has a spontaneous, natural look.

Press the individual stems together just below the base of the wheat ears. A thin ribbon of dough can then be wrapped around the stems at this point to form a decorative bow. The stems protruding from beneath the bow should flare out from side to side to give a decorative effect.

Cut the base of each stem with a paring knife. Be sure to cut at an angle for a more natural appearance.

Do not use egg wash to hold the stems together. A better effect is obtained by moistening the stems at the points where they touch with a fingertip dipped in cold water.

Baking

Bake at 170°C (350°F) for approximately 30 minutes. Do not use steam in the oven during baking.

The baked wheat sheaves are best displayed in pastry shop windows attached to a mirror or a piece of wood with flour paste.

221

Leaves

Equipment

Baking sheet
Paring knife
Rolling pin

Wheat Leaves

Procedure

Roll a 100-gram (3.5-ounce) piece of decorating dough into a very thin sheet. The sheet of dough should be approximately 1 millimeter (1/16 inch) thick. Avoid flouring the work surface unless the dough sticks.

Cut the sheet of decorating dough into thin, elongated leaves with a paring knife. Save the trimmings from the leaves. Cover the leaves with plastic wrap.

Work with one leaf at a time. Cover each leaf again with a small sheet of plastic and press around its edges with the thumb so that the dough is as thin as possible all around the perimeter.

Make a vein in the center of each leaf through the plastic wrap with a paring knife. Then make the remaining veins.

Carefully remove the plastic wrap from the surface of the leaf. Gently lift one edge of the leaf off the work surface with the end of the paring knife. Pick it up between two fingers and transfer it to an egg carton, to give it a natural-looking wavy shape.

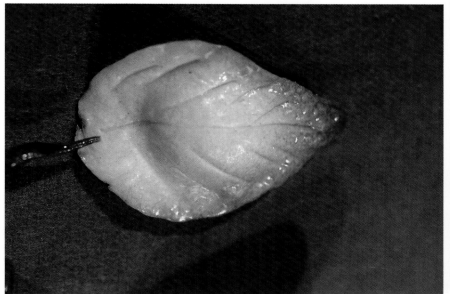

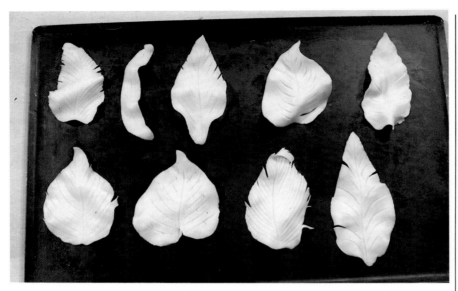

Baking

Bake for several minutes in a 180°C (350°F) oven without steam. Do not let the leaves brown excessively: they should be pale beige.

Note

Because the leaves are so thin, they must be checked constantly during baking to prevent them from getting too brown.

Remove the leaves from the oven and let them cool. Carefully remove any small pieces of aluminum foil used to help them keep their shape.

The leaves are best stored on baking sheets in a dry place.

Shaping the Leaves

Decorative leaves can be shaped in several ways:
1. They can be left flat.
2. They can be folded slightly, with a mound in the middle.
3. They can be made very narrow and elongated.
4. They can be curved or folded slightly over themselves.
5. Small cuts can be made along the sides for a more natural effect.

Note

To help hold the leaves in the desired shapes, it is sometimes necessary to prop them up with small pieces of aluminum foil. Place them in the refrigerator overnight without covering them. This will dry them out and help them to keep their shape during baking.

Attaching Decorative Leaves to Large Loaves

Before Baking

Advantages

- saves time
- leaves adhere better to loaves
- leaves hold better after baking
- no need to use flour paste

Disadvantages

- less attractive
- leaves sometimes change shape during baking
- leaves may brown excessively
- loaves may sag after baking

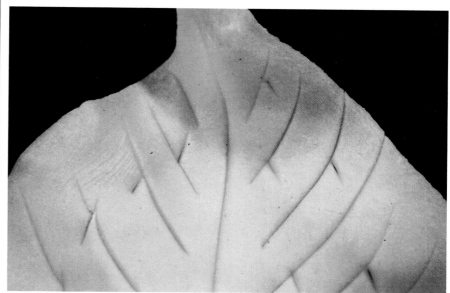

After Baking

Advantages

- very attractive
- leaves hold their shape
- color can be more closely controlled
- loaves are less likely to sag after baking

Disadvantages

- prebaked leaves are very fragile and sometimes hard to work with—they break easily
- flour paste is needed to attach the leaves to the loaves

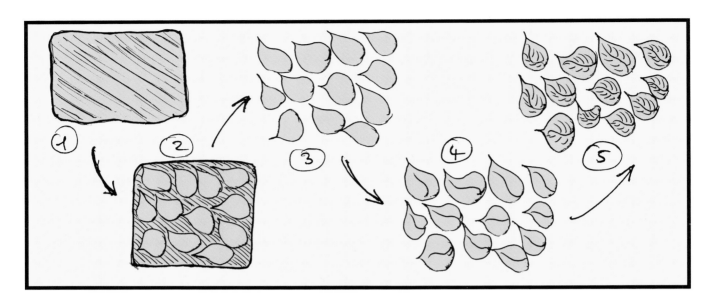

Rose Leaves

The method used for preparing rose leaves is essentially the same as that used for wheat leaves.

Once the leaves have been shaped and the veins have been drawn with a paring knife, the edges of the leaves should be thinned by gently pressing with the thumb. The leaves should then be allowed to dry in cardboard egg cartons that fit their shape perfectly.

The minimum drying time is 24 hours.

Bake in a 250°C (475°F) oven for several minutes. The leaves should be baked while they are still in the egg cartons. Simply place the egg cartons directly on the baking sheets. Use only cardboard egg cartons for this—Styrofoam will melt in the oven. Keep checking the leaves to prevent them from getting too brown or from burning.

Ribbons and bows

Ribbons are rarely made, even in France, where elaborately decorated breads are far more common than in the United States. They are fairly easy to make and provide a decorative touch to artistic pieces or elaborate breads. Ribbons can be used as the only decoration on a particular loaf or can be used to complement other more complicated decorations.

Ingredients

Several types of decorating dough can be used to make ribbons:

- decorating dough made with either wheat or rye flour plus butter or shortening
- decorating dough made with either wheat or rye flour with no butter or shortening

Ingredients should also include:

- egg wash
- caramel
- coffee extract
- flour paste
- edible varnish made especially for this purpose (optional)

If the decorative ribbons are being used in loaves that are to be eaten, they are best prepared with decorating dough

that contains butter or shortening. This dough is softer and more tender.

For presentation pieces, it is better to use dough that contains no butter or shortening. Such dough is easier to work with and lends itself to delicate workmanship. It also has the advantage of a longer shelf life and can be worked more quickly because it tends to dry and hold its shape once formed.

Preparation

Dough that contains butter or shortening should be prepared at least 24 hours before it is needed. Dough without butter or shortening, on the other hand, can be prepared up to an hour before it is needed.

Equipment

Baking sheet
Rolling pin
Paring knife
Chef's knife
Pastry brush (for egg wash)
Thin, wooden rolling pin (a section of broom handle works well)

Procedure

Roll the dough into a thin, even layer with a standard rolling pin. The layer should be about 2 millimeters (1/16 inch) thick. Use as little flour as possible to prevent the dough from sticking to the work surface.

Cut the dough into strips with a chef's knife. Make sure to cut carefully so the ribbons are of even width. Cut the strips about 5 centimeters (2 inches) longer than needed to form the bows.

The edges of the ribbons should be beveled for added decorative effect. Separate the ribbons and cover them with a sheet of plastic wrap. Gently press along both edges of the ribbons with either the thumbs or the rolling pin.

Trim the edges of the ribbons with a chef's knife if they are not perfectly even. Cut the corners off both ends of the ribbons.

Place the ribbons on a baking sheet. Be sure to leave about 2.5 centimeters (1 inch) between each of the ribbons. This helps them bake more evenly and makes them easier to handle once they come out of the oven.

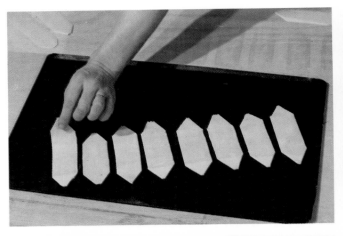

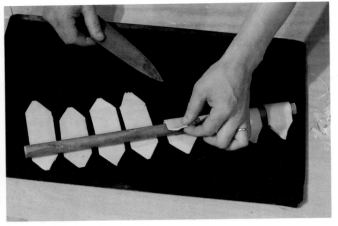

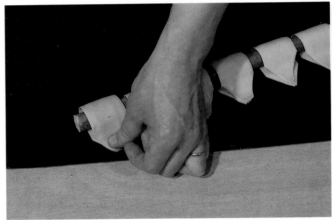

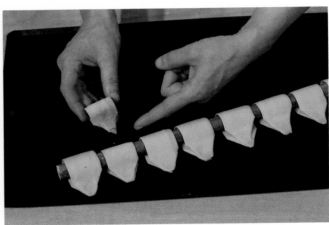

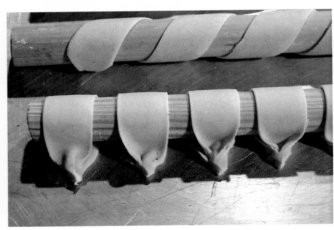

Place a thin rolling pin (or broom handle) across the ribbons. The diameter of the finished loops will correspond to the thickness of the rolling pin.

Lightly moisten the ends of the ribbons. Fold the ribbons over the rolling pin and attach the two moistened ends by pressing them gently against one another and against the side of the rolling pin. Do not press the loops too firmly against the rolling pin, or they might stick to it. Pinch the ends of the ribbons together so they are not too wide when it comes time to assemble them into bows.

Note

Decorative ribbons can be given a variety of shapes by wrapping them around a rolling pin or by placing them in an upside-down mold for tuiles.

Drying the Ribbons

Allow the ribbons to dry for 12 to 24 hours if the dough contains butter or shortening, and from 1 to 2 hours if it contains no fat. The individual ribbons should be assembled in a cool, dry place. If the temperature of the work area is greater than 20°C (68°F), they should be assembled in the refrigerator.

Baking

Decorative ribbons and bows are baked in the same way as rose leaves (page 224) if dough containing butter or shortening is used. If the dough contains no butter or shortening, a slightly lower oven, 200°C (400°F), should be used. In either case, steam should not be introduced into the oven during baking.

The ribbons should be brushed with caramel coloring and egg wash immediately after they come out of the oven while they are still hot. They should be placed back in the oven for a few seconds to set the coloring and glaze.

Assembling the Bows

The individual loops are assembled into bows using flour paste.

Assemble the base of the bow first by attaching the pinched ends of the loops together in the center.

Do not try to make the bows perfectly symmetrical. It is a good idea, however, to arrange the loops in the most appealing shape before attaching them with the flour paste.

Once the loops have been assembled into bows with flour paste, they should be baked in a low oven to dry the flour paste.

The bows can be further reinforced by adding more flour paste under the base in the center after baking.

Note

Because bows usually have a large, flat bottom surface, they are easy to attach to loaves of bread. Decorative bows can be brushed with edible varnish to give them added sheen.

Storing Ribbons and Bows

Finished ribbons and bows should be stored in tightly sealed containers away from moisture and dust. If the ribbons or bows are meant to be eaten, they should be stored for no more than a week. Bows used only for presentation, however, can be stored for several months.

Scrolls

Equipment

Rolling pin
Paring knife
Mixing bowl
Heavy baking sheet
Plastic wrap

Procedure

Rolling Out the Scrolls

Roll a 100-gram (3.5-ounce) piece of decorating dough into a thin, even sheet, 1 millimeter (1/16 inch) thick. If possible, avoid flouring the work surface while rolling.

Cut irregular shapes for the scrolls out of the sheet of dough with a paring knife. Keep in mind the shape and size of the loaves to be decorated so the scrolls will look even once on the surface of the bread.

Pull the trimmings away from the dough cutouts.

Cover the cutouts with plastic wrap so they do not dry out while others are being completed.

Take one cutout at a time, place it in front of you, and cover it again with plastic wrap. Press along the edges of the cutout over the plastic wrap with the tip of the thumb. Work from center outward.

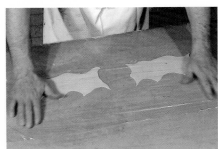

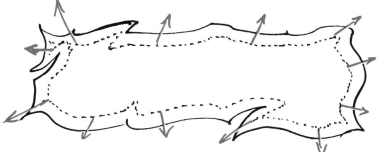

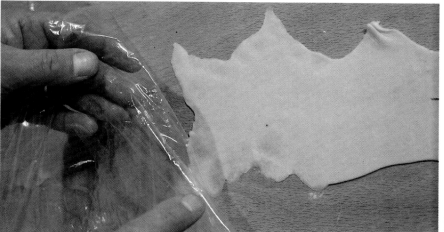

strands, or the writing may become illegible. The only time overlapping should be used is when loops are made, as shown circled in red in the diagram below.

Preparing the Letters and Writing on the Scroll

Use from 30 to 50 grams (1 to 2 ounces) of decorating dough for each strand. The dough can be colored with coffee extract if desired.

Moisten a section of the work surface with cold water. This will make it easier to work with the strands of dough used to form the letters. In no case should flour be used.

Writing on the Scrolls

As an example, to write the name Valerie, ten strands of dough are needed, as

the drawings show. Plan the number of strands needed for any inscription in a similar manner.

Regardless of the inscription to be made, it is best not to overlap the

Roll the dough into a thin strand on the moistened section of the work surface. The strand should be from 2 to 3 millimeters (about 1/8 inch) thick.

Cut the strand into lengths for the individual letters. Be careful to anticipate the lengths of the different sections; for example, capital letters will require longer lengths than small letters.

Dip the strands in cold water, one at a time, before placing them on the scrolls.

To apply each strand, hold it directly above the scroll so that it hangs vertically. Slowly lower the strand onto the scroll, guiding it to form the letters.

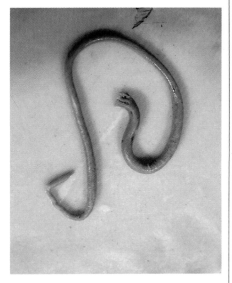

Tips on Making Letters

The appearance of the lettering is improved if the tips of those strands used for the ends of the letters are rolled so that they come to a point.

Make sure that the strands are moist before applying them to the scroll. The moisture is essential to ensure that the lettering adheres to the scroll.

If the lettering appears uneven, the strands can be adjusted by gently lifting them with the tip of a paring knife.

Coffee extract can be used to color the dough used for the strands, but remember that the contrast between the colored letters and the finished scrolls will be diminished after baking because the scroll itself will be browned.

Once the lettering has been applied to the surface of the scroll, carefully lift up one corner of the scroll with the tip of a paring knife, grip it between the thumb and the forefinger and transfer it to:

- an egg carton for a scroll with an undulated surface
- a baking sheet for a flat scroll
- a baking sheet for baguettes for a concave scroll

If the scrolls are being dried on baking sheets, it is advisable to wedge pieces of aluminum foil under different sections of the scroll to give it a more natural, undulating effect.

Drying the Scrolls

The scrolls should be dried on cooling racks or in the refrigerator for 24 hours. They should not be covered during drying.

Baking

Bake the scrolls in a 240°C (500°F) oven with the vents (if available) open. Do not use steam in the oven. The scrolls should not be glazed.

Watch the scrolls constantly during baking. Only the edges of the scrolls should be allowed to brown. Allow 4 to 5 minutes for baking.

Remove the scrolls from the oven when the edges are dark brown, almost black. The center of the scroll should be pale beige. The difference in coloring between the center and edges of the scroll is caused by the difference in thickness.

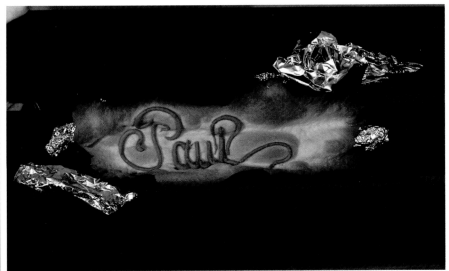

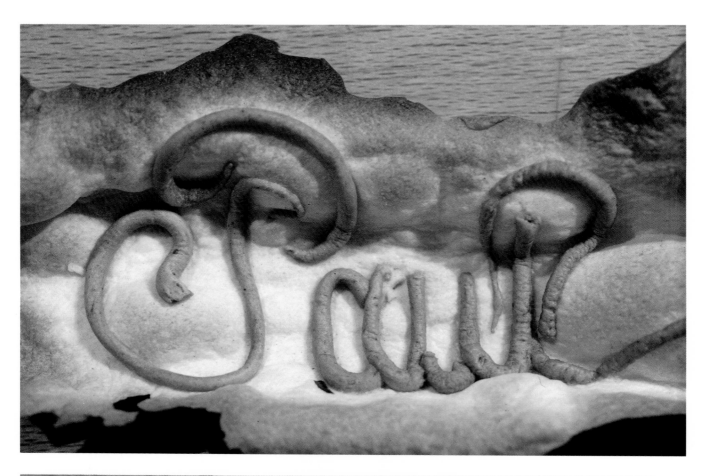

After Baking

Carefully transfer the baked scrolls to cooling racks. Paint the lettering with coffee extract, using a small pastry brush. This helps the lettering to stand out more clearly against the background of the scroll.

Uses

Attach the finished scrolls to baked loaves of bread with flour paste. Bread decorated in this way can be served on special occasions such as weddings, birthdays, and anniversaries.

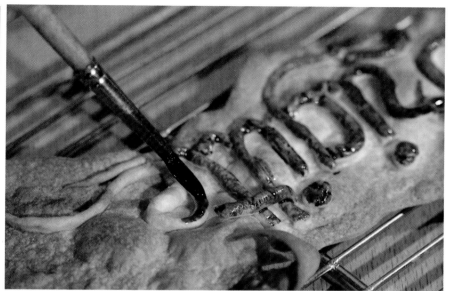

Examples of Lettering

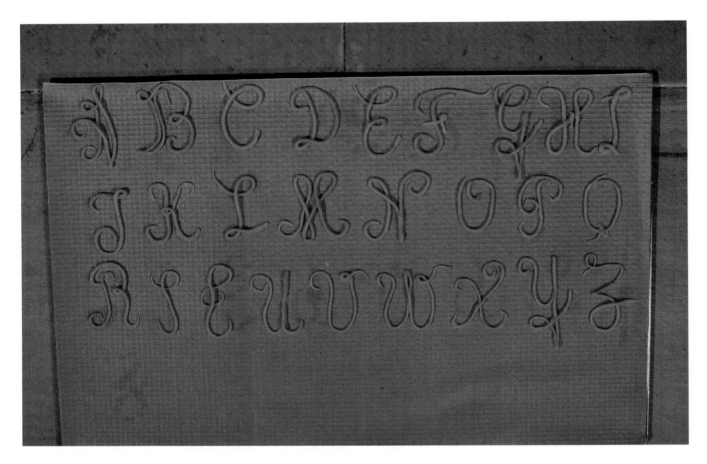

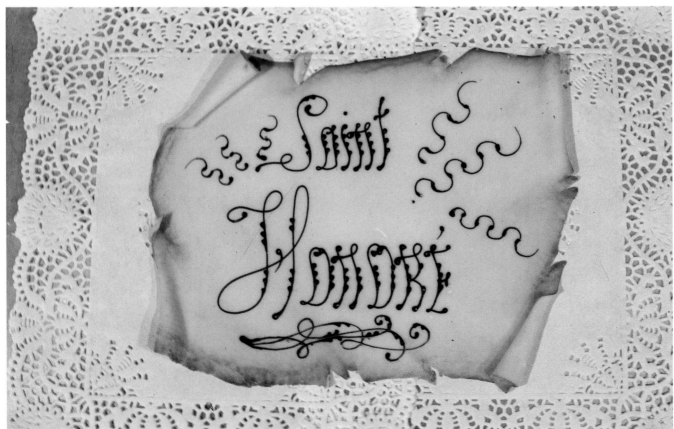

Assorted decorations

Easy-to-make Decorations

A large variety of motifs and decorations can be made with decorating dough and applied to decorate loaves of bread. Although the tradition of specially decorated breads is far more prevalent in France than it is in the United States, certain classic designs such as grape clusters, roses, and sheaves of wheat will always be appealing if presented in the proper setting. This type of elaborate decoration has enabled bakers to perfect their skills and develop pride in their profession.

Presented on the following pages are four classic examples of decorations made from decorating dough: rose-shaped candle holders, rose flowers and branches, vines, and sheaves of wheat.

In France decorative candle holders are traditionally used for baptisms, first communions, and weddings. They can also hold the candles for a romantic dinner.

Rose flowers and branches, vines, and sheaves of wheat made of decorating dough make attractive decorations for a bakery window. An appealing and constantly changing display is important for a popular baker who has regular customers. This is especially true in France, where regular customers go to the bakery every day to pick up their bread.

Wooden Plaques for Hanging Decorative Pieces

Equipment

Wooden Plaque

Plywood 1 centimeter (½ inch) thick; a yardstick, a pencil, a small handsaw or jigsaw, and medium-grit sandpaper are needed to make the wooden base.

Cloth Covering

Felt or satin, a staple gun and staples or small upholstery tacks and a small hammer or upholstery glue, scissors, and a screwdriver are needed to cover the wooden base.

Assembling the Plaque

Preparing the Plywood

Cut the piece of plywood to the desired size. If the support is small enough, plywood trimmings can sometimes be used. Sand the edges of the plywood smooth with sandpaper.

Preparing the Cloth Covering

Cut the cloth so that it can fit over the plywood plaque, allowing an extra 5 centimeters (2 inches) of cloth on all four sides, to wrap around the wooden base. Wrap the cloth tightly over the surface of the plywood and attach it to the back with staples, upholstery tacks, or glue. Make sure the cloth is taut over the surface of the base. Insert screws in the back side of the plaque for hanging. The bread is mounted on the cloth-covered plaque.

237

Candle holders

Simple Candle Holders

Candle holders can be prepared using a straightforward method that is especially easy once the technique of preparing roses has been mastered. The only difference is that the roses are constructed around a wooden dowel, such as a section of broom handle, that has been cut into 8-centimeter (3-inch) lengths.

When constructing the roses, be especially careful to moisten the base of each petal to ensure the petals hold together.

Elaborate Candle Holders

These candle holders include both roses and rose branches; they are miniature versions of the decorative roses discussed on pages 241 to 243.

First Stage

Roll from 200 to 400 grams (7 to 14 ounces) of decorating dough into a cylinder. Roll the cylinder so that it tapers slightly at one end. It is not essential that the dough be worked into a perfectly even shape. In fact, small irregularities help give it a realistic look.

Cut the dough in half lengthwise from the center toward the tapered end. Cut each of these sections down the middle from the tapered ends halfway to where the first cut began so four branches are formed. (See photos on pages 241 to 243.)

Roll each of the four branches with the palms of the hands to round off the edges. Do not try to make the branches look too perfect, or their natural appearance will be lost.

Second Stage

Cut the ends of each of the four branches in two. Roll each of these stems slightly to give them a natural, rounded appearance. Make sure that the ends taper to a point. Shape the thick end of the dough by bending it over a cardboard cylinder taken from a roll of paper towels.

Place the branches and stems on a cardboard egg carton. Cross the branches and stems over one another on the egg carton. If necessary, different sections can be supported with pieces of aluminum foil.

Make small cuts into the thickest parts of the base with the tip of a scissors, similar to making grains of wheat on a wheat ear. Keep the scissors at a 45-degree angle while making the cuts. Gently roll the protruding cut pieces of dough so they have a natural look, resembling thorns. Arrange the rose branches in the egg cartons so all the branches are well supported during the drying stage.

If the rose branches have unnatural looking edges or protrusions, smooth them off with the tip of a finger dipped in cold water.

Let the rose branch candle bases dry for 24 to 48 hours before baking.

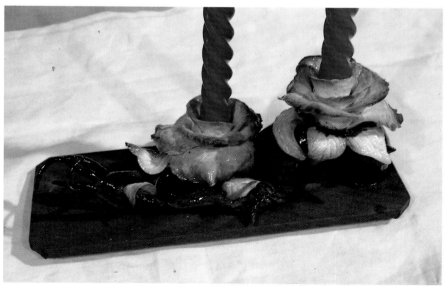

Working with Decorating Dough

First Day		Second Day (rest) ·	Third Day
First Stage	*Second Stage*		*Third Stage*
Same for all 3 objects	*Different, depending on the object*	*Refrigerate (5°C/42°F), without covering to dry designs*	*Same for all 3 objects*
Shape cylinders of decorating dough	**1. Candle holders**		**Do not use egg wash** **Bake at 170°C (350°F) with vents open for 45 minutes to 1 hour**
	2. Rose branches		*After baking*
Separate branches with a paring knife	**3. Grapevines**		**Predry in the oven for 2 to 3 minutes** **Stain while hot with coffee extract**
Fourth Day: Brush with lacquer			**Dry for 24 hours on cooling racks**

Rose branches

First Stage

Follow the procedure used in the first stage of preparing the miniature rose branches for candle holders.

Second Stage

This stage is also the same as when preparing candle holders, except more dough is used. When preparing larger branches it is possible to cut one or two more small branches.

Place the shaped rose branches on baking sheets. Extra support should be given to the branches by placing small pieces of aluminum foil under different sections of the branches to help them keep their shape.

Make incisions in alternating rows along the base of the branches to give the appearance of thorns.

Arrange the branches and stems in their final shape. Let the branches dry for 24 to 48 hours in the open air before baking.

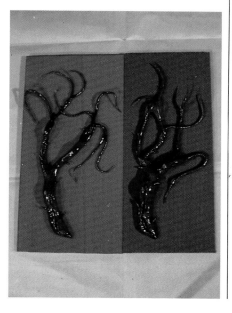

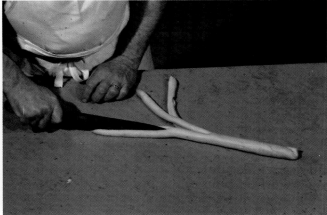

Final Assembly and Application of Bread Decorations

Construction

Assembling the Pieces

Presentation pieces should be worked out before the different sections of a decoration are glued together or mounted on a loaf of bread.

Arranging the Decorations

Experiment with different arrangements of leaves and flowers in different positions on the loaves to get a sense of the most attractive arrangement.

Attaching the Decorations

Make sure that you have decided on the exact arrangement of the components before attaching them with flour paste. The flour paste should be colored with coffee extract so it will match the baked loaves.

Note

Use as little flour paste as possible and try to apply it so that it will be hidden from view.

The Aesthetics of Decoration

Arrange each element of the decoration so the finished loaf has a light, uncluttered look. Always resist the temptation of adding too much decoration to a loaf of bread. Otherwise, it will have a heavy, unpleasant appearance.

Carefully balance the various decorating elements on top of the loaf of bread before attaching them with the flour paste.

When Are the Decorations Attached?

Before Baking

Decorations are seldom attached before baking because they weigh down the loaves while they are baking, preventing the loaves from rising completely and making them heavy.

Certain lighter decorations, such as G clefs and musical notes written on a loaf's surface, do not interfere with the final baking. These decorations should be attached to the loaves with water.

During Baking

This commonly used method involves placing the decoration on top of the loaf 10 minutes before baking is finished. The decoration can be attached to the top of the loaf with flour paste or plain water. This method works well for a wide variety of decorations, such as bunches of grapes,

grape leaves, roses, rose leaves, and sheaves of wheat.

This method does, however, have certain disadvantages:

- If the crust on the loaf's surface is insufficiently baked and so too thin, it may sag under the weight of the decoration.
- Interrupting the baking to place the decoration on top of the bread will cause it to cool before it has finished baking and may leave it heavy and too moist.
- The decoration itself may droop slightly if it is not baked in advance with the proper supports, such as wedges of aluminum foil and cardboard egg cartons.

After Baking

This is by far the preferred method. It has several advantages

over the other methods:

- The bread is completely baked before being decorated so there is no danger that it will sag or become heavy because of the weight of the decoration.
- The decorations can be assembled several days before the bread is baked, so the workload is easier to organize.
- The bread can be allowed to cool before the decoration is attached, and excess moisture will thus not accumulate under the decoration.
- The flour paste used to attach the decoration to the loaves can be colored more accurately with coffee extract, matching exactly the tint of the baked loaves.
- The decoration can be more three-dimensional because it is baked in advance on egg carton or aluminum foil supports.

Rose Branches

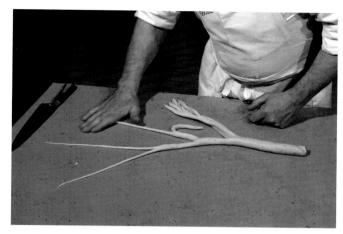
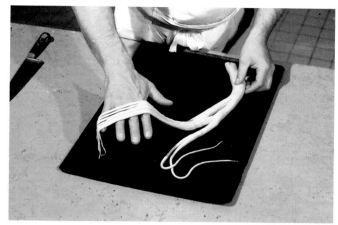

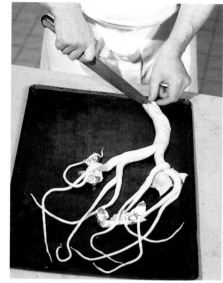
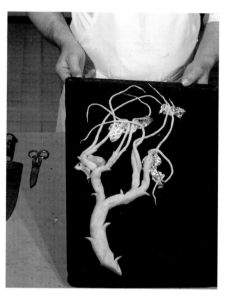

Grapevines

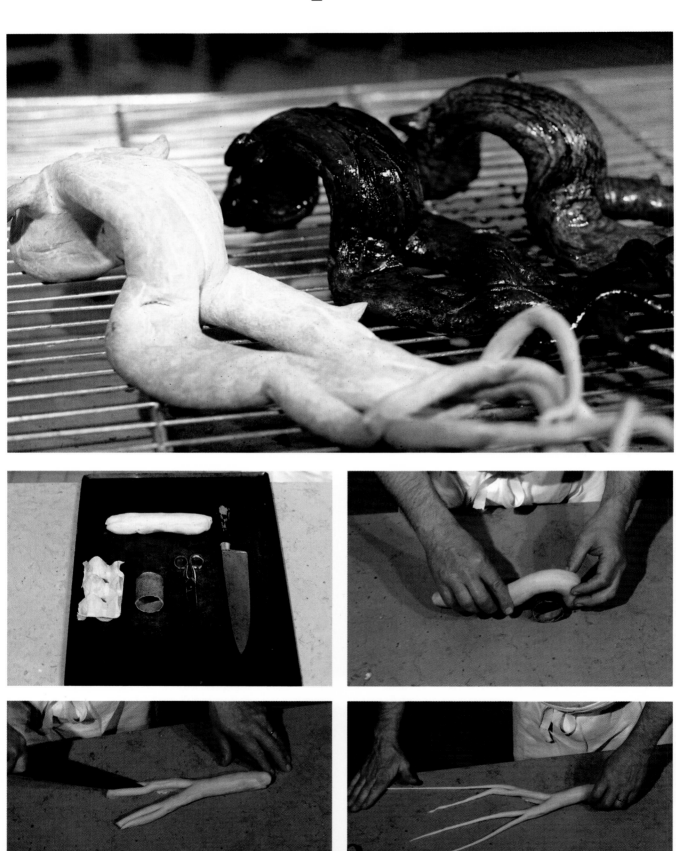

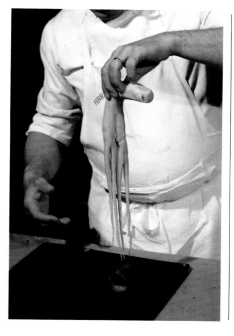

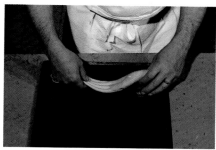

The shaping of grapevines requires considerable manual dexterity and familiarity with bread dough. Once the vines have been formed, they should be arranged and given their final shape on cardboard egg cartons. Remember that the grapevines are three-dimensional, so do not hesitate to bend them to a full, natural shape. Be sure to let them dry for 24 to 48 hours before baking.

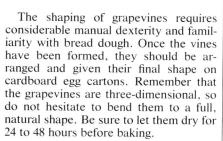

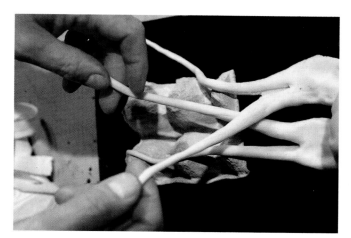

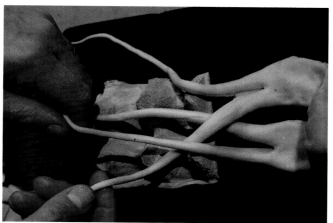

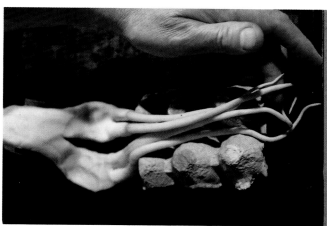

Procedure

Equipment

Baking sheet
Chef's knife
Scissors
Cardboard cylinder from a roll of paper
  towels
Small section of cardboard egg carton

Day One

Prepare a 300-gram (10.5-ounce) section of decorating dough.

Cut a section of cardboard cylinder about 5 centimeters (2 inches) long. Hang the thick base of the vine over the cardboard cylinder just under the point where the branches will separate.

Cut one end of the dough in two lengthwise, forming two branches. Cut each of these branches again in two so that four branches are formed. Gently roll each of the branches between the palms of the hands so that they thin to a point at the ends.

Arrange the grapevine so that the base is bent over the cardboard cylinder while the branches are supported by the section of egg carton.

Make several cuts into the base of the vine with the scissors. The small segments of dough now protruding can be shaped into tendrils or thorns. If a tendril is formed, attach it to the side of the vine by moistening it with water.

Set the grapevine in a dry area of the kitchen, protected from moisture and dust. The vine can also be dried in the refrigerator. The various branches can be supported during the drying with pieces of crumpled aluminum foil. Allow 24 to 48 hours for the vine to dry before baking.

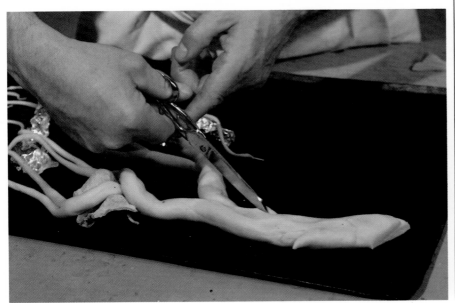

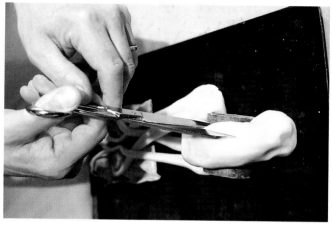

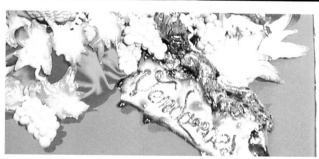

Day Two

Bake the grapevine in a 180°C (350°F) oven. Do not brush it with egg wash.

The photo on page 248 shows four stages of coloring the vine: before baking, baked without coloring, stained with coffee extract, lightened with gelatin-based sealer.

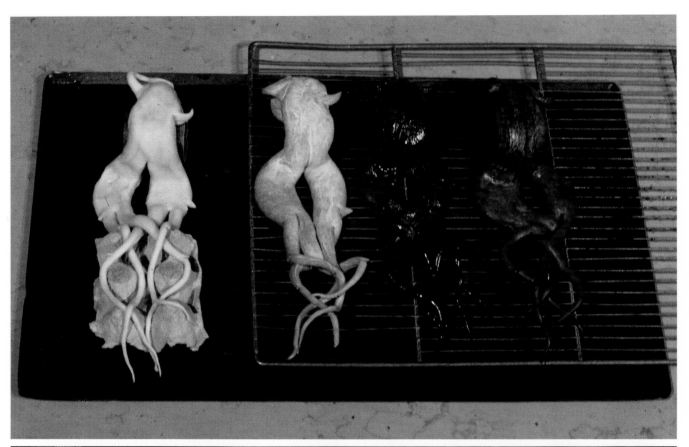

Sheaves of wheat

Sheaves of wheat can be used not only to decorate loaves of bread but can also be mounted on plaques and used as decorative murals.

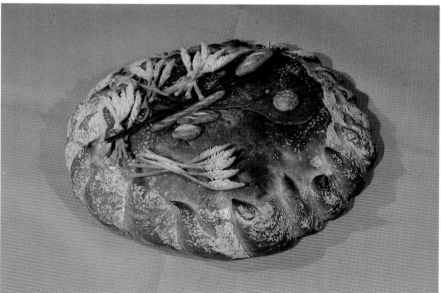

Sheaves of Wheat

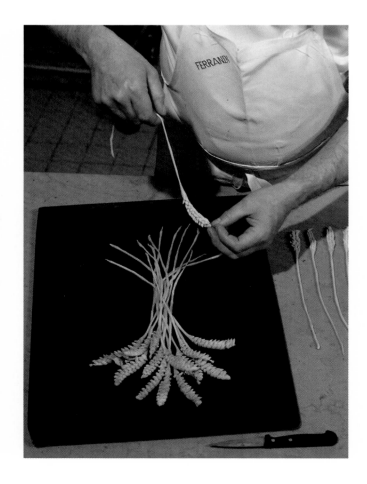

Chapter 5
Presentation pieces

The History of Presentation Pieces

Prior to the twentieth century, French food was arranged and presented in a more elaborate style than it is today. Decorative pieces, called "pièces montées," were prepared and placed on the dining tables during the lavish dinners of the times. Today chefs and diners prefer food presented in simpler ways, and many of these elaborate arrangements have fallen into disuse. Elaborate presentations are still popularly used in food shows, competitions, and bakery window displays in France and are increasingly common in the United States. This is especially true in the realm of baking bread and pastry, where the ingredients keep well.

Guidelines for Constructing Presentation Pieces

Because they will never be eaten, presentation pieces are often prepared exclusively with decorating dough. They are usually composed of a collection of smaller decorative pieces that are carefully assembled to give an impression of abundance. The visual impact of presentation pieces depends on how closely each of the components resembles the object being represented.

Presentation pieces are usually assembled on some kind of support, usually made of wood that has been covered with cloth. They may also be enclosed in a glass case to protect them from dust. Although presentation pieces may attract customers to a bakery, they are never profitable in themselves. Be sure to keep the following points in mind:

- Be patient and do not hurry the process.
- Think about each of the components before beginning.
- If money is an issue, budget a given amount beforehand.
- Improvise and be inventive.

Constructing presentation pieces

Because presentation pieces are time consuming to prepare, carefully plan the design and the basic dimensions of the piece before actually beginning the piece. It is a good idea to divide the work into three distinct stages:

1. Constructing the pedestal or base
2. Preparing the various components, which should all convey one distinct theme
3. Constructing the glass showcase

The Pedestal

Find a suitable place to work where woodworking will not interfere with the baking routine. Be especially careful to avoid getting sawdust near any bread or dough. It is probably best to work at the end of the work shift to avoid this.

Saw the wood to the desired dimensions. Prepare any brackets or supports for the pedestal before screwing or nailing it together.

Covering the Wooden Pedestal with Cloth

Select a clean work space for this task so that no dust ends up on the cloth.

The cloth should be cut large enough to be wrapped behind the wooden frame and attached at the back with heavy staples or small nails (brads). Make sure that the cloth is taut over the pedestal's surface so that there are no wrinkles or irregularities. The wooden pedestal should not be visible anywhere when the presentation piece is completed.

To give the presentation piece a three-dimensional effect, small pieces of wood can be placed on the cloth-covered pedestal. These are then covered with cloth, giving the pedestal a natural, undulating appearance (see the photo above). These irregularities in the pedestal's surface will also make it easier to arrange the breads.

Arranging the Decorative Breads

Each of the decorative pieces should be constructed with decorating dough and carefully varnished to give them sheen and help them to keep.

Arrange and rearrange the various elements of the piece until you come up with a suitable design. At this point, it is a good idea to photograph the arrangement with an instant camera to get a sense of how to glue the pieces together. Carefully disassemble the arrangement, and begin attaching the pieces with flour paste.

The Glass Showcase

If the presentation piece is to be entered in a competition, it must be enclosed in a glass case. This keeps people from touching it and also protects it from dust. Constructing a showcase can be a difficult operation, especially when the presentation piece is large and you are working with large panes of glass.

Carefully clean the glass panes. Have handy a large roll of Scotch tape.

Align the first pane of glass with the base of the pedestal. Have someone hold the first pane of glass in place while placing the second pane next to it at a 90-degree angle. Attach the corners of the glass panes with the Scotch tape. Continue in this way until all four panes have been assembled, with the corners attached with Scotch tape. Make sure that someone holds the case during the first stages of the taping.

The trickiest part of the assembly is attaching the top pane. Do not try to do this alone. Carefully place it on the top of the showcase, even with edges of the other four panes. Finish attaching the top with Scotch tape.

Reinforce the showcase with at least three more strips of Scotch tape along each of the corners.

Avoiding Problems

Keep a clear image of the finished presentation piece in your mind at all times while working. Use drawings, measurements, and even photographs if you find them useful. Beginners often find that the finished presentation piece has a completely different size and appearance than originally expected. Try to avoid this as much as possible.

Construction Procedure

Dimensions

Try to plan the dimensions of the pedestal as accurately as possible. It is better to prepare too large a pedestal and showcase than one that is too small. The materials below are for a pedestal that is 70 by 70 centimeters (27.5 by 27.5 inches).

Materials

1 piece of plywood 70 by 70 by 2 centimeters (27.5 by 27.5 by 1 inch) for the base
2 strips of wood 50 by 3 by 5 centimeters (19.5 by 1.5 by 2 inches) for the feet
quarter-round wooden molding for the molding around the base
2 pieces of cloth, 1 that is 90 by 90 centimeters (35 by 35 inches), to cover the wooden support and 1 that is 90 by 150 centimeters (35 by 60 inches), to cover it again; select rich-colored cloths such as maroon or forest green
1 strip of decorative cloth, to the dimensions of the base, to be attached around the sides of the cloth-covered base
1 tube upholstery glue
upholstery tacks or staples and staple gun to attach the cloth to the wooden frame
5 panes of glass, 3 millimeters (¼ inch) thick—be sure to consider the thickness of the glass when calculating the dimensions of the piece. The dimensions of the panes should be as follows:
  2 should be 68 by 100 centimeters (27 by 39.5 inches)
  2 should be 67.5 by 100 centimeters (26.5 by 39.5 inches)
  1 should be 68 by 68 centimeters (27 by 27 inches) for the lid
1 roll of Scotch tape for attaching the panes
Small saw, hacksaw, scissors, yardstick, pencil, hammer, sandpaper

Glass Showcase

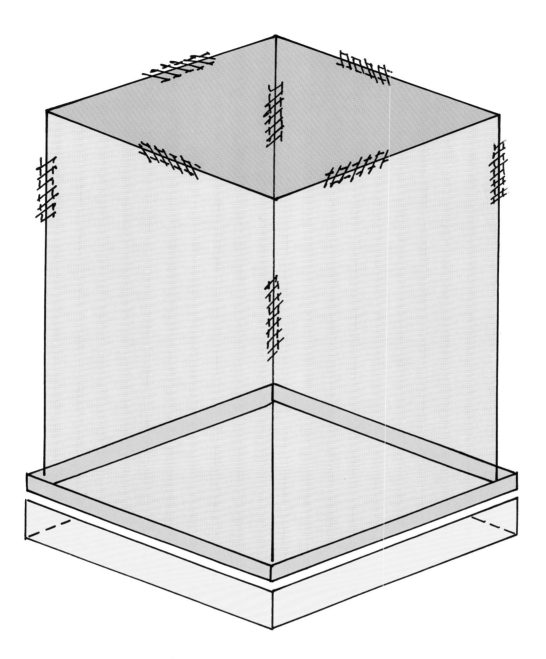

Summary of Dimensions

Pedestal: 70 by 70 centimeters (27.5 by 27.5 inches)

Feet: 50 by 3 by 5 centimeters (19.5 by 1.5 by 2 inches)

Molding: 1-centimeter-diameter (½-inch) quarter-round wooden molding

Panes: 2 should be 68 by 100 centimeters (27 by 39.5 inches)
2 should be 67.5 by 100 centimeters (26.5 by 39.5 inches)
1 should be 68 by 68 centimeters (27 by 27 inches), for the lid

Attach the panes by applying strips of Scotch tape to the corners.

Judging presentation pieces

Grading Criteria for Competition Presentation Pieces

In France bakers and other artisans often enter into contests and other shows where their entries are judged. Six typical criteria for judging competition entries are:

1. *Consistency of theme and dimensions*
2. *Elegance and lightness*
3. *Use of color*
4. *Balance*
5. *Detail and quality of individual components*
6. *Overall quality of workmanship*

Grading criteria (1 to 10)	Piece no.21	Piece no.34	Piece no.36	Piece no.42
1. Theme/dimensions	9	6	8	8
2. Elegance/lightness	7	6	9	3
3. Color	8	5	7	6
4. Balance	6	8	7	4
5. Quality of components	4	9	5	5
6. Workmanship	5	9	3	4
Total (60 points maximum)	39	43	39	30

Example 1

Example 2

Example 3

Weaving

Possible Designs

Decorating dough can be worked in much the same way as wicker. For this reason, a wide variety of woven designs are used in presentation pieces. For a detailed diagram of weaving technique, see page 273.

Bread Baskets

Bread baskets, either long or round, are decorative and appealing in presentation pieces. They can be prepared raw and allowed to dry, or they can be baked. In either case, they should be stained with coffee extract and then brushed with gelatin sealer to give them sheen and natural-looking color.

Straw Hats (see page 262)

Once woven, straw hats made from decorating dough can be baked for different lengths of time to give a wide range of tints and shades.

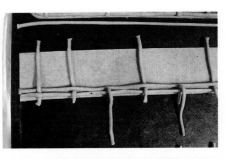

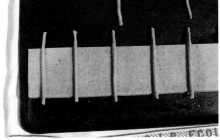

Straw hats

Peels

The baker's peel has long been a symbol of the baking profession. When one of the first bakers' guilds was formed in Paris during the early part of the fifteenth century, a silver baker's peel appeared on the coat of arms along with the portrait of the profession's patron saint, Saint Honoré.

French bakers have long made decorative peels out of decorating dough and used them in elaborate presentations.

Because of their flat shape, peels are easy to make. It is best to make cardboard templates of the peels in advance and keep them on hand to be used when needed. Make separate templates for the flat part and the handle of the peel. Construct and bake the flat section of the peel and the handle separately and then piece them together when needed.

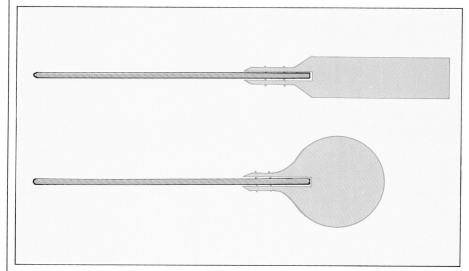

Note

Bake the cutout sections of dough in a 180°C (350°F) oven until they are completely dry and pale beige. Remove them from the oven, and while they are still hot, brush them with coffee extract. Return them to the oven for 2 to 3 minutes to fix the coloring.

After the two sections of the peel have cooled, brush them with gelatin sealer to lighten their color and give them the appearance of natural wood.

Harvest scenes

The presentation piece shown above is an assembly of different elements that have been described in earlier chapters.

1. *Sheaves of wheat*

2. *Ears of corn*

3. *Bread baskets*

4. *Grape bunches*

5. *Grape leaves*

6. *Frame*

7. *Baker's peel and miniature breads*

Preparing the Frame

The sides of the frame are cut separately using a cardboard template. The frame is constructed with three layers of dough, which are layered to reinforce the frame. They are then baked and attached with flour paste.

When layering the dough for the frame, put each of the layers in the freezer for at least 10 minutes before attaching them with the flour paste. This will help them hold their shape.

The frame should be glazed at least twice with egg wash before baking. Designs are then worked into the dough with a small paring knife. These designs should then be stained with coffee extract to help them stand out.

Details of the harvest presentation piece

Bread baskets, lanterns, and people

Bread Baskets

Decorating dough is used to make the baskets. In addition to the usual equipment for baking, have a mixing bowl and parchment paper on hand.

Turn the mixing bowl upside down and moisten it by sprinkling it with cold water. Cover the moistened underside of the bowl with parchment paper. The dough should then be placed over the parchment paper. Brush the dough with egg wash, and bake in a 180°C (350°F) oven until lightly browned.

Lanterns

Lanterns are made by installing a light bulb between two attached bread baskets. The lanterns provide an appealing, muted light that can be used in presentation pieces.

People

Almost life-size people can be prepared with regular dough, allowed to rise, and baked in the usual way. They are best presented in the traditional baker's work clothes.

Wall Plaques

Wall plaques are especially practical because they can be used to decorate the work area or the front room of a bakery. They can also be designed around traditional themes and sold to customers for special celebrations such as anniversaries, birthdays, and holidays.

Making the Support

Wall plaques consist of a piece of plywood that has been covered with felt. The decorative bread is then attached.

A piece of plywood about 60 by 25 by 1 centimeter (24 by 10 by ½ inch) is usually the best size for mounting these pieces.

Finishing the Plaque

Carefully position and attach a rose branch or other decoration to the felt-covered plywood frame using flour paste. Position the rose branch before attaching the flowers.

Other Decorations for Wall Plaques

Sheaves of wheat
A grapevine with bunches of grapes and
   grape leaves

The method is the same as for mounting rose branches.

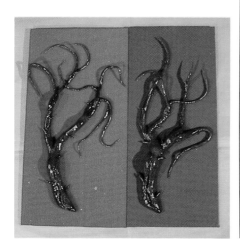

The grape harvest

The grape harvest has long been a time for special celebration in the French countryside. It is so much a part of French tradition that it is almost treated as folklore. Because of its importance to the French, it is often used as a theme for traditional presentation pieces. The presentation illustrated on the following pages won the grand prize for artistic presentation in one of France's competitions for bakers.

Opposite page: grapevines
grape bunches

Following pages: traditional grape harvester's basket
wine press

Traditional grape harvester's basket

Because this part of the presentation piece requires several time-consuming stages, it is best to plan to work over a three-day period.

Day 1

The traditional grape harvester's basket has one flat side, which rests against the harvester's back, and one curved side. The basket is handwoven around a frame constructed with two long wooden supports (which form each side of the flat side of the basket), five shorter, straight supports, which form the flat surface of the basket, and nine curved supports, shorter still, which support the curved side. When preparing these sections with bread dough, anticipate breakage and prepare extra pieces of each section. A bottom section is also required.

Prepare the base for the basket by rolling out a 5-millimeter (¼-inch) sheet of decorating dough.

Cut 26 thin strips from another sheet of decorating dough to form the supports. Four should be longer, eight less long, and fourteen shorter still—see the photo. Each of these sections should be about 4 millimeters (¼ inch) wide. They should then be gently rolled so they have about the thickness of pencils. It is essential that the curved supports have exactly the same shape, so it is advisable to draw the curve on a sheet of cardboard so each of the supports can be curved to the same degree. Then shape the fourteen shortest pieces, following the curve.

Place the floured cutouts for the base and the supports in the refrigerator overnight. Do not glaze any of the pieces.

Day 2

Bake the flour base and supports in a 180°C (350°F) oven. Leave the oven vents (if available) open while baking. Bake the sections thoroughly but do not allow them to brown.

When the sections are baked and have cooled, drill 16 holes around the perimeter of the base to hold the supports: 7 along the straight side and 9 along the curved side. Work carefully so the holes are evenly spaced.

Carefully work the holes to the appropriate size with the drill. Be gentle—it is easy to break the base. It is for this reason that extra pieces should be baked.

Gently work the ends of the supports into the holes drilled into the base. Place the two longest supports in the outside holes in the straight side, the five shorter straight supports along the straight side between the two longer supports, and the nine curved supports in the holes along the curved side. (The remaining pieces are extras, in case of breakage.) If necessary, file the bottom tips of the supports or gently scrape them with a paring knife. Attach the tips of the supports to the base with flour paste.

Place the base with the vertical supports on a baking sheet.

The next stage consists of weaving strips of dough between the vertical supports. Be sure to brush the vertical supports with water before beginning to weave, to help the strands of dough adhere to the supports and to each other. Continue weaving the strips of dough around the basket until you reach the tops of the supports.

Chill the basket overnight in the refrigerator. The weaving should not be brushed with egg wash at this point.

Day 3

Bake the baskets in the same way as the supports, in a 180°C (350°F) oven until the dough is cooked completely through but has not browned.

While the basket is still hot, brush it with coffee extract to give it the color of wicker. Place it back in the oven for 2 to 3 minutes to help fix and dry the stain. After the basket comes out of the oven the second time, brush it with gelatin sealer to give it a sheen.

Let the gelatin sealer dry for several hours before finishing the basket.

When the basket has dried, partially fill it with crumpled aluminum foil to take up space, so that you do not have to fill it entirely with baked grapes.

To improve the final appearance of the basket, spray it and the grapes with three coats of varnish, allowing the varnish to dry completely between applications.

Harvester's basket

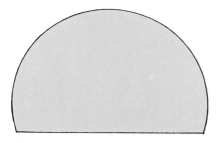

Base

**Sheet of decorating dough
5 millimeters (¼ inch) thick—
make one or two extra**

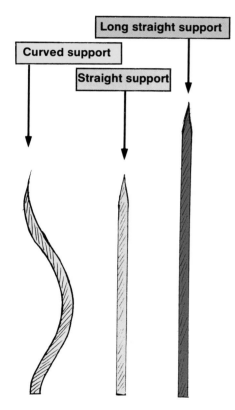

Curved support

Straight support

Long straight support

In case of breakage, prepare:

*14 curved supports instead of 9
8 straight supports instead of 5
4 long straight supports instead of 2*

Be sure that each type of support is exactly the same size and shape. The supports should be well rounded and have about the same thickness as a pencil, 5 millimeters (¼ inch).

For the curved supports, prepare a cardboard template to help guarantee that they will have the same curve.

When the base for the basket is baked, drill 16 holes in the base for the supports. Drill gently to avoid breakage.

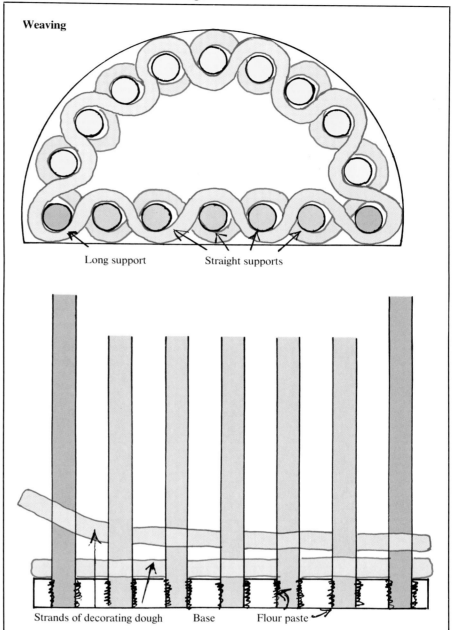

Weaving

Long support   Straight supports

Strands of decorating dough   Base   Flour paste

Gently insert the supports into the base. Each hole should contain a small amount of flour paste. The basket can now be woven with strands of decorating dough.

273

Wine press

Each section of the wine press is made with decorating dough and baked before the final assembly.

Each piece is:

- prepared and baked separately
- dried before baking
- stained with coffee extract (only the visible sections)
- coated with gelatin sealer (only the visible sections)
- attached with flour paste

The sections of the wine press are as follows:

- 1 base, composed of two thicknesses of raw decorating dough that are attached with egg wash before baking; the top section of dough has a cove that forms the drain.
- 2 large disks of dough, used to attach the outer slats—one disk at the bottom and one at the top
- 6 medium-size disks, placed on the inside of the press and surrounded with grapes (see diagram)
- 25 "wooden" slats
- 1 central screw, which should be twisted or threaded
- 1 lever
- grapes

Assembly

The Base

Attach the upper and lower sheets of dough with egg wash to form the base. Cut a cove along the outer rim with a paring knife to form a drain around the inside perimeter of the base. Give the drain a smooth, natural appearance by working over it with a hand moistened with cold water. Let the base dry overnight before baking.

Medium-size Inner Disks

Prepare the disks with decorating dough and allow them to dry. Attach them with egg wash to form a cylinder. Coat the outside of the cylinder with flour paste and attach the grapes. Attach the cylinder to the center of one of the two larger disks.

Attaching the Cylinder to the Base

Make sure the cylinder is well centered on the base. Attach it with flour paste.

Attaching the Slats to the Top of the Press

Glue two rows of slats to the second large disk. Attach this disk to the top of the cylinder. Make sure that small spaces evenly separate the slats.

Attaching the Central Screw

Attach one end of the screw to a small indentation made in a vertical section of dough attached to the top of the press. A small hole should be drilled into one side of the central screw for attaching the lever.

Attaching the Vertical Slats

Make sure the slats are separated by small, even spaces.

Attaching the Lever

Attach the lever with flour paste in the small indentation on the top of the press.

Varnishing the Press

Coat the press with three coats of a colorless commercial spray varnish. Allow the varnish to dry thoroughly between coats. The wine press will keep for several years if protected in a glass case.

274

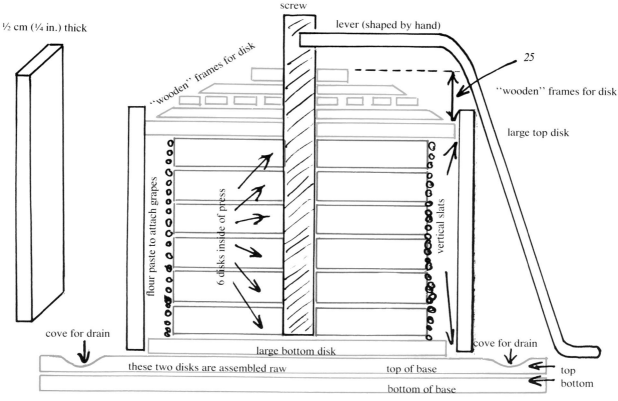

½ cm (¼ in.) thick

screw

lever (shaped by hand)

"wooden" frames for disk

25

"wooden" frames for disk

large top disk

flour paste to attach grapes

6 disks inside of press

vertical slats

cove for drain

large bottom disk

cove for drain

these two disks are assembled raw

top of base

top

bottom of base

bottom

base is 1 cm (½ in.) thick

6 disks, 4 cm. (2 in.) thick, with a hole cut in the middle of each. They should be baked separately and attached with flour paste.

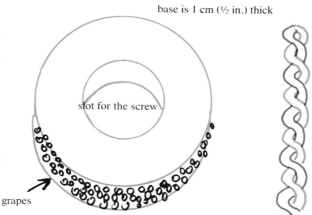

slot for the screw

Prepare 30 slats 2 cm (1 in.) wide, 20 cm (8 in.) long, and ½ cm (¼ in.) thick

grapes

central screw

Roosters

Procedure

To shape the dough for the body of a rooster, a mold is first prepared with papier-mâché and modeling clay. Two sheets of decorating dough are then pressed against this mold until they assume the correct shape. The sheets of dough are then baked (they are supported with crumpled aluminum foil) and eventually attached together. The rooster's tail is formed from large feathers cut from a section of dough with a paring knife and attached with flour paste.

The feathers are cut out with a small cookie cutter and elongated slightly. The size of the feathers can be varied by using different-sized cookie cutters and sheets of dough with different thicknesses. The color of the feathers can also be adjusted by using dough that has been tinted with coffee extract.

The effect is enhanced by painting the large feathers of the tail with coffee extract or egg yolk.

When the rooster is completely assembled, it should be dried in a proof box.

Preparing the Mold

The rooster is prepared by forming sections of dough in two identical half-molds.

Draw an outline of a rooster on a piece of plywood. Prepare papier-mâché by working shredded newspaper with water until it has a stiff, claylike consistency. Work the papier-mâché within the outline on the plywood until it has a natural shape. The papier-mâché can be attached to the plywood at this point with glue to make it easier to work with. When the papier-mâché has the general shape of a rooster, coat it with modeling clay. Smooth the surface of the clay with a trowel or a putty knife. Give the surface as smooth and natural a texture and shape as possible. Repeat this process for the other half of the mold.

Allow the two halves of the mold to dry. They should be the exact same size. It may be necessary to file certain sections to get an exact fit.

275

Assembling the Rooster

Step 1: When the two half-molds have dried, roll out two sheets of decorating dough, and press one over each mold. Cut off the excess with scissors. Allow the dough to harden over the molds. Gently lift them off the molds, fill them with crumpled pieces of aluminum foil to support them during baking, and transfer them to baking sheets. Bake them in a 180°C (350°F) oven without steam, with the vents (if available) left open. When the molds are finished baking and have cooled, attach them with flour paste.

Step 2: Cut the large tail feathers from a sheet of decorating dough, using a paring knife. Place them on a baking sheet and bake them in a 180°C (350°F) oven. When they have cooled, they can be attached to the main body of the rooster with flour paste.

Step 3: The small feathers should be cut from a thin sheet of decorating dough with a cookie cutter. Press gently on the rounds to elongate them. They should then be attached, while still raw, to the rooster body. Overlap them by starting first at the tail and working toward the head. The feathers closer to the head should be smaller.

Step 4: Dry the assembled rooster in a 120°C (250°F) oven for approximately 2 hours.

Windmills
(see pages 267, 282, 288, and 289)

Windmills can be prepared in a variety of shapes and sizes. There are several techniques for finishing both the base and the blades. When preparing the different sections of the windmill, working from a photograph or an engraving is helpful. It is especially important to maintain the correct proportions between the blades and the base.

The base for the mill is prepared by wrapping a sheet of dough around a paint can (with handles removed) that has been first coated with a sheet of moistened parchment paper. It is important at this stage that the dough completely cover and adhere evenly to the sides of the can. The conical top to the base can be fashioned from decorating dough shaped over a cardboard template covered with parchment paper or over a special kind of mold used for croque-en-bouches.

The blades for the windmill are best cut out of a single sheet of decorating dough. Be very careful to cut the blades in accurate proportion to the base. A small piece of dough should also be prepared to resemble the axle holding the blades to the base.

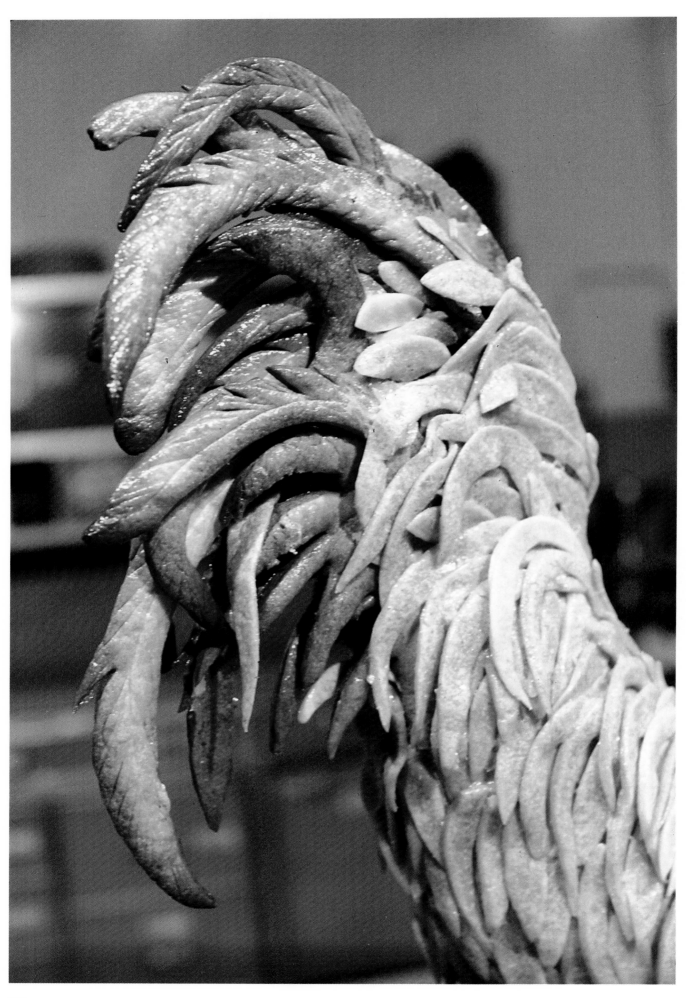

Examples of presentation pieces

The pages that follow contain photographs and short descriptions of some of the winners of the Concours d'Arpajon, one of France's most prestigious food shows.

The preparation of the parchment scrolls shown above is relatively straightforward. It is important, however, to give them an antique appearance.

Cut an uneven rectangle from a sheet of decorating dough. Make several small cuts in the edges of the sheet to help give it a tattered, aged appearance. The letters should also be cut from a sheet of decorating dough and attached to the scroll with a small amount of cold water.

The scroll should be allowed to dry slightly and then placed directly on top of a bread loaf before baking.

Large Decorated Country Loaf

Claude Mesnier

This highly decorative loaf is prepared by attaching small pieces of decorating dough to the loaf after it is three-quarters baked. When using this technique, it is especially important to cut the decorations from a very thin sheet of dough. If the dough cutouts are too thick and too heavy, their weight can cause the bread to sag during the last quarter of the baking.

Notice the texture of the interiors of the loaves shown on the following page. This coarse texture with relatively large holes is characteristic of bread that has been prepared using traditional methods and contains no additives.

This method of decorating loaves with small decorative cutouts gives the baker enormous versatility in designing special loaves for holidays, birthdays, and other special events.

Farmer's Field and Windmill

Gérard Thiou

This presentation shows a bucolic scene presented atop a loaf of bread. The base of the windmill is prepared by wrapping a sheet of decorating dough over half of a tin can coated with moistened parchment paper.

The blades of the windmill are composed of two pieces cut from a sheet of decorating dough. These two sections are then attached directly to the base while it is still attached to the tin can, before baking. The door and window frames are made to look like stone by attaching small pieces of dough to the base with water. After the windmill has been assembled, it is baked in a 175°C (350°F) oven for approximately one hour. No steam should be used, and the oven vents (if available) should be left open.

The most delicate stage consists of removing the wind mill from the tin can support. Make sure the dough has cooled completely before proceeding with this step.

The miniature pieces—the farmer, the plow, and the horses—are cut from decorating dough, using cardboard templates prepared in advance. The tree trunk is stained with coffee extract. The leaves are prepared by intertwining thin strips of decorating dough or spaghetti.

Bean-shaped Loaf

Nicole Robine

This comical presentation is simple to prepare. The bean shape of the loaf is obtained by working the dough over a cardboard template that has been cut to the appropriate shape.

The face and lettering are made on the loaf using a stencil that has been cut out ahead of time. The stencil should be placed over the loaf just before baking. Flour is then sprinkled over the loaf through the stencil by holding a drum sieve or a flour sifter over the stencil. Be careful to distribute the flour evenly so the letters and face have the same amount of flour. Carefully remove the stencil from the surface of the loaf. The loaf can then be baked in the usual way.

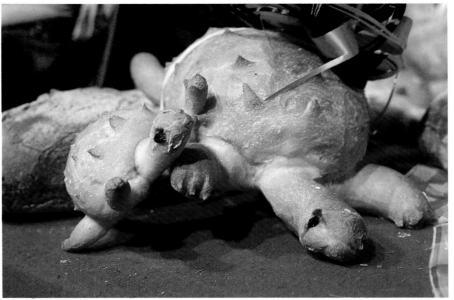

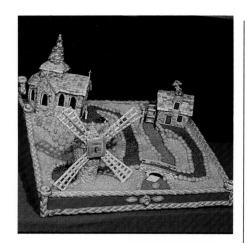

In the pages that follow, additional presentation pieces are shown. Credit goes to André Beaudron, Jean-Louis Clément, Jacques Herbaut, Denis Mottier, Marcel Montagne, Christophe Pitman, and Moïse Trohel.

Country Scene

This scene is particularly original because each structure is covered with tiny pieces of dough that resemble tiles. Each of these "tiles" is baked separately and then meticulously attached to a flat surface of dough to form the roofs of these miniature buildings.

The stones used for the bridge and walls of the buildings are made by slicing a cylinder of decorating dough, baking each of the miniature disks, and then carefully attaching them to one another with flour paste.

Because these elaborate constructions require familiarity with certain building techniques, it is often useful to work from a drawing or photograph.

Decorative Breads Made with Brié Dough

Jacques Bazin

Brié dough has an extremely firm consistency, which makes it especially malleable and easy to mold into decorative shapes. Because of its claylike consistency, it is fun to work with. The small animals shown on the following pages are especially appealing to children.

The primary disadvantage to preparing decorative breads with brié dough is that it is very perishable, making it necessary to prepare the breads fresh each day.

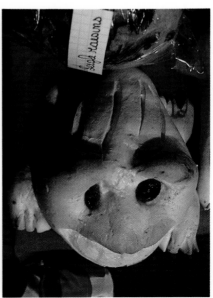

Miniature Animals

Patrick Brouard

Templates for miniature animals should be prepared by drawing the design on the cardboard. The templates can then be used over and over again as needed.

Cut the decorations from a sheet of decorating dough approximately 3 millimeters (⅛ inch) thick, using the cardboard templates as guides. Bake the dough cutouts in a 180°C (350°F) oven

with the vents (if available) left open.

Note: The horse's mane is prepared by attaching thin strips of dough to the cut-out with water. The rest of the horse should consist of a single cutout.

The sheep is finished by attaching miniature balls of decorating dough to the cutout with water or egg wash.

Chapter 6
Marketing breads

Marketing your Breads

You have learned to:

- make special and decorative breads
- design fanciful Viennese breads
- prepare presentation pieces

Now that you are on your way to mastering the methods and techniques used for preparing a wide range of appealing breads, an added challenge remains: marketing your breads to an appreciative clientele. This last chapter summarizes a few essential points to help the traditional baker sell the breads he or she has worked so hard to prepare.

Practical tips for marketing breads

1. Give advance notice

If you are planning to prepare special or elaborate loaves for an upcoming holiday or feast day, be sure to let your customers know in advance. Not only will this prepare your customers and encourage them to return to your bakery, but it will give you an opportunity to determine what types of breads most interest your customers and give you an idea of how much of each type to prepare.

2. Keep your customers informed

It is not always possible to display the entire selection of breads prepared by your bakery. For this reason, a list of what is available should be clearly visible from the street. Traditional French bakeries often write a list of breads directly on the window in white grease pencil. Hang a complete list of your breads on the bakery wall and in the front window. Another good idea is to wrap your breads in paper with not only your name and logo, but a list of the types of breads you sell.

3. Display your breads

Make your breads as visible as possible. Label the breads clearly so customers know what they are. For some special breads, a few words of explanation are also helpful.

Take advantage of the natural beauty of breads. When displayed carefully, the interplay of the loaves' subtle brown hues becomes an irresistible temptation for many a customer. This is probably the most effective method of marketing your breads.

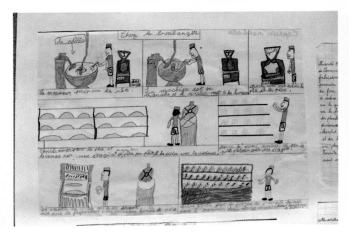

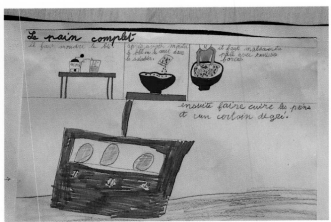

4. Give samples

When introducing a new type of bread, it is a good idea to place a basket of samples somewhere in the bakery for customers to taste. This is especially important in the United States, where customers are less likely to be familiar with traditional French breads and will be eager to learn as well as try something new.

5. Advise and explain

Don't let your customers struggle with indecision because they are uncertain of how the different breads taste or how they are best served. Make yourself available to the customer and do not hesitate to make suggestions.

Some customers will have more questions than others. Take your time and explain what you feel is necessary. Some customers will even want to know what types of flours are used or how breads are shaped and baked.

6. Vary your selections

Always try to have something new for your customers. Some bakers promote a "specialty" of the week or even of the day. You may even want to have a special day devoted to special fanciful breads for children. Keep changing special items on your list of breads. In this way, you will be able to pinpoint your clientele's preferences and adapt to their needs.

7. Adapt to the needs of your customers

Listen to your customers' comments. If your customers are reserved about telling you what they like, do not hesitate to ask their advice. This also provides you with the opportunity to get to know your customers. Once you have developed rapport and they trust you to cater to their needs, your customers will return regularly and will tell others about the quality and selection of breads that you offer.

By following these practical tips, your customers will:
- rediscover the pleasure and satisfaction of eating old-fashioned freshly baked bread
- realize that bread is a wonderfully complex and varied food that they can serve in new and different ways.

Units of Measure and Conversions

All measures are rounded to the nearest ½ ounce or ½ fluid ounce.

Weight Measures

16 ounces = 1 pound

1,000 grams = 1 kilogram

30 grams = 1.0 ounce
50 grams = 1.5 ounces
100 grams = 3.5 ounces
125 grams = 4.5 ounces
150 grams = 5.0 ounces
200 grams = 7.0 ounces
250 grams = 9.0 ounces
300 grams = 10.5 ounces
350 grams = 12.5 ounces
400 grams = 14.0 ounces
450 grams = 16.0 ounces
500 grams = 17.5 ounces
550 grams = 19.5 ounces
600 grams = 21.0 ounces
650 grams = 23.0 ounces
700 grams = 24.5 ounces
750 grams = 26.5 ounces
800 grams = 28.0 ounces
850 grams = 30.0 ounces
900 grams = 31.5 ounces
950 grams = 33.5 ounces
1,000 grams = 35.0 ounces

Liquid Measures

3 teaspoons = 1 tablespoon
2 tablespoons = 1 fluid ounce
8 fluid ounces = 1 cup
2 cups = 1 pint
2 pints = 1 quart
4 quarts = 1 gallon

1,000 milliliters = 1 liter

5 milliliters = 1 teaspoon
15 milliliters = 1 tablespoon
30 milliliters = 1.0 fluid ounce
50 milliliters = 1.5 fluid ounces
100 milliliters = 3.5 fluid ounces
150 milliliters = 5.0 fluid ounces
200 milliliters = 6.5 fluid ounces
250 milliliters = 8.5 fluid ounces
300 milliliters = 10.0 fluid ounces
350 milliliters = 12.0 fluid ounces
400 milliliters = 13.5 fluid ounces
450 milliliters = 16.0 fluid ounces
500 milliliters = 17.0 fluid ounces
550 milliliters = 18.5 fluid ounces
600 milliliters = 21.0 fluid ounces
650 milliliters = 22.0 fluid ounces
700 milliliters = 23.5 fluid ounces
750 milliliters = 25.5 fluid ounces
800 milliliters = 27.0 fluid ounces
850 milliliters = 28.5 fluid ounces
900 milliliters = 30.5 fluid ounces
950 milliliters = 33.0 fluid ounces
1,000 milliliters = 34.0 fluid ounces

Linear Measures

12 inches = 1 foot
3 feet = 1 yard

1,000 millimeters = 100 centimeters = 1 meter

1 millimeter = .04 inch
1 centimeter = .4 inches
1 meter = 39.37 inches

Index

abaisse, 12
accoler, 12
allonger, 12
almond bread, 102–3
apple bread, 75–76
apprêt, 12
apricot bread, 75–76
Auvergne-style loaves, 120

bacon
    bread, 104–5
    onion/, bread, 104–5
barley
    bread, 107
    flour, 16
bassiner, 12
bear claws, 128
bows. *See* Ribbons
braids, 124, 170–74
bran, 17
    bread, 112
bread baskets, 260, 267
bread making
    baking, 37–39
    cooling, 39
    fermenting, 30–31
    by hand, 22–25
    kneading, 22–25, 28–29
    old-fashioned methods
        for, 42–43
    proofing, 31
    scoring, 36
    shaping/rounding loaves,
        34, 35
    summary of techniques
        for, 20–21
    techniques for country-
        style bread, 43
    techniques for white
        bread, 42
    weighing/sectioning
        dough, 33
breads. *See also* Bread
        making; Elaborately
        shaped loaves
    almond, 102–3
    apple, 75–76
    apricot, 75–76
    bacon, 104–5
    barley, 107
    bran, 112
    brié, 80
    brown, 79
    carrot, 84
    carrot-herb, 86
    chorizo, 82
    corn, 95
    country-style, 43, 47, 48–
        51, 52–53, 54–55, 56–57
    cumin, 83
    fougasse, Provençale,
        108–9
    four-grain, 81

gruau, 92
hazelnut, 102–3
herb, 85
high-gluten, 90–91
Italian, 94
low-gluten, 91
méteil, 96–97
Normandy cider, 100–101
olive, 106
onion, 104–5
onion/bacon, 104–5
oyster, 93
prune, 75–76
pullman, 98–99
rye, 58–59, 60–62, 63, 64,
    65, 66
seaweed, 78
sesame-seed, 109–10
soy, 111
surprise, 113
Viennese, 114–15, 118,
    119, 142–74
walnut, 102–3
wheat-germ, 89
white, 42
whole-wheat, 69–71, 72–
    73, 74
whole-wheat, with dried
    fruits, 88
brié bread, 80
brown bread, 79
buckwheat, 16
buée, 12

candle holders, 238–39
caps, 123
carrot
    bread, 84
    -herb bread, 86
chorizo bread, 82
clé, 12
cider bread, Normandy,
    100–101
contrefraser, 12
cornmeal, 16
    bread, 95
corn-shaped loaves, 189–90,
    210–13
    leaves for, 214–17
corps, 12
corser, 12
country-style breads, 43, 47
    with a mixed starter, 48–
        51
    with a natural (sourdough)
        starter, 52–53
    with a sponge starter, 56–
        57
    with a yeast starter, 54–55
crescents, 132
crowns, 126
    Lyons-style, 127
cumin bread, 83

decorating doughs, 179–81
    cutting, 193–98
    hand-shaping, 191–92
    molding, 189–90
dessécher, 12
donner un tour, 13

ebarber, 12
elaborately shaped loaves,
    118–19. *See also*
        Viennese breads
    Auvergne-style loaves,
        120
    bear claws, 128
    braids, 124
    caps, 123
    country-style flat bread,
        133
    crescents, 132
    crowns, 126, 127
    cut with scissors, 134–37
    folded loaves, 131
    horseshoes, 130
    Pithiviers, 125
    pouches, 121
    ropes, 125
    spirals, 125
    split loaves, 129
    tricorns, 122
    twists, 130
etuver, 12

façonner, 12
fermentation, 13, 30–31, 48,
    49, 55
fermented dough starter, 60–
    62
ferrer, 12
flour paste, 183
flours
    ash content of, 14
    barley, 16
    buckwheat, 16
    composition of, 14
    cornmeal, 16
    dusting, 118
    extraction ratio of, 13, 14
    gray, 118
    high-gluten, 15
    judging quality of, 15
    oat, 15
    patent, 15
    rice, 16
    rye, 16
    rye/wheat (méteil), 16
    soy, 17
    white-wheat, 15
    whole-wheat, 15
flowers, 206–8
folded loaves, 131
force, 12
fougasse, 133
    Provençale, 108–9

four-grain bread, 81
fraser/frasage, 12, 22
fruits, dried, whole-wheat
    bread with, 88

glazes
    colored, 118
    egg, 118
gluten
    flour, 15
    high-, bread, 90–91
    low-, bread, 91
grape harvester's basket,
    272–73
grapes, 199–201
    leaves for, 203–5
    vines for, 245–47
grigne, 12
gruau bread, 92

hazelnut bread, 102–3
herb
    bread, 85
    carrot-, bread, 86
horseshoes, 130
hydratation, 13
hygrometers, 26

inciser, 13
Italian bread, 94

kneading
    by hand, 22–25
    by machine, 28–29

lanterns, 267
leaves
    attaching, 225
    corn, 214–17
    grape, 203–5
    rose, 226
    wheat, 222–24
levain, 13
levain-levure, 13
levure biologique, 13

marketing, 295–97
méteil (rye/wheat)
    bread, 96–97
    flour, 16
milk bread dough, 138–41
mixed starter, 33, 48, 63
modeler, 13
''mother,'' 32
moulage, 13
moulure, 13

natural yeast starter. *See*
    Sourdough starter

oat flour, 15
olive bread, 106

onion
   /bacon bread, 104–5
   bread, 104–5
ovens, 37–39
oyster bread, 93

peels, 38
   decorative, 263
people (bread), 267
Pithiviers, 125
polka cut, 36
plaques, wooden, 237, 269
pointage, 13
poolisch, 13
pouches, 121
pousse, 13
presentation pieces
   assembling and attaching
      components of, 242, 254
   examples of, 264–66, 279–
      93
   glass showcase for, 254–
      55
   guidelines for constructing,
      253
   judging, in competition,
      256
   pedestal for, 254–55
proofing, 12, 31
prune bread, 75–76
pullman bread, 98–99
punching down, 13

raisins, rye bread and rolls
   with, 66–67
ressuage, 13

retention power, 31
ribbons, 227–29
rice flour, 16
rompre, 13
roosters, 275–77
ropes, 125
rose
   branches, 240, 243
   leaves, 226
rounding, 34
round loaves, cut with
      scissors, 137
rye. *See also* Méteil
   bread, 58–59
   bread, light, 65
   bread with a fermented
      dough starter, 60–62
   bread with a mixed
      starter, 63
   bread with a sponge
      starter, 64
   bread with raisins, 66
   rolls with raisins, 67

sabler, 13
sausage cut, 36
scissors, cutting loaves with,
   134–37
scoring, 13, 36
scrolls, 230–36, 279
sealer, gelatin-based, 184–86
seaweed bread, 78
sesame-seed bread, 109–10
shaping. *See also*
   Elaborately shaped
      loaves; Viennese breads

long loaves, 34
round loaves, 35
soudure, 12
sourdough starter, 13, 32,
soy
   bread, 111
   flour, 17
spirals, 125
split loaves, 129
sponge starter, 13, 33, 56–
   57, 64
stains, 186–87
stars, 136–37
starter doughs
   fermented, 60–62
   mixed, 33, 48, 63
   refreshing, 32, 33, 48, 52–
      53
   sourdough, 32, 52–53
   sponge, 33, 56–57, 64
   yeast, 32, 54
steam, 12, 39
straw hats, 260, 262
surprise breads, 113

taux d'extraction, 13
temperatures, base, for
   calculating water
      temperature, 22, 29
tolerance, 13, 31
tourner, 12
tricorns, 122
tulips, 206–8
twists, 130

Viennese breads, 114–15,

118, 119, 142
displaying, 168
shaped by hand, 158–59,
   160–67
shaped with templates,
   143–44, 145–57
walnut bread, 102–3
water
   content, as percentage of
      flour, 27
   temperature of, 22, 29
weaving, 260
weighing, 33
wheat (bread) flour, 15
wheat germ, 17
   bread, 89
wheat-shaped loaves
   ears, 134–35, 218–19
   leaves for, 222–24
   sheaves, 220–21, 249–50
   stalks, 220
wheelbarrow, 197
whole-wheat
   bread with a fermented
      dough starter, 74
   bread with a mixed
      starter, 69–71
   bread with a sponge
      starter, 72–73
   bread with dried fruit, 88
windmills, 277
wine press, 274–75

yeast, 13, 17–19, 30. *See
   also* Starter doughs
yeast starter, 32, 54–55